Visual Basic .NET
For Dummies

Cheat Sheet

D0783138

Objects That Store Data from the User Interface

Object	Data Type	Object Property
Check box	Boolean	Checked
Checked list box (currently highlighted item)	String	Text
Checked list box (checked items)	Boolean	Checked
Color dialog box	System.Drawing.Color	Color
Combo box (single items)	String	Text
Combo box (multiple items)	Collection	SelectedItems.Item
DateTimePicker	Long	Value
DomainUpDown	String	Text
Font dialog box	System.Drawing.Color	Color
	Boolean	Font.Bold
	Boolean	Font.Italic
	Boolean	Font.StrikeThru
	Boolean	Font.Underline
	String	Font.Name
	Single	Font.Size
List box (single items)	String	Text
List box (multiple items)	Collection	SelectedItems.Item
NumericUpDown	Decimal	Value
Open dialog box	String	Filename
Radio button	Boolean	Checked
RichTextBox	String	Text
Save As dialog box	String	Filename
Scroll bars	Integer	Value
Text box	String	Text
TrackBar	Integer	Value

Type Declaration Characters

Data Type	Character	Example	Equivalent to
Decimal	@	Dim Money @	Dim Money As Decimal
Double	#	Dim Fraction#	Dim Fraction As Double
Integer	%	Dim Count%	Dim Count As Integer
Long	&	Dim Big Num&	Dim BigNum As Long
Single	!	Dim Small	Dim! Dim SmallNum As Single
String	$	Dim MyString$	Dim MyString As String

For Dummies: Bestselling Book Series for Beginners

Visual Basic .NET For Dummies®

Shortcut Keys for Using Visual Basic .NET

Key(s)	What the Shortcut Does
Ctrl+B	New breakpoint
Ctrl+N	Creates a new file
Ctrl+O	Opens an existing file
Ctrl+P	Prints
Ctrl+S	Saves selected items
Ctrl+Shift+S	Saves all
F4	Displays the Properties window
F7	Displays the code window for the currently selected object
Shift+F7	Displays the object for a particular event procedure
F10	Steps over
F11	Steps into
Ctrl+Alt+L	Displays the Solution Explorer window
Ctrl+Alt+X	Displays the Toolbox
Ctrl+Shift+A	Adds new item
Ctrl+F5	Starts without debugging
F5	Starts (your Visual Basic .NET program)

Object Naming Conventions for Common User Interface Controls

Object	Prefix	Example
Button	btn	btnYourLip
Check box	chk	chkTheMail
Combo box	cbo	cboSandwich
Form	frm	frmAStraightLine
Horizontal scroll bar	hsb	hsbTemperature scroll bar
Image	img	imgDirty
Label	lbl	lblGraffiti
List box	lst	lstPotentialDates
Menu	mnu	mnuFileExit
Radio button	rad	radRock101
Picture box	pic	picAndShovel
Text box	txt	txtWarning
Vertical scroll bar	vsb	vsbVoltage

Declaring and Calling a Function

```
Public Function
FunctionName(ArgumentList)As
DataType

   FunctionName = SomeValue
End Function
```

or

```
Public Function
FunctionName(ArgumentList)As
DataType

   Return SomeValue
End Function
```

```
Variable =
FunctionName(ArgumentList)
```

Declaring and Calling a Procedure

```
Public Sub
ProcedureName(ArgumentList)
   ' Instructions to run
End Sub


ProcedureName (ArgumentList)
```

or

```
Call ProcedureName
(ArgumentList)
```

Hungry Minds™

Copyright © 2002 Hungry Minds, Inc.
All rights reserved.

Cheat Sheet $2.95 value. Item 0867-9.

For more information about Hungry Minds,
call 1-800-762-2974.

For Dummies: Bestselling Book Series for Beginners

TM

BESTSELLING BOOK SERIES

References for the Rest of Us! ®

Are you intimidated and confused by computers? Do you find that traditional manuals are overloaded with technical details you'll never use? Do your friends and family always call you to fix simple problems on their PCs? Then the For Dummies® computer book series from Hungry Minds, Inc. is for you.

For Dummies books are written for those frustrated computer users who know they aren't really dumb but find that PC hardware, software, and indeed the unique vocabulary of computing make them feel helpless. For Dummies books use a lighthearted approach, a down-to-earth style, and even cartoons and humorous icons to dispel computer novices' fears and build their confidence. Lighthearted but not lightweight, these books are a perfect survival guide for anyone forced to use a computer.

> *"I like my copy so much I told friends; now they bought copies."*
> — Irene C., Orwell, Ohio

> *"Quick, concise, nontechnical, and humorous."*
> — Jay A., Elburn, Illinois

> *"Thanks, I needed this book. Now I can sleep at night."*
> — Robin F., British Columbia, Canada

Already, millions of satisfied readers agree. They have made For Dummies books the #1 introductory level computer book series and have written asking for more. So, if you're looking for the most fun and easy way to learn about computers, look to For Dummies books to give you a helping hand.

Hungry Minds™

Visual Basic® .NET

FOR

DUMMIES®

Visual Basic® .NET FOR DUMMIES®

by Wallace Wang

Hungry Minds™

Best-Selling Books • Digital Downloads • e-Books • Answer Networks • e-Newsletters • Branded Web Sites • e-Learning

New York, NY ◆ Cleveland, OH ◆ Indianapolis, IN

Visual Basic® .NET For Dummies®

Published by
Hungry Minds, Inc.
909 Third Avenue
New York, NY 10022
www.hungryminds.com
www.dummies.com

Library of Congress Control Number: 2001089346

ISBN: 0-7645-0867-9

Printed in the United States of America

10 9 8 7 6 5 4 3 2 1

1B/QR/RR/QR/IN

Distributed in the United States by Hungry Minds, Inc.

Distributed by CDG Books Canada Inc. for Canada; by Transworld Publishers Limited in the United Kingdom; by IDG Norge Books for Norway; by IDG Sweden Books for Sweden; by IDG Books Australia Publishing Corporation Pty. Ltd. for Australia and New Zealand; by TransQuest Publishers Pte Ltd. for Singapore, Malaysia, Thailand, Indonesia, and Hong Kong; by Gotop Information Inc. for Taiwan; by ICG Muse, Inc. for Japan; by Intersoft for South Africa; by Eyrolles for France; by International Thomson Publishing for Germany, Austria and Switzerland; by Distribuidora Cuspide for Argentina; by LR International for Brazil; by Galileo Libros for Chile; by Ediciones ZETA S.C.R. Ltda. for Peru; by WS Computer Publishing Corporation, Inc., for the Philippines; by Contemporanea de Ediciones for Venezuela; by Express Computer Distributors for the Caribbean and West Indies; by Micronesia Media Distributor, Inc. for Micronesia; by Chips Computadoras S.A. de C.V. for Mexico; by Editorial Norma de Panama S.A. for Panama; by American Bookshops for Finland.

For general information on Hungry Minds' products and services please contact our Customer Care Department within the U.S. at 800-762-2974, outside the U.S. at 317-572-3993 or fax 317-572-4002.

For sales inquiries and reseller information, including discounts, premium and bulk quantity sales, and foreign-language translations, please contact our Customer Care Department at 800-434-3422, fax 317-572-4002, or write to Hungry Minds, Inc., Attn: Customer Care Department, 10475 Crosspoint Boulevard, Indianapolis, IN 46256.

For information on licensing foreign or domestic rights, please contact our Sub-Rights Customer Care Department at 212-884-5000.

For information on using Hungry Minds' products and services in the classroom or for ordering examination copies, please contact our Educational Sales Department at 800-434-2086 or fax 317-572-4005.

For press review copies, author interviews, or other publicity information, please contact our Public Relations Department at 317-572-3168 or fax 317-572-4168.

For authorization to photocopy items for corporate, personal, or educational use, please contact Copyright Clearance Center, 222 Rosewood Drive, Danvers, MA 01923, or fax 978-750-4470.

Hungry Minds™ is a trademark of Hungry Minds, Inc.

About the Author

The author is an anonymous figure to well over 99 percent of the total world's population. This sobering thought alone helps to remind him to stay humble, despite any modicum of fame and wealth this book may generate during its short publication cycle until Microsoft unleashes another version of Visual Basic on an unsuspecting public, solely to generate additional revenue for Microsoft and its collective band of stockholders.

When not writing computer books, the author enjoys indulging in sky-diving, mountain-climbing, hang-gliding, spelunking, working as a mercenary in Third World countries, tracking Big Foot across the Northwest wilderness, communicating with UFOs, mining the rich mineral deposits on the second moon of Saturn, and weaving other tales of fiction and imagination to keep himself amused while writing computer books that need to be updated every few years.

In his spare time, the author can often be found staring in utter disbelief as Windows 98 and Windows Millennium Edition crashes on him for the fourth time that day.

Dedication

This book is dedicated to a variety of people who had nothing whatsoever to do in the creation of this book, but who like to see their name in print anyway:

Steve Schirripa and Don Learned, for giving me my first Las Vegas gig at the Riviera Comedy Club, located in the Riviera Hotel & Casino (www.theriviera.com). The next time you're in Las Vegas, drop by, see a show, and dump some money in one of the many Riviera Casino slot machines. Who knows? Maybe you'll win enough money to buy yourself a new computer.

Patrick DeGuire, who helped me put together Top Bananas Entertainment (www.topbananas.com), our company devoted to providing clean comedy around San Diego. Thanks also goes to Chris (the Zooman) Clobber, Bob Zany, Tony Vicich, Kip Addotta, Ron Pearson, Willie Farrell, and Leo (the man, the myth, the legend) Fontaine. None of these people helped with the book but they made me laugh a lot while I was doing all the hard work so they should at least get credit for something.

Final thanks go to all my relatives who keep bugging me to put their names in print because they get tired of seeing my cats get more publicity than they do: Ruth and Herbert (my mom and dad), Wayne (my brother), and Gail (my sister). I'm not quite sure why they want to see their names in a book that they'll never use in a million years, but since this makes them happy, maybe this will help make their lives more complete and fulfilling somehow.

Acknowledgments

Nobody writes and publishes a book without the help of other people, and this book is no exception. It goes without saying (although I'm going to say it anyway) that two of the most important people responsible for this book are Matt Wagner and Bill Gladstone of Waterside Productions. Thanks, guys. I'd give you more than your usual 15 percent cut, but if I did, then I wouldn't have anything left over to pay for my groceries.

Two other people who deserve thanks include Colleen Esterline (the friendly editor) and Allen Wyatt (the friendly technical editor, who made sure everything in this book really does work the way it's supposed to) of Discovery Computing, Inc.

Next, I have to acknowledge Cassandra (my wife), Jordan (my son), along with Bo, Scraps, Tasha, and Nuit (my cats) for their support during the long hours I've spent glued to my computer instead of doing anything else around the house.

Naturally, I need to acknowledge all the trees that sacrificed themselves in front of the lumber mill cutting saw so that their essence of life could be snuffed out and smashed flat to make the paper that this book is printed on. An additional round of acknowledgments must also go to any horses that may have given up their hooves and bones to make the glue that binds these pages together.

Finally, I must acknowledge all the people who break their backs every day, hauling boxes of these books around the country and stacking them on shelves so you can stand in the air-conditioned comfort of a bookstore and browse through these pages at your leisure. Support your local bookstore, and show your support by buying three more copies of this book in the process.

Publisher's Acknowledgments

Some of the people who helped bring this book to market include the following:

Acquisitions, Editorial,
and Media Development

Project Editor: Colleen Williams Esterline

Acquisitions Editor: Bob Woerner

Technical Editor: Discovery Computing, Inc.

Editorial Manager, Freelance:
Constance Carlisle

Media Development Manager: Laura VanWinkle

Media Development Supervisor:
Richard Graves

Editorial Assistants: Amanda Foxworth,
Jean Rogers

Production

Project Coordinator: Jennifer Bingham

Layout and Graphics: LeAndra Johnson,
Gabriele McCann, Heather Pope,
Jacque Schneider, Jeremey Unger

Proofreaders: Laura Albert, David Faust,
John Greenough, TECHBOOKS Production
Services

Indexer: TECHBOOKS Production Services

Special Help
Chris Webb

General and Administrative

Hungry Minds Technology Publishing Group: Richard Swadley, Senior Vice President and
Publisher; Mary Bednarek, Vice President and Publisher, Networking; Joseph Wikert,
Vice President and Publisher, Web Development Group; Mary C. Corder, Editorial Director,
Dummies Technology; Andy Cummings, Publishing Director, Dummies Technology; Barry
Pruett, Publishing Director, Visual/Graphic Design

Hungry Minds Manufacturing: Ivor Parker, Vice President, Manufacturing

Hungry Minds Marketing: John Helmus, Assistant Vice President, Director of Marketing

Hungry Minds Production for Branded Press: Debbie Stailey, Production Director

Hungry Minds Sales: Michael Violano, Vice President, International Sales and Sub Rights

Contents at a Glance

Cartoons at a Glance

By Rich Tennant

page 365

page 7

page 335

page 49

page 305

page 121

page 269

page 165

Cartoon Information:
Fax: 978-546-7747
E-Mail: richtennant@the5thwave.com
World Wide Web: www.the5thwave.com

Table of Contents

Chapter 7: Boxes and Buttons for Making Choices 87

Chapter 8: Text Boxes and Labels for Typing and Showing Words 95

Chapter 9: Showing Choices with List and Combo Boxes 105

Chapter 10: Fine-Tuning the Appearance of Your User Interface 115

Introduction

● ●

Welcome to computer programming using Visual Basic .NET, Microsoft's programming language designed to help you create programs quickly and easily. If the idea of writing your own program intrigues you but also intimidates you, relax. If you can write step-by-step instructions to give someone directions to where you live, you can discover how to write a program in Visual Basic .NET. (Seriously!)

To help you master Visual Basic .NET programming, this book uses honest-to-goodness English explanations and explains how to use the more common features that you're likely to need when writing programs in Visual Basic .NET.

Contrary to popular belief, programming doesn't have to be difficult — it actually can be lots of fun. As a reminder to enjoy yourself, this book keeps up a spirit of playfulness. After all, that's why most people buy a computer in the first place — to have fun. (Admit the truth. Does anyone really buy a computer just to balance a budget?)

About This Book

Think of this book as a friendly guide and reference to Visual Basic .NET. Some sample topics in this book include the following:

- ✔ Saving your program
- ✔ Designing a user interface
- ✔ Creating pull-down menus
- ✔ Killing bugs in your program
- ✔ Writing large programs

Although mastering the intricate details of Visual Basic .NET can take years, you can still discover how to use Visual Basic .NET well enough to create your own programs fairly quickly. The purpose of this book is to show you all the steps you need to write a Visual Basic .NET program so you can start programming with Visual Basic .NET as soon as possible.

How to Use This Book

This book shows you step by step how to create a real-life working Windows program using Visual Basic .NET. To help you understand what may appear to be cryptic instructions, this book displays certain information using the following conventions.

All code appears in monospaced type, like this:

```
Printer.DrawWidth = Value
```

In case a line of code is too wide for the margins of this book, some long lines of code wrap to the next line. So whenever you see the underscore character at the end of a line, that means that the code really should appear on your computer as one single line:

```
Private Sub Button_Click(ByVal sender As System.Object,_
        ByVal e As System.EventArgs) Handles Button.Click
```

Visual Basic .NET doesn't care if you type everything in UPPERCASE, lower-case, or any coMBinaTioN of both. However, to make what appears on your screen match the figures in this book, use uppercase and lowercase, as shown throughout the book's examples.

When you're designing your program's user interface, you may also run across cryptic-looking tables such as:

Object	*Property*	*Setting*
Form	Name	frmHello
	Text	Hello, world!
Button	Name	btnClickMe
	Visible	True

These tables help you define the way you want your user interface to look. The Object column identifies the type of item on your user interface to modify, such as a form or button. The Property column tells you which characteristic of the object to change. The Setting column tells you what to type.

Because some people don't feel comfortable learning anything unless they get tested afterwards, this book contains several quizzes sprinkled throughout. Rather than focus on making people miserable, these multiple-choice quizzes emphasize boosting your self-esteem. All choices but one will be so outrageously wrong that choosing the right one will be easy. Not only will these questions reinforce what you need to know, but (hopefully) they'll keep you amused in the process of learning Visual Basic .NET.

Foolish Assumptions

Assuming that you already know how to turn a computer on and off and use a mouse and a keyboard — and that you want to write your own programs for fun, profit, or work (work isn't always fun or profitable) — you're ready to start finding out how to program in Visual Basic .NET.

In addition to your computer, you also should have a copy of Visual Basic .NET. In case you're still feeling self-conscious about your programming abilities, consider Albert Einstein (the famous physicist who came up with the theory of relativity). Einstein once had an elementary-school teacher who thought he was such a slow learner that he must be retarded.

Perhaps in response to this, Albert Einstein said, "Imagination is more important than knowledge." (Some people claim that Einstein also said, "If my elementary-school teacher is so smart, where is his Nobel Prize?" However, this latter statement has yet to be confirmed.)

So if you have imagination, a personal computer, and a copy of Visual Basic .NET, you're ready to get started writing programs in Visual Basic .NET.

How This Book Is Organized

This book contains eight major parts. Each part contains several chapters, and each chapter contains several modular sections. Anytime you need help, just pick up this book and start reading. Following is a breakdown of the eight parts and what you'll find in them.

Part 1: Creating a Visual Basic .NET Program

Part I contains a brief introduction to using Visual Basic .NET and writing a Visual Basic .NET program so you can see how easy, fun, and simple programming can really be.

Part II: Creating User Interfaces

This is the fun part, where you can make your user interface look as ugly or as beautiful as you want. The whole point of creating a user interface is to display information on the screen and to give users a way to communicate with your program, so this part of the book shows you how to create a user interface for your Visual Basic .NET programs.

Part III: Making Menus

Most programs offer pull-down menus to organize groups of commands in one place. If you want your program to impress your friends and influence people, this part of the book explains how to make pull-down menus for your own Visual Basic .NET creations.

Part IV: The Basics of Writing Code

This part of the book explains how to write honest-to-goodness BASIC commands that tell your computer what to do next. Although you may already know how to tell your computer what to do (using four-letter words), this is where you find out how to tell your computer what to do using the BASIC programming language.

Part V: Making Decisions and Getting Loopy

Besides showing you how to write programs that can react to different types of data, this part of the book also explains how to make your programs repeat one or more commands over and over again in something called a loop. Loops, combined with commands for making decisions, can make your program appear to act (somewhat) intelligently.

Part VI: Writing Subprograms (So You Don't Go Crazy All at Once)

Writing a short program is easy. Writing a large program can be time-consuming, intimidating, and downright troublesome even for experienced programmers. So this part of the book explains different techniques for breaking a large program up into several smaller programs, called subprograms. Theoretically, after you write a bunch of smaller programs that work, you can paste them together to create one large program that also works (also theoretically).

Part VII: Understanding Object-Oriented Programming

One of the latest techniques for writing and managing large programs is to use something called object-oriented programming. In case you don't know what it is or why you should even consider using it, this part of the book answers those questions for you so you can decide whether to use object-oriented programming techniques in your next Visual Basic .NET program.

Part VIII: The Part of Tens

This part of the book contains miscellaneous information that you may find useful and interesting, including tips about add-ons for Visual Basic and where to find more information about Visual Basic .NET programming.

Icons Used in This Book

This icon identifies technical details that are informative (and often interesting) but not necessary. Skip these sections if you want.

This icon flags useful or helpful information that can make programming more fun and less troublesome.

These gentle reminders offer important information that can reinforce what you've discovered and help make Visual Basic .NET programming easier and more enjoyable at the same time.

Be careful when you encounter this icon because it warns you of things that can ruin your day (not to mention wiping out or wrecking your program) if you're not careful.

This icon points out step-by-step instructions that explain exactly how certain Visual Basic .NET commands work.

Where to Go from Here

If you've read this far, the next step to go from here is to turn the page and keep reading. To help you master Visual Basic .NET, you may want to allocate small chunks of time every day (such as 15 minutes) to investigate Visual Basic .NET. Just sit in front of your computer, prop this book nearby, and load Visual Basic .NET so you can start experimenting right away.

Take your time learning Visual Basic .NET. It's often better to discover a little bit at a time and experiment with your newfound knowledge rather than plow through the entire book and wind up forgetting 90 percent of what you've read. Remember, the more you play with Visual Basic .NET, the more comfortable you will get and the more the various nuances of Visual Basic .NET will seem like second nature to you.

Like any skill, learning may appear to go slowly at the beginning. However, if you stick with the topic, you'll soon find that your knowledge gradually increases and learning becomes easier and more interesting at the same time. Just take your time, go at your own pace, and find as many ways as possible to use Visual Basic .NET to meet your own needs. Before you know it, you can become proficient at writing your own programs in Visual Basic .NET.

Part I
Creating a Visual Basic .NET Program

The 5th Wave   By Rich Tennant

Re'al Pro·gram·mers

Real Programmers code in pen.

In this part . . .

Writing your own program isn't hard. If you've always been curious about computer programming but were intimidated by the hard-to-read books, less-than-useful software, or obtuse and convoluted "explanations" from "experts," then this book is for you.

Rather than impress you with mathematical proofs and theoretical background about computer programming, this book (with the help of Visual Basic .NET) lets you jump right in and start finding out about programming on your own computer all by yourself. Here you will learn how Visual Basic .NET helps you create programs, how to design a user interface, and how to write BASIC code to make programs do something useful.

So grab some snack foods, a few carbonated beverages, a comfortable seat, and get ready to program your computer and make it finally do what you want it to do. . . .

Chapter 1

How Visual Basic .NET Works

*T*he whole purpose of programming is to write commands to make your computer do something useful such as print a report, calculate a budget, or launch nuclear missiles at your next-door neighbor.

In the old days, programming meant writing two sets of commands: one set to display the data on the screen (known as the user interface) and the second set to manipulate the data itself, such as adding or multiplying numbers.

Unfortunately, programming presents two difficulties for most people. First of all, most programming languages (such as C/C++) are cryptic and difficult to master. Trying to learn C/C++ can seem as alien as a native English speaker trying to read and write in Arabic or Japanese. Secondly, writing commands to create a user interface takes time away from writing commands that actually make your program do something useful.

To solve both of these problems, Microsoft developed Visual Basic .NET, which combines the BASIC programming language with the ability to create user interfaces quickly and easily. Unlike programming languages such as C/C++, the BASIC programming language is specifically designed to teach beginners how to program. As a result, you can find out how to write programs in BASIC faster than you can if you use any other programming language.

The visual part of Visual Basic .NET refers to the ability to draw your user interfaces on the screen without having to write a single command. That way, you can spend your time writing commands to make your program work and then design your user interface visually without writing a single command to do so.

Writing a Visual Basic .NET Program

The first step in writing any program is deciding what you want that program to do. When you know what you want your program to do, you have to figure out how to write commands that tell the computer how to do what you want.

There is no one correct way to write a program. Theoretically, you can write the same program in a million different ways. Two people can write a program that works exactly the same, yet that program can contain entirely different commands. The point isn't how a program is written but whether it works as it's supposed to.

Typically, programming requires three steps before you even touch a computer:

1. Decide what you want your program to do.

2. Define all the specific steps that the computer must follow to do what you want it to do. (If you want your program to calculate the value of all the office supplies you've stolen from work, you need to write commands that tell the computer how to count all your office supplies, assign a value to each item, and total the final result.)

3. Decide how your program will look on the screen.

Steps 2 and 3 are actually independent of each other. You can decide how your program will look on the screen before defining the specific steps to make your program work or vice versa.

When you know what you want your program to do, how it will accomplish this task, and what it will look like on the screen, you're ready to sit in front of your computer and actually write your program.

Deciding what you want your program to do can be the hardest and most important step in writing any program. Programming is just a matter of writing the right commands to coerce the computer into doing what you want.

Drawing a user interface

Visual Basic introduced the idea of rapid-application development (RAD), which is just a fancy term that means you can draw your user interface in much the same way that you can draw smiley faces, squiggly lines, or circles in a painting program such as Microsoft Paint.

The user interface serves two purposes: to display information and to accept commands and additional data from the user. In Visual Basic .NET, a user interface consists of two items: forms and objects (which are sometimes also called controls).

A form is nothing more than a rectangular window that appears on the screen. Objects are items that appear on a form to display or get information from the user such as text, buttons, or check boxes, as shown in Figure 1-1.

Form

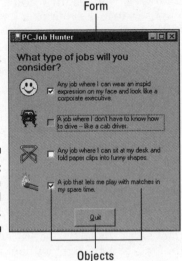

Figure 1-1:
Identifying a
form and
objects.

Objects

Not all programs need a user interface. If you're going to write a program that needs to get information from people, your program will need a user interface of some sort.

Defining properties to make your user interface unique

After you've created a form and sprinkled various objects on it, the next step is to customize that form and those objects for your particular program. In the world of Visual Basic .NET, every form and object has *properties,* which define how they look or behave. For instance, properties can control attributes such as an object's size, position on the screen, or color.

Different objects have different properties. Each time you draw a form or object on a form, Visual Basic .NET assigns your form or object with default property values. Unless you want to create a generic-looking program, you absolutely must modify some (but not all) of the properties for every form or object that you draw for your user interface.

Writing BASIC code

Unlike traditional programming languages such as C/C++, Visual Basic .NET separates your user interface from the actual commands (which programmers refer to as *code*) needed to make your program work. In the world of Visual Basic .NET, commands provide two purposes: to make your user interface work and to manipulate any data to calculate a useful result.

Once you design your user interface in Visual Basic .NET, your user interface won't do a thing until you write commands that tell it what to do if the user clicks on a button. Any time a user presses a key, moves the mouse, or clicks the mouse button, that activity is called an *event*. Whenever an event occurs, your computer frantically looks for BASIC commands to tell it how to respond, such as by displaying a dialog box, making a beeping sound, or storing data from the screen into the computer's memory.

Besides writing BASIC commands to make your user interface work, you still need to write additional BASIC commands to calculate some useful result, such as adding numbers and displaying the total on the screen.

By dividing a program into three distinct parts, Visual Basic .NET allows you to focus on getting one part of your program to work right without worrying that changing one part may interfere with another part. As a result, Visual Basic .NET can help you write even the most complicated programs faster than any other programming language in the world.

Getting to Know Visual Basic .NET

Visual Basic .NET is the latest version of Visual Basic. To understand the changes that Microsoft made to the Visual Basic language, you need to understand what Microsoft is trying to accomplish with its .NET creation in the first place.

From a programmer's point of view, hundreds of different programming languages exist to solve a variety of different tasks. Yet most programs are still written using a single programming language such as C or BASIC. One big problem is that programming languages aren't designed to work together.

Even programming languages from the same company, such as Microsoft, had problems working together. Trying to write a program in older versions of both Visual C++ and Visual Basic was often an exercise in frustration because both languages save data, such as strings and numbers, differently. Because trying to discover all the particular ways each programming language saves and manipulates strings and numbers can be tedious, most programmers simply wrote programs using a single programming language, even when a second programming language may be better suited for solving a particular problem.

So Microsoft invented something called the .NET framework, which acts as an intermediary layer sandwiched in between the operating system and any programs that you write. This manages to solve two major problems simultaneously.

The first problem the .NET framework solves is getting different programming languages to cooperate with one another. Instead of allowing each programming language direct access to the computer's operating system (where they might store strings and numbers in different ways), the .NET framework forces all programming languages (which are designed to work with the .NET, that is, Visual Basic .NET) to store strings and numbers in exactly the same way. That way, you can write a single program using a variety of different languages without worrying that one programming language may store and handle data differently than another programming language.

A second problem the .NET solves involves program distribution. Currently most people run programs stored on their hard disks. However the .NET will allow programs to run over the Internet or a network, which Microsoft has dubbed "Software as a service." The idea is that you store one copy of a program on a single computer and allow multiple computers to run that one program through the Internet or local area network (LAN). Now if you want to update a program, you just have to update the program on a single computer instead of updating it on multiple computers scattered throughout a corporate office. Best of all, any Internet programs you create with the .NET can sport fancy graphical user interfaces just like ordinary desktop programs.

Once you write a program that works with the .NET framework, your program will (theoretically) run on any other computer that also uses the .NET framework. At the time of this writing, the only operating system that supports the .NET framework is Microsoft Windows, but if Microsoft (or someone else) eventually ports the .NET framework to other operating systems such as Linux or the Macintosh, you will be able to write a Visual Basic .NET program and run it on different operating systems.

Knowing the Drawbacks of the .NET

Knowing that every computer crashes periodically should have already taught you that applying more technology will rarely solve today's technological woes. So although the promises of the .NET framework may sound wonderful, don't be seduced by the marketing hype from Microsoft.

The .NET framework itself is software, which means it's prone to all sorts of bugs and glitches that make using a computer such a frustrating experience in the first place. Even worse is that the .NET framework is only available for newer versions of Windows, such as Windows XP. If you want to write a program to run on older versions of Windows such as Windows 95 (or non-Windows operating systems such as Macintosh or Linux), you can't use the .NET framework or any programming languages that use the .NET such as Visual Basic .NET. (To write programs for older versions of Windows, you'll have to use an older version of Visual Basic such as Visual Basic 6.0.)

Another problem is that not all programming languages work with the .NET. Microsoft provides Visual C++, Visual Basic, and C# (their own updated version of C++) for the .NET framework, but they're relying on outside companies to develop other programming languages to work with the .NET. If your favorite programming language can't work with the .NET, you won't be able to work with the .NET framework either.

For programmers already familiar with Visual Basic, the biggest drawback of the .NET is that Microsoft changed the Visual Basic language fairly drastically to make Visual Basic .NET handle numbers and strings in the same way that the C++ language does. This means that any programs you've already written in Visual Basic 6.0 or earlier may not be able to run on the .NET (or Visual Basic .NET) without extensive modification.

So if you're going to use Visual Basic .NET, be aware of its limitations. In exchange for the ability to coexist peacefully with other programming languages such as Visual C++, you sacrifice backwards compatibility with older versions of Visual Basic. Despite these problems, Visual Basic .NET is still a fast and easy way to create professional-quality programs in the shortest amount of time possible.

Chapter 2

Using the Visual Basic .NET User Interface

. . . .

In This Chapter

▶ Loading Visual Basic .NET

▶ Getting to know the Visual Basic .NET user interface

▶ Opening, closing, and moving windows around

▶ Quitting Visual Basic .NET

. . . .

*T*he first step to writing programs using Visual Basic .NET is to understand how to use its user interface, which consists of commands buried inside pull-down menus, windows that pop up around the screen to show you different information about your program, and toolbars that display icons representing the more common commands you need to write a Visual Basic .NET program.

(In the world of Visual Basic .NET, writing a Visual Basic .NET program means creating a *project*. A project consists of one or more files stored in a separate folder. Each time you create another project, Visual Basic .NET creates a new folder to store all your files. That way, you can make sure files belonging to one project don't accidentally get mixed up with files belonging to another project.)

To use Visual Basic .NET, you need to know the following three functions:

> ✔ How to load Visual Basic .NET
>
> ✔ How to use Visual Basic .NET to write your own programs
>
> ✔ How to exit out of Visual Basic .NET

Loading Visual Basic .NET

To load Visual Basic .NET, just follow these simple steps:

1. **Click on the Start button of the Windows taskbar.**

   A pop-up menu appears.

2. **Click on Programs, click on the Microsoft Visual Studio.NET, and then click on Microsoft Visual Studio.NET.**

   Visual Basic .NET displays a Start Page window, as shown in Figure 2-1.

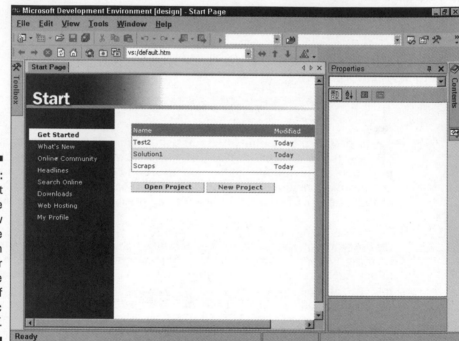

Figure 2-1: The Start Page window is where you can create or customize your copy of Visual Basic .NET.

When the Start Page appears, you can:

✔ Create a brand new project (in case you want to create a new program).

✔ Load an existing project (so you can modify a program you already created).

✔ Customize the user interface of Visual Basic .NET

Starting a new project

In the world of Visual Basic .NET, a *project* describes a collection of one or more files that work together to create a single program.

To create a new Visual Basic .NET project:

1. **Choose one of the following methods:**

   • Click on the New Project button on the Start Page.

   • Choose File⇨New⇨Project.

   • Press Ctrl+Shift+N.

   No matter which method you use, Visual Basic .NET displays the New Project dialog box, as shown in Figure 2-2.

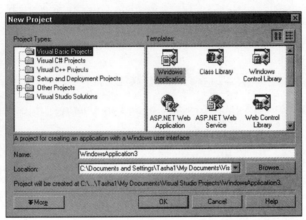

Figure 2-2:
The New
Project
dialog box
gives you
different
options for
creating a
Visual Basic
.NET
program.

2. **Click on the Visual Basic Projects folder in the Project Types box.**

   A list of different Visual Basic .NET templates appears in the Templates pane.

3. **Click on the template that you want to use for creating your Visual Basic .NET program.**

   For practicing with this book, click on the Windows Application template.

   Creating an ASP.NET Web Service or Windows Control Library is fairly advanced, so don't worry about such files until you figure out how to create a simple (Windows Application) Visual Basic .NET program first.

4. **Click in the Name box and type a name for your project.**

   You can skip Steps 5–7 if you don't want to specify a folder to store your new project.

5. **Click on the Browse button.**

   A Project Location dialog box appears.

6. **Click on the folder where you want to store your newly created Visual Basic .NET project.**

   Besides storing your project in an existing folder, you can also create a new folder in which to store your project.

7. **Click Open.**

   The New Project dialog box appears again.

8. **Click OK.**

   Visual Basic .NET displays a blank form so you can start drawing the user interface for your program.

Loading an existing project

Most of the time you are going to want to load an existing project so you can modify it. To load an existing project:

1. **Choose one of the following methods:**

   • Click on the Open Project button on the Start Page.

   • Choose File⇨Open ⇨Project.

   • Press Ctrl+Shift+O.

   No matter which method you use, Visual Basic .NET displays the Open Project dialog box.

2. **Double-click on the folder containing the project you want to open.**

   A list of files that make up your project appears.

3. **Click on the project file that you want to open.**

   When you move the mouse pointer over each file, a tiny window appears, listing the type of file you're pointing at such as Visual Basic .NET Project file.

4. **Click Open.**

   At this point, you're ready to start modifying your Visual Basic .NET project.

To speed up the process of opening an existing project, Visual Basic .NET offers these two options:

✔ The Start Page displays your most recently saved projects. Just click on the project name you want to load and Visual Basic .NET kindly opens that project for you.

✔ Choose File⇨Recent Projects to list the last projects you've opened. Just click on the project name that you want to load and your project magically appears on the screen.

Welcome to the Visual Basic .NET User Interface

Whether you create a new project or open an existing one, you still must face the task of using the Visual Basic .NET user interface. The main parts of the Visual Basic .NET user interface appear in Figure 2-3, although all parts may not be visible at any given time.

✔ **Pull-down menus:** Provide access to every available Visual Basic .NET command, although these menus can be confusing and intimidating to use.

✔ **Toolbars:** Display icons that represent the most commonly used Visual Basic .NET commands — which may still be confusing and intimidating to use.

✔ **Form:** Provides a window where you can draw objects to design your program's user interface.

✔ **Solution Explorer window:** Displays all the files that make up your Visual Basic .NET project.

✔ **Toolbox:** Displays the types of objects (such as a command button or check box) that you can draw on a form.

✔ **Properties window:** Displays the properties of the currently selected form or object.

✔ **Design tab:** Displays forms so you can design your program's user interface.

✔ **Code tab:** Displays the code window so you can write BASIC code, as shown in Figure 2-4.

Toolbars   Design tab

Toolbox   Pull-down menus   Code tab   Solution Explorer window

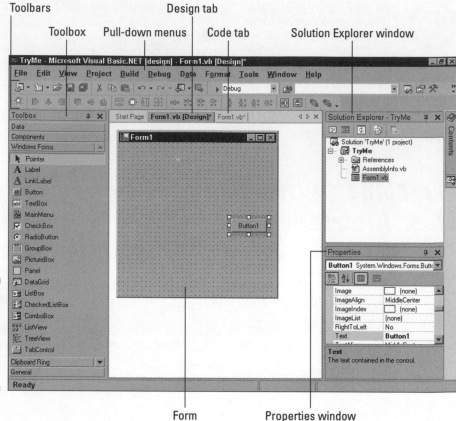

Figure 2-3:
Common
parts of the
Visual Basic
.NET user
interface.

Form   Properties window

If an asterisk (*) appears on the Design or Code tab, you haven't saved your work yet.

When you're designing your user interface, you use the Toolbox to draw objects on a form. After you draw your objects, the next step is to customize the appearance of each object by using the Properties window. Finally, when you're happy with the way your user interface works, you can switch to the code window to write BASIC commands to make your user interface actually work.

Figure 2-4:
By clicking
on the Code
tab, you can
view and
edit the
BASIC code
that makes
that form's
user
interface
objects
(buttons,
check
boxes, and
so on) work.

Manipulating your windows

Visual Basic .NET gives you three ways to display windows on the screen, as shown in Figure 2-5:

- ✔ **Floating:** Windows appear like disembodied heads that can appear anywhere on the screen.

- ✔ **Dockable:** Windows appear smashed along the top, bottom, or sides of the screen.

- ✔ **Auto hide:** Windows automatically tuck themselves out of view as soon as you move the mouse pointer off the window.

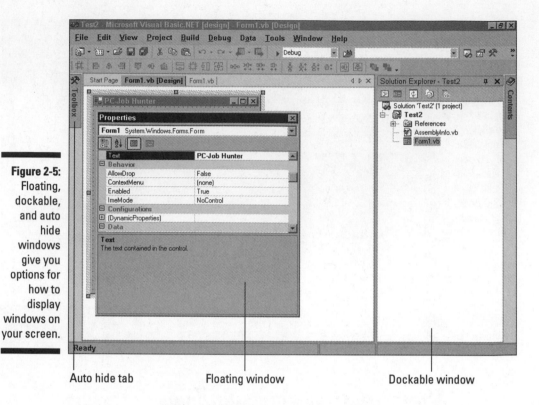

Figure 2-5:
Floating, dockable, and auto hide windows give you options for how to display windows on your screen.

Auto hide tab   Floating window   Dockable window

Making a floating window

To turn any window into a floating window, follow these steps:

1. **Open the window you want to view by choosing View and then the window name (such as Properties Window or Solution Explorer).**

   Your chosen window appears.

2. **Move the mouse pointer over the title bar of the window, hold down the left mouse button, and drag the mouse to the middle of the screen.**

   Visual Basic .NET displays the gray outlines of your window so you can see its position on the screen.

3. **Release the left mouse button.**

   Congratulations! You've just created a floating window.

If you double-click on the title bar of a floating window, you can instantly dock it to one side of the screen.

Making a dockable window

To turn any window into a dockable window, follow these steps:

1. **Open the window you want to view by choosing View and then the window name (such as Solution Explorer or Toolbox).**

   Your chosen window appears.

2. **Move the mouse pointer over the title bar of the window, hold down the left mouse button, and drag the mouse to any side of the screen.**

   Visual Basic .NET displays the gray outlines of your window so you can see its position on the screen.

3. **Release the left mouse button when the gray outline of the window appears to "snap" into place.**

   You've just created a dockable window.

If you double-click on the title bar of a dockable window, you can turn it into a floating window that appears in the middle of the screen.

Auto hiding a window

Auto hiding temporarily tucks a window out of sight and displays the window as a tab that appears on one side of the screen. When you want to view the window, move the mouse over the tab and Visual Basic .NET magically "slides" your window from the side and in full view so you can see it again.

To auto hide a window, follow these steps:

1. **Follow Steps 1 and 2 in the previous section "Making a dockable window."**

   When your chosen window appears docked to one side of the screen, the Auto Hide (a pushpin) icon appears in the window's upper-right corner.

2. **Click on the Auto Hide icon.**

   Visual Basic .NET displays your window as a tab on one side of the screen.

3. **Move the mouse pointer over this tab to display your window at any time.**

You can auto hide all your dockable windows (but not floating windows) by choosing Window⇨Auto Hide All.

Closing a window

Whenever you want to close a window completely, click on its Close box.

Quitting Visual Basic .NET

No matter how much you may love using Visual Basic .NET, eventually you need to turn off the computer and go to sleep (or at least pass out on the keyboard for an hour or two). To exit Visual Basic .NET, use one of these three methods:

- ✔ Choose File➪Exit.
- ✔ Press Alt+F4.
- ✔ Click on the Close box of the Visual Basic .NET user interface window.

If you haven't saved the currently displayed Visual Basic .NET program, Visual Basic .NET displays a dialog box, giving you one last chance to save your work before your work is gone for good. Just click on Yes to save your work (or No to lose any changes you have made since the last time you saved the file).

As long as your computer hasn't crashed, Visual Basic .NET smoothly exits and dumps you back to the Windows desktop.

Chapter 3

Designing Your First User Interface

. . . .

In This Chapter

▶ Understanding the common parts of a user interface

▶ Drawing a user interface

▶ Changing the properties of a user interface

. . . .

The user interface displays information on the screen and accepts data from the user. Make your user interface easy to understand, and your program will appear easy to use. Make your user interface complicated and hard to understand, and you can often sell your program to others and prompt publishers to produce 500-page books to explain how "easy" your program is to use.

To give you a quick introduction to the power of Visual Basic .NET, this chapter (along with Chapter 5) guides you through the fundamental steps to creating a user interface:

⌨ Drawing the user interface

⌨ Defining the user interface properties

⌨ Writing BASIC code to make your user interface work (which Chapter 4 explains)

Common Parts of a User Interface

A standard user interface consists of a window that displays text or pictures. A window can fill the entire screen or just part of it. Two or more windows can appear on the screen at the same time, overlapping like cards or side by side like tiles. In the world of Visual Basic .NET programming, a window is called a *form*.

When you first create a form, it's entirely blank. To make your form useful, you have to draw objects on it. An *object* can be a button, text box, picture, or radio button. People can then communicate with your program by clicking, typing, or manipulating the objects displayed on a form.

Drawing objects with the Toolbox

To draw objects on a form, you need to use the Toolbox, which normally appears on the left side of the screen (unless you move it somewhere else). The Toolbox contains icons along with descriptive names (such as Button) to identify the different types of objects you can draw on a form, as shown in Figure 3-1.

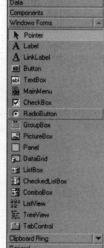

Figure 3-1:
The Toolbox
contains all
the different
types of
objects you
can draw on
a form.

To draw any object on a form, you always have to follow these steps:

1. **Click on the object in the Toolbox to tell Visual Basic what you want to draw on a form, such as a command button or a check box.**

2. **Move the mouse pointer onto the form where you want to draw the object.**

3. **Hold down the left mouse button and drag the mouse to draw your chosen object on the form.**

If you double-click an object (such as Button or TextBox) in the Toolbox, Visual Basic .NET draws your chosen object on the currently displayed form automatically.

Drawing your first user interface

To get acquainted with Visual Basic .NET right away, the following are some steps you can use to create a real-life user interface:

1. **Start Microsoft Visual Basic .NET and then choose File⇔New⇔Project.**

   Visual Basic .NET displays a New Project dialog box, asking you what type of program you want to create.

2. **Click on the Windows Application icon.**

3. **Click in the Name box, type** Hello, **and click OK.**

   Visual Basic .NET displays a blank form titled Form1.

4. **Move the mouse cursor over the bottom-right corner of the form (directly over the small rectangle, called a handle, that appears in the corner of the right edge) so the mouse cursor turns into a left- and right-pointing arrow. Hold down the left mouse button and drag the mouse to resize the form.**

5. **Choose View⇔Toolbox to make the Toolbox appear on the left side of the screen.**

   (Skip this step if the Toolbox is visible already.)

6. **Click on the Button icon in the Toolbox.**

7. **Move the mouse over the form and then drag the mouse to draw a button (see Figure 3-2).**

   Don't worry about the exact placement of objects on the form. Just try to make it look somewhat similar to what you see in Figures 3-2, 3-3, and 3-4.

8. **Click on the PictureBox icon in the Toolbox and draw a picture box.**

   Repeat this process two more times to draw three picture boxes. Figure 3-3 shows how the three picture boxes should be placed on the form. (Note that Figure 3-3 shows all three picture boxes highlighted to make them easier to see. Your screen won't look this way unless you select all three picture boxes.)

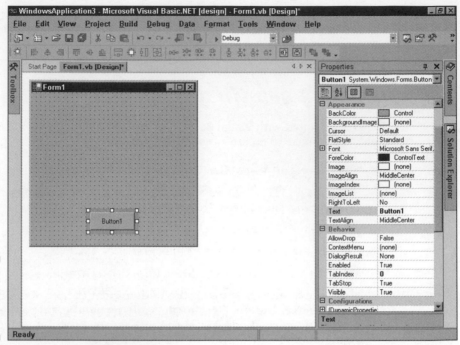

Figure 3-2:
Drawing a button on a form.

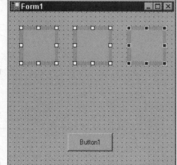

Figure 3-3:
Drawing picture boxes on a form.

9. **Click on the Label icon and draw a label on the form (see Figure 3-4).**

10. **Choose File⇨Save All.**

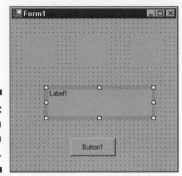

Figure 3-4:
Drawing a
label on a
form.

11. **Press F5 (or choose Debug⇨Start).**

    Visual Basic .NET runs your program so you can see what your user
    interface looks like. Because you haven't modified any properties of
    your user interface, your user interface looks pretty dull and boring
    right about now. The next section, "Defining the Properties of Your User
    Interface," explains how to make your user interface more presentable.

12. **Click the Close box on your form (named Form1).**

    Visual Basic .NET stops running your program. At this point you can
    start modifying your program once more.

Defining the Properties of Your User Interface

Drawing your user interface creates the initial appearance of your Visual
Basic .NET program. To finish defining your program's user interface, you
need to define the properties for each object on your user interface as well.

While each object typically has multiple properties that you can change, you
don't have to modify every single property. Most of the time, you just need to
modify two or three properties of each object.

What properties do

Properties define the characteristics of an object such as its location, size,
shape, and color on the screen. Because most objects have dozens of different properties you can modify, Microsoft conveniently organizes properties
into different categories, as shown in Figure 3-5.

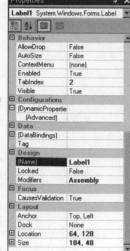

Figure 3-5:
The
Properties
window
organizes
properties
into
different
categories.

Each object may display different categories. Some of the more common property categories include:

- **Appearance:** Defines colors, alignment, and text that appear on the object.

- **Behavior:** Defines the way the object behaves when the user clicks the mouse or presses a key.

- **Data:** Links the object to information stored in a database.

- **Design:** Defines the object's name, whether it can be moved or not, and the visibility of this object to other parts of your program.

- **Focus:** Defines how the object acts when the user chooses it.

- **Layout:** Defines the object's size and location on the screen.

One property that you will almost always change will be the Name property, located in the Design category in the Properties window. Visual Basic .NET automatically gives all objects boring names like Text1 or Button3. However, when you need to refer to specific objects, it's much easier if you have descriptive names for each object.

Changing property settings

You can change the property settings of an object at two separate times:

- During design time
- During run time

Design time is when you're drawing your user interface but before you actually run your program. Changing an object's properties at design time allows you to define the initial size, color, or position of an object.

Most of the time, you want to change an object's property settings at design time. The most important property to change at design time is the Name property of the object.

Run time is when your program uses BASIC code to change an object's properties while your program is actually running. Changing an object's property during run time allows you to change an object while the user is running your program, such as displaying a message on the screen or moving an object to another part of the screen.

Changing property settings at design time

To change the property of an object at design time, just follow these simple steps:

1. **Click on the object whose properties you want to change, such as a button or a form.**

2. **Open the Properties window and click on the property that you want to change.**

    If the Properties window isn't visible, press F4 to make it appear.

3. **Type or choose a new setting for the property.**

Simple, don't you think? As you are working through the examples in this book, you will often need to make changes to object properties. When you need to change multiple properties for one or more objects, this book displays a table similar to the following:

Object	Property	Setting
Form	Text	Hello, world!

The following steps explain what this table is telling you to do:

1. **Click on the form object.**

2. **Click on the Text property in the Properties window.**

3. **Type** Hello, world! **in the Text property.**

Test your newfound knowledge

1. What are the two common parts of almost every user interface?

   a. The easy-to-use interface and the 500-page manual that explains how easy the interface is to use

   b. Menus that nobody can understand and commands that nobody can use

   c. Useless icons that don't make any sense and text that doesn't explain anything

   d. Forms and objects

2. How can you change property settings of an object?

   a. You can't. Property settings have to want to change first.

   b. Use constant threat and intimidation.

   c. Use the Properties window while designing the user interface (known as design time) or write BASIC code to change the properties while the program is running (known as run time).

   d. Stick a magnet next to your monitor and watch the images warp and wreck your computer screen.

Defining the properties of your first user interface

To define the properties of your user interface, follow these steps:

1. **Load Microsoft Visual Basic .NET. (Skip this step if Visual Basic .NET is already running.)**

   This displays the Start Page.

2. **Choose File⇨Recent Projects⇨Hello.sln.**

   In Step 3 of the previous section "Drawing your first user interface," you named your project Hello. If you chose a different name during that step, you will need to choose that name from Step 2 above. Depending on where you stored your project, the Hello.sln file may be buried underneath several folders such as C:\...Visual Studio Projects\Hello\ Hello.sln.

3. **Click on the picture box in the upper-left corner of the form.**

4. **Press F4 to open the Properties window.**

5. **Double-click on the Name property (in the Design category) and type** picSmile.

6. **Click on the Image property (in the Appearance category).**

   A gray button with three dots (. . .) appears.

7. **Click on the gray button with the three dots (. . .).**

   An Open dialog box appears.

8. **Open the Icons folder. (Visual Basic .NET usually buries the Icons folder within the Programs\Microsoft Visual Studio.NET\ Common7\Graphics folder.)**

9. **Click on the Misc folder within the Icons folder.**

   Visual Basic .NET displays the icons stored in the Misc folder.

10. **Click on the FACE02 icon and click Open.**

    Visual Basic .NET displays a smiley face in the picture box. At this point, the smiley face appears as a tiny image.

11. **Click on the SizeMode property (in the Behavior category), click on the downward-pointing arrow and choose StretchImage.**

    Visual Basic .NET makes the smiley face expand to fit the entire size of the picture box.

12. **Click on the Label1 label.**

13. **Click on the BorderStyle property (in the Appearance category), click on the downward-pointing arrow, and choose Fixed3D.**

    Visual Basic .NET displays your label with a 3-D visual effect.

14. **Double-click on the Name property (in the Design category) and type** lblMessage.

15. **Double-click on the Text property (in the Appearance category) and press Backspace to clear the Text property so no text appears.**

16. **Finish changing the properties for the rest of the objects according to Table 3-1.**

17. **Choose File⇨Save All, or press Ctrl+Shift+S.**

Congratulations! You just defined all the necessary properties for your first user interface. By the time you finish defining all the properties, your user interface should look like Figure 3-6.

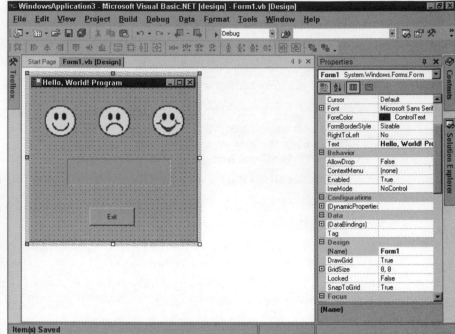

Figure 3-6:
The completed user interface with all the necessary properties defined.

Table 3-1	Properties to Change to Finish Designing Your User Interface	
Object	**Property**	**Setting**
Form	Text	Hello, World! Program
PictureBox2	Name	picFrown
	Image	FACE04
	SizeMode	StretchImage
PictureBox3	Name	picHappy
	Image	FACE03
	SizeMode	StretchImage
Button1	Name	btnExit
	Text	Exit

Chapter 4

Writing BASIC Code

• •

In This Chapter

▶ Finding out what BASIC code can do

▶ Writing an event-handling procedure

▶ Writing BASIC code for your program

• •

To have your computer do anything, you have to give it step-by-step instructions. If you skip a step or give unclear instructions, your computer doesn't know what to do. (Actually, the computer knows what to do — it just won't do what you want it to.)

Programmers call a single instruction a *command*. A typical BASIC command looks like the following:

```
Taxes = Income * FlatTaxRate
```

Programmers refer to a series of commands as *code*. If you want to speak the language of programmers (even though programmers are notorious for never saying much of anything), you have to know programming etiquette.

You never write a program; you write code. Heaven forbid if you say, "Let me look at your series of commands." Cool programmers are likely to blush at your faux pas. Instead, you ought to say, "Let me look at your code."

The following is a typical example of code:

```
Income = 90000
FlatTaxRate = .95
Taxes = Income * FlatTaxRate
```

A collection of code that makes your computer do something useful (such as play a game, calculate your taxes, or display flying toasters on your screen) is called a *program*.

What Is BASIC Code?

To get your computer to do anything, you have to give it instructions that it can understand. Because you're using Visual Basic .NET, any commands you give the computer must be written using the BASIC programming language.

Like all computer languages, BASIC has special commands called reserved keywords. Some examples of reserved keywords are as follows:

Loop	Function	Sub	End
Do	Integer	Case	If
Else	Select	Then	For

BASIC code consists of nothing more than BASIC reserved keywords creatively strung together to form a program. Whenever the computer sees a reserved keyword, it automatically thinks, "Oh, this is a special instruction that I already know how to obey."

A program can be as short as a single reserved keyword or as long as several million reserved keywords. Short programs generally don't do anything more interesting than display something such as Hello, world! on the screen. Long programs usually do much more, but these programs are often as confusing to read as an IRS tax form.

Theoretically, you can write one long program consisting of a million or more reserved keywords. However, any programmer attempting to do so is likely to go insane long before completing the task.

To make programming easier, most programmers divide a large program into several smaller ones that (hopefully) work together. In the world of Visual Basic .NET, a program typically consists of three distinct parts, as shown in Figure 4-1:

- **The user interface:** Gets stored in a file with the extension .VB, such as GAME.VB. (You don't need to write any BASIC code to design your user interface.)

- **Event-handling procedures (also called event handlers):** Get stored in the same file as your user interface file. (Event-handling procedures contain BASIC code to display information and retrieve data from the user interface.)

- **Module and class files:** Contain BASIC code to calculate or manipulate any data retrieved from the user interface. Visual Basic .NET stores module and class files with the .VB file extension.

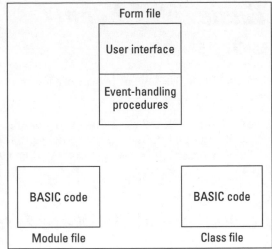

Form file

User interface

Event-handling procedures

BASIC code

Module file

BASIC code

Class file

Figure 4-1:
The typical parts of a Visual Basic .NET program.

Module files contain BASIC code called general procedures, which are explained in Part VI of the book. Programs don't necessarily have to use module or class files, but using them can help organize related BASIC code together.

You don't have to use module or class files; you can always store your BASIC code that manipulates data in your user interface files. However, cramming both BASIC code to make your user interface work and to manipulate your data can make your program harder to read, understand, and modify later on.

Most programs will use multiple forms so you may want to store BASIC code in a form file if that BASIC code is only useful to that form. Then if you have BASIC code that can be used by two or more forms, store that BASIC code in a module or class file.

The rest of this chapter explains how to create event-handling procedures. A typical event procedure may tell the computer what to do if the user clicks on an object, such as a button, with the mouse or if the user presses a certain key while an object, such as a check box, is highlighted.

Not every object needs event-handling procedures. The only objects that need event-handling procedures are those that the user can click on or choose in some way, such as buttons or check boxes. For more information about event-handling procedures, refer to Part IV of the book.

Writing Visual Basic .NET Event-Handling Procedures

Before you can write a Visual Basic .NET event procedure for an object, you have to draw the object on a form first.

Next, you have to change the properties of each object to give them unique names you can remember. If you don't do this, you're stuck with the generic names that Visual Basic .NET provides by default for everything, such as RadioButton1 or TextBox3.

Creating an event-handling procedure the fast way

Many objects, such as a button or check box, need to respond to the user clicking on them. To make these objects respond to the user, you need to write BASIC code. For example, the most common event that a button needs to respond to is an event called the Click event, which occurs whenever the user clicks on that particular button.

To create an event-handling procedure for responding to the most common event for a particular object, follow these steps:

1. **Display the form that contains the objects that need BASIC code to make them respond to the user.**

   To display a form, you can choose View➪Designer, press Shift+F7, or click on the Design tab. If you still can't see your form, choose View➪Solution Explorer and double-click on the form that you want to view. Visual Basic .NET displays your chosen form.

   When Visual Basic .NET displays a form, this is called the *Design View*.

2. **Double-click on the object that you want to write an event procedure.**

   If you want to write an event-handling procedure for a button, double-click on that button. Visual Basic .NET displays an empty event-handling procedure that looks something like the following:

```
Protected Sub Button1_Click(ByVal sender As Object,_
        ByVal e As System.EventArgs)

End Sub
```

When Visual Basic .NET displays BASIC code, this is called the *Code View*. At this point, don't worry about the garbage that appears in parentheses.

3. Write any BASIC code you want for your event-handling procedure, sandwiched between the first and last lines, such as:

```
Protected Sub Button1_Click(ByVal sender As Object,_
        ByVal e As System.EventArgs)
    Me.Close ()
End Sub
```

Creating an event-handling procedure the slower way

Each time you draw an object on a form (your user interface), Visual Basic .NET stores the name of that object in a list called the Class Name list, as shown in Figure 4-2.

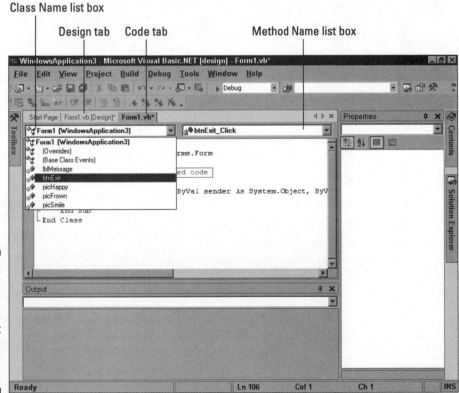

Figure 4-2: Choosing an object from the Class Name list box in the code window.

To create an event procedure for an object, you have to tell Visual Basic

- ✔ The name of the object to use
- ✔ The event you want the object to respond to

To choose the name of the object to use and the event that you want the object to respond to, follow these steps:

1. **Switch to the Code View.**

   To switch to the Code View, choose View➪Code, press F7, or click on the Code tab. Visual Basic displays the BASIC code that makes your user interface work.

2. **Click in the Class Name list box and click on the object for which you want to write an event-handling procedure.**

   If you want to write an event-handling procedure for a button, click on that button's name in the Class Name list.

If you write an event-handling procedure for an object and then later change that object's name, Visual Basic .NET gets confused and thinks that you've created a brand-new object, which means that the renamed object won't have any event-handling procedures attached to it. So rename all objects before writing any event-handling procedures for that object.

Test your newfound knowledge

1. What are reserved keywords?

   a. Words you say when you have a reservation in a fancy restaurant where water costs $25 a glass.

   b. What shy people want to say.

   c. Special instructions that every programming language has.

   d. Words that you want to say to the face of someone you don't like.

2. What do event-handling procedures do?

   a. They tell the computer when an upcoming event, like a concert or baseball game, is coming to town.

   b. They wipe out all the data stored on the hard disk to punish the user for not knowing more about computers.

   c. You mean I was actually supposed to pay attention to this chapter?

   d. They tell an object on your user interface how to respond to a particular event such as a mouse click.

3. **Click in the Method Name list box and click on the event that you want your object to respond to such as Click or CheckChanged.**

   Visual Basic .NET creates an empty event-handling procedure.

4. **Write any BASIC code you want for your event-handling procedure.**

What can BASIC code do?

After you've created an empty event-handling procedure, you need to fill it with BASIC commands to make the event-handling procedure do something. BASIC code is generally used to do the following:

- Calculate a result
- Modify the properties (appearance) of another object on the user interface

If you want to calculate the number of people who live in wooden cabins, subscribe to *Soldier of Fortune,* and own cats, Visual Basic .NET can calculate this if you provide all the necessary data. An example of a BASIC calculation might be the following:

```
PayThis = 5000 * 0.5
```

After you calculate a result, you probably want to show the result on the screen. To do so, you have to modify the properties of an object (such as a text box or label) on your user interface. For example, if you want to display a message on the screen, you first need to draw a text box object on a Visual Basic .NET form.

You then have to name this text box with something such as txtMessage. Finally, to display anything in this text box, you have to modify the Text property of the txtMessage text box, such as:

```
txtMessage.Text = "Display Me!"
```

This command displays the message Display Me! in the txtMessage text box on the screen. This is equivalent to modifying the Text property of the txtMessage text box at design time, as shown in Figure 4-3.

BASIC code can't change all the properties of an object. You can change some properties (such as the Name property) only during design time using the Properties window.

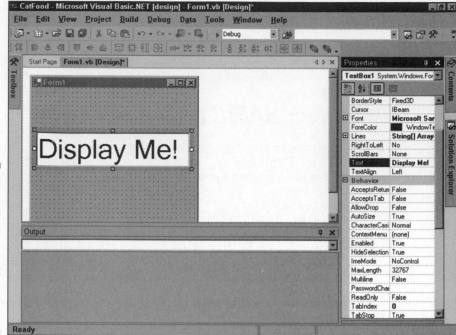

Figure 4-3:
When you
modify the
properties
of an object,
you change
the way it
appears on
the user
interface.

How Visual Basic .NET event-handling procedures work

The instructions in an event-handling procedure run only when a specific event occurs, such as when the user clicks on an object. The same set of instructions can run over and over again each time the user clicks on an object. The only time a Visual Basic .NET program ends is when an object's event-handling procedure specifically tells the program to end.

To stop your Visual Basic .NET program from running, you need to include an event-handling procedure that looks like the following:

```
Protected Sub Button1_Click(ByVal sender As Object, ByVal_
          e As System.EventArgs)
  Me.Close()
End Sub
```

As soon as the user clicks on the Button1 object, this is what the computer does:

1. Visual Basic .NET asks, "Hey, what's the name of this object that the user just clicked?"

2. In a huff, Visual Basic .NET quickly notices that the object that the user clicked on is named Button1.

3. Thinking quickly, Visual Basic .NET asks, "Are there any instructions here that tell me what to do if the user clicks on the Button1 object?" Happily, Visual Basic .NET finds the `Protected Sub Button1_Click()` event-handling procedure that contains instructions to follow the moment the user clicks on the Button1 object.

4. Visual Basic .NET examines the first instruction of the `Button1_Click()` event-handling procedure. In this case, the only instruction is `Me.Close()`, which tells Visual Basic .NET to close the form identified by the Me keyword, which is the currently displayed form. When your Visual Basic .NET program closes all its forms, the program stops running.

5. Visual Basic .NET stops running the program and removes it from the screen and memory. Naturally, all this happens in the blink of an eye, and your computer looks as though it's responding instantly.

Writing BASIC Code for Your First Visual Basic .NET Program

Because experience is always the best teacher, the following steps show you how to write real-life BASIC code that you can use to impress your friends. The following steps explain how to write BASIC code for the Visual Basic .NET program you created in Chapter 3.

Don't worry about understanding everything you're typing. The purpose of this exercise is just to show you how simple creating a program in Visual Basic .NET can be.

1. **Start Microsoft Visual Basic .NET if you haven't already done so. (Or choose File➪Open➪Project if Visual Basic .NET is already running.)**

   Visual Basic .NET displays an Open Project dialog box.

2. **Click on the Hello Visual Basic .NET Project, and click on Open.**

   (You can skip this step if you already have the form displayed on the screen from Chapter 3.)

3. **Double-click on the smiley face icon in the upper left-hand corner.**

   Visual Basic .NET displays an empty event-handling procedure for the picSmile picture box.

4. **Type in the following** `picSmile_Click` **event-handling procedure:**

```
Private Sub picSmile_Click(ByVal sender As_
        System.Object, ByVal e As System.EventArgs)_
        Handles picSmile.Click
    picSmile.BorderStyle =_
        System.Windows.Forms.BorderStyle.FixedSingle
    picFrown.BorderStyle =_
        System.Windows.Forms.BorderStyle.None
    picHappy.BorderStyle =_
        System.Windows.Forms.BorderStyle.None
    lblMessage.Text = "Hello, world!"
End Sub
```

To save time and typing, Visual Basic .NET displays a pop-up list of acceptable commands, as shown in Figure 4-4, that you can use while writing BASIC code. So rather than type everything yourself, you can just highlight the command you want to use and Visual Basic .NET types it in your BASIC code automatically.

Figure 4-4:
Pop-up
lists of
acceptable
commands
appear as
you type
BASIC
code.

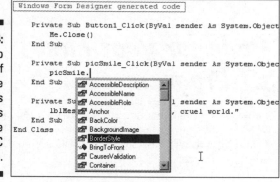

5. **Click on the Design tab, choose View⇨Designer, or press Shift+F7 to view your form.**

6. **Double-click on the picFrown picture box. (This is the picture box in the middle.)**

   Visual Basic .NET displays an empty `picFrown` event-handling procedure.

7. **Type in the following** `picFrown` **event-handling procedure:**

```
Private Sub picFrown_Click(ByVal sender As_
        System.Object, ByVal e As System.EventArgs)_
        Handles picFrown.Click
  picSmile.BorderStyle =_
        System.Windows.Forms.BorderStyle.None
  picFrown.BorderStyle =_
        System.Windows.Forms.BorderStyle.FixedSingle
  picHappy.BorderStyle =_
        System.Windows.Forms.BorderStyle.None
  lblMessage.Text = "Good-bye, cruel world!"
End Sub
```

8. **Click on the Design tab, choose View⇨Designer, or press Shift+F7 to view your form.**

9. **Double-click on the picHappy picture box. (This is the picture box that appears in the upper-right corner.)**

   Visual Basic displays an empty `picHappy` event-handling procedure.

10. **Type in the following** `picHappy` **event-handling procedure:**

```
Private Sub picHappy_Click(ByVal sender As_
        System.Object, ByVal e As System.EventArgs)_
        Handles picHappy.Click
  picSmile.BorderStyle =_
        System.Windows.Forms.BorderStyle.None
  picFrown.BorderStyle =_
        System.Windows.Forms.BorderStyle.None
  picHappy.BorderStyle =_
        System.Windows.Forms.BorderStyle.FixedSingle
  lblMessage.Text = "I'm going to DisneyWorld!"
End Sub
```

11. **Click on the Design tab, choose View⇨Designer, or press Shift+F7 to view your form.**

12. **Double-click on the btnExit button. (This is the button that says "Exit.")**

    Visual Basic .NET displays an empty `btnExit` event-handling procedure.

13. **Type in the following** `btnExit` **event-handling procedure:**

```
Protected Sub btnExit_Click(ByVal sender As_
        System.Object, ByVal e As System.EventArgs)_
        Handles btnExit.Click
  Me.Close()
End Sub
```

14. Press F5 to run your program, or choose Debug⇨Start.

If you typed everything correctly, Visual Basic displays your user inter-face on the screen, as shown in Figure 4-5.

Figure 4-5:
The Hello,
World!
Program
running.

15. Click on the smiley face picture in the upper-left corner of the form.

Visual Basic .NET displays the message Hello, world!, as shown in Figure 4-6.

Figure 4-6:
What
happens
when you
click on the
Smiley face
picture box.

16. Click on the frowning face in the middle of the form.

Visual Basic .NET displays the message Good-bye, cruel world!, as shown in Figure 4-7.

Figure 4-7:
What
happens
when you
click on the
Frowning
face picture
box.

17. **Click on the happy face in the upper-right corner of the form.**

    Visual Basic displays a really happy face on the screen, along with the
    message I'm going to Disney World!, as shown in Figure 4-8.

Figure 4-8:
What
happens
when you
click on the
Happy face
picture box.

18. **Click on the button labeled Exit.**

    Visual Basic .NET quits running your program and returns you to the
    Visual Basic .NET user interface.

You finally completed the Hello, World! example. Now, you can see how you
can use Visual Basic .NET to create a friendly user interface quickly and
easily.

Part II

Creating User Interfaces

The 5th Wave   By Rich Tennant

HISTORY WAS ABOUT TO REPEAT ITSELF AS CHARLIE VAN GOGH, VISUAL BASIC PROGRAMMER AND GREAT-NEPHEW OF VINCENT VAN GOGH, IS ASSIGNED THE JOB OF DESIGNING A USER INTERFACE FOR HIS COMPANY'S NEW DATABASE PROGRAM.

Sorry Chuck-management is still rejecting your latest designs.

In this part . . .

A user interface allows other people to use your program. The clumsier the user interface, the harder your program is to use. So if you make your user interface simple and logical, you can bet that more people will be able to use your program.

This is the fun part of the book. You aren't forced to type any bizarre code, study arcane commands, or memorize ridiculous keystrokes. In this part of the book, you get to doodle on your computer screen while actually finding out how to write your own programs at the same time.

Chapter 5

User Interface Design 101

To make oneself understood to the people, one must first speak to their eyes.
— Napoleon Bonaparte

First of all, nobody really wants to use your program. Most people would rather play at the beach, watch TV, or make out. However, people do want the results that your program can produce. If they could get these same results by other means with less work, they would. But because they can't, they're willing to use your program.

This means that people really want your program to read their minds and then magically do all their work for them automatically. Because that's not possible, the best you can hope for is to make your program as easy to use as possible. If an idiot can use your program, then most other people are going to be able to use your program as well.

Before You Create Your User Interface

Creating a user interface doesn't mean just slapping together some pretty pictures in a colorful window and hoping that the user can figure out how your program works. Your program's user interface must make your program easy to use. To help you create a user interface, here are some points to keep in mind.

Know your user

Before designing your user interface, ask yourself who is going to use your program. Are your typical users data-entry clerks who understand computers, or managers who understand only paper procedures and are learning to use a computer for the first time?

When you decide who your users are, design your user interface so that it mirrors the way the users already work, regardless of whether the user interface seems totally inefficient or alien to anyone else. Accountants readily accept spreadsheets because the row-and-column format mimics green sheets of ledger paper. Likewise, typists prefer word processors because a word processor mimics a blank sheet of paper.

But imagine if all word processors looked like spreadsheets with rows and columns. Any typist trying to use this kind of word processor would quickly feel lost and confused (although accountants may feel right at home with such a word processor).

The more a programmer understands the user, the more likely the interface is going to be used and accepted. Ultimately the only person the user interface really has to satisfy is the user.

Orient the user

Not surprisingly, people get lost wandering through today's supermalls, which contain multiple levels and two different time zones. How do you feel when you have no idea where you are and no idea where you can go from your current position?

This feeling of helplessness is the reason why lost kids cry uncontrollably and confused computer users curse under their breath. (This is also the reason why malls install directories with the big red X that says, "You are here.")

A good user interface must orient people so that they know where they are in your program and how to get out if they want. Some user interfaces display a message at the bottom of the screen, such as "Page 2 of 5." In this case, the user knows exactly how many pages are available for viewing and which page currently appears on the screen.

Your user interface is a map to your program. Make sure that your user interface shows just enough information to orient users but not too much to confuse them.

Make the choices obvious

In addition to letting users know where they are in a program, a good user interface must also make all choices obvious to the user. If your user interface displays "Page 4 of 25" at the bottom of the screen, how can the user know what to do to see the next or previous page? One solution may be to show forward- and backward-pointing arrows in each bottom corner of the page. Another solution may be Next Page and Previous Page buttons.

As long as your program shows the user which options are available next and which keys to press or where to click the mouse, she feels a sense of control and confidence when using your program.

Be forgiving

The key here is useful feedback. If your program takes an arrogant attitude and displays scolding messages like "File MPR.DLL missing" whenever the user presses the wrong key or clicks the mouse in the wrong area, he may feel intimidated if your program doesn't explain what the error message means and how he can avoid the error in the first place.

So be kind. Have your program hide or dim any buttons or menu commands that are unavailable to the user. If the user does press the wrong key or click the mouse in the wrong area, have your program display a window and explain what the user's options are. Users love a program that guides them, which means you can spend a lot less time answering phone calls for technical support.

Keep it simple

Most programs offer users two or more ways to choose a specific command. You can click on a button, choose a command from menus, or press certain keystroke combinations (Ctrl+F2, for example). Of these three methods, clicking directly on the screen is the easiest procedure to remember and pressing bizarre keystroke combinations is the hardest.

Make sure that users can access commonly used commands quickly through a button or a menu. Not all commands must be or need to be accessed through a keystroke combination.

Although keystroke combination commands are faster to use, they are harder to learn initially. Make keystroke combinations easy to remember whenever possible. For a Save command, Ctrl+S is easier to remember than something totally abstract like Shift+F12. People can easily remember that S stands for Save, but who has any idea what F12 represents?

Designing Your Visual Basic .NET User Interface

A Visual Basic .NET user interface consists of forms and objects. Forms define the size, position, and background color of the windows that make up your program. Objects consist of items such as buttons and check boxes that make your user interface display and retrieve information for the user. Figures 5-1 and 5-2 show a typical user interface consisting of:

✔ Forms (also known as windows)

✔ Buttons (such as radio buttons)

✔ Boxes (such as text boxes and check boxes)

✔ Labels

✔ Pictures (such as icons and decorative graphics)

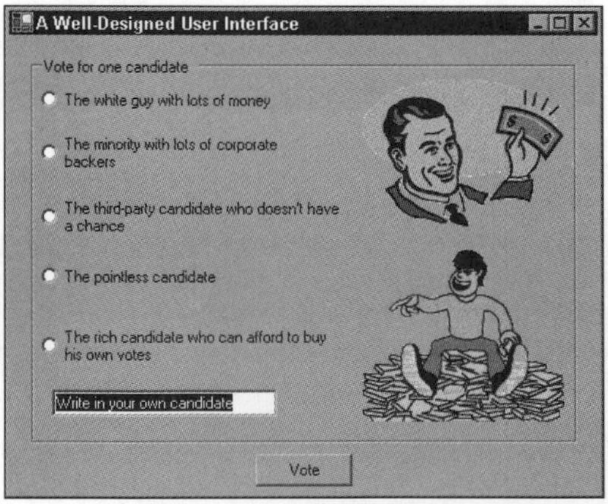

Figure 5-1:
A well-designed user interface makes choices easy to understand.

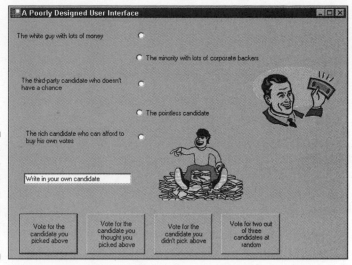

Figure 5-2:
A poorly
designed
user
interface
confuses
the user.

Creating a form

The first part in designing a user interface is to create a form, which acts like a window for displaying or accepting information from the user. When you create a new Windows application, Visual Basic .NET automatically creates one form for you. But because most programs consist of more than one window, you will probably need to create additional forms (windows).

To create a form, choose Project➪Add Windows Form (or click on the Add New Item icon, click Windows Form, and click Open). Visual Basic .NET creates a new form.

Visual Basic .NET can actually create a variety of different forms, but Windows Forms are the most common when using Visual Basic .NET to create a Windows program such as a game or accounting program.

Drawing objects on a form

After you've created a form, the next step is to draw user interface objects on that form by following these steps:

1. **Choose View➪Toolbox, or press Ctrl+Alt+X. (Skip this step if the Toolbox is already visible.)**

   The Toolbox appears, as shown in Figure 5-3. You may need to click on the Windows Forms button to display all the user interface objects available for creating a Windows user interface.

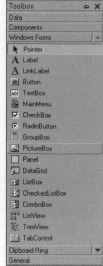

Figure 5-3:
The Toolbox
contains
user
interface
objects that
you can
draw on a
form.

2. **Click on the user interface object that you want to draw, such as a TextBox or RadioButton. (Table 5-1 lists the user interface objects you can choose from the Toolbox.)**

   The mouse pointer turns into a crosshair shape.

3. **Move the mouse over the form where you want to draw your object, hold down the left mouse button, and drag the mouse. Then release the left mouse button.**

   Visual Basic .NET draws your chosen user interface object on the form.

Table 5-1	Tools in the Visual Basic .NET Toolbox
Tool Name	*What This Tool Does*
Pointer	Selects objects
Label	Draws a box to display text
LinkLabel	Draws a box to display a hyperlink
Button	Draws a rectangular-shaped button
TextBox	Draws a box that can display text and let the user type in text
MainMenu	Creates pull-down menus

Tool Name	What This Tool Does
CheckBox	Draws a check box
RadioButton	Draws a radio button
GroupBox	Draws a box for enclosing multiple objects, such as radio buttons or check boxes
PictureBox	Draws a box for displaying a graphic image
Panel	Draws a rectangular box to organizing multiple objects on a form
DataGrid	Draws a table of rows and columns for displaying data stored in a database file
ListBox	Draws a list box
CheckedListBox	Draws a list box that displays check boxes next to each item
ComboBox	Draws a combo box
ListView	Draws a box that displays text in a list
TreeView	Draws a box that displays text in a tree that users can expand or collapse
TabControl	Draws one or more tabbed pages that can display additional user interface objects such as buttons

To draw an object on a form in a hurry, double-click on the object in the Toolbox. For example, if you want to draw a button quickly, just double-click on Button in the Toolbox and Visual Basic .NET draws a button on your form automatically.

Changing the properties of an object

After you draw an object on a form, the next step is to define the properties for that object, which can define the object's color, size, or any text to appear on the object. Every object contains several properties, but you don't need to modify all the properties of an object to make your Visual Basic .NET program.

The two properties you need to modify on most objects are the Name and Text properties. The Name property uniquely identifies each object on your user interface. The Text property displays text that appears on the object, such as the words OK or Cancel that appear on a button.

To change the properties of an object, follow these steps:

1. **Choose one of these methods to open the Solution Explorer window:**

   • Press Ctrl+Alt+L.

   • Choose View⇨Solution Explorer.

   • Click on the Solution Explorer icon in the toolbar.

2. **Click on the form that contains the object whose properties you want to modify.**

   Visual Basic displays your chosen form and any objects displayed on that form.

3. **Click on the object that you want to modify.**

   The Properties window displays all the properties available for your chosen object. If the Properties window is not visible, press F4.

4. **Click on the property you want to change.**

   Depending on the specific property, changing a property may require you to do one of the following:

   • Type text (such as when changing the Text property of an object) or a number (such as when defining the Size or Location properties of an object).

   • Click on a downward-pointing arrow to choose from a list of available property options (such as True or False when changing the Visible property of an object).

   • Click on the button that displays three dots, which opens a dialog box for choosing multiple options, such as defining the Font property of an object.

Naming objects

Every object has a Name property, which Visual Basic .NET uses to identify that particular object. (That's the same reason your parents gave you a name — so people don't say, "Hey, you!" all the time to get your attention.) The Name property, which Visual Basic .NET displays as (Name), appears in the Design category in the Properties window.

Every Visual Basic .NET object on a form must have a unique name. If you try to give the same name to two different objects on the same form, Visual Basic .NET complains and refuses to let you make such a horrid mistake. (However, you can give the same name to objects stored on different forms. Just remember that doing so could make your program more confusing to read and understand.)

When you create an object, Visual Basic .NET automatically gives your object a boring, generic name. For example, the first time you create a button, Visual Basic .NET names the button Button1. The second time you create a button, Visual Basic .NET names this new button Button2, and so on.

The name of an object never appears on the screen. Names can be up to 40 characters long, but they cannot contain punctuation marks or spaces. You can name your objects anything you want, but many Visual Basic .NET programmers use three-letter prefixes, as shown in Table 5-2, to make it easy to identify specific objects.

Table 5-2	Suggested Prefixes for Naming Objects	
Object	*Suggested Prefix*	*Example Name*
Button	btn	btnYourLip
CheckBox	chk	chkYourZipper
ComboBox	cmb	cmbBLT
DataGrid	dat	datFanOverThere
Form	frm	frm1040Tax
Label	lbl	lblFakeName
ListBox	lst	lstCandidates
MainMenu	mnu	mnuHamAndEggs
PictureBox	pic	picPrettyPictures
RadioButton	rad	radStation101
TextBox	txt	txtReadStuffHere

To change the name of a form, follow these steps:

1. **Open the Solution Explorer.**

   To do so, press Ctrl+Atl+L, choose View➪Solution Explorer, or click on the Solutions Explorer icon on the toolbar.

2. **Click on the form that you want to name.**

3. **Open the Properties window.**

   To do so, press F4, choose View➪Properties Window, click on the Properties Window icon in the Solution Explorer window, or right-click on a form and choose Properties. The Properties window appears.

4. **Double-click on the Name property (in the Design category) and type a new name.**

To change the name of any object, such as a radio button or check box, follow these steps:

1. **Click on the object that you want to name.**

   Handles appear around the object.

2. **Open the Properties window.**

   To do so, press F4, choose View⇨Properties Window, or click on the Properties Window icon on the toolbar.

3. **Double-click on Name property (in the Design category) and type a new name.**

Displaying text on an object

In addition to a name, most (but not all) objects can also display text through its Text property, which appears under the Appearance category in the Properties window. The most common objects used to display text include:

- ✔ Buttons
- ✔ CheckBoxes
- ✔ CheckedListBoxes
- ✔ Labels
- ✔ GroupBoxes
- ✔ RadioButtons
- ✔ TextBoxes

The Text property for a form displays text in the title bar of that form. For other objects, the Text property displays text directly on that object such as a button or a check box.

By default, an object's Text and Name properties are the same until you change them. So the moment you draw a check box on a form, the check box's Text and Name properties are something dull like Check1.

To change the Text property of an object, follow these steps:

1. **Click on the object that you want to name.**

   Handles appear around the object.

2. **Open the Properties window.**

   To do so, press F4, choose View⇨Properties Window, or click on the Properties Window icon on the toolbar.

3. **Double-click on Text property (in the Appearance category) and type any text.**

   Visual Basic .NET displays your text on your chosen object.

You can make your text look extra special (or just really annoying) by changing the Font property under the Appearance category. Just choose your fonts carefully to make sure your text is still easy to read.

Changing the size of objects

After creating an object, you may want to change the size of your object. Visual Basic .NET provides two ways to change the size of an object:

- Use the mouse.
- Change the Width and Height properties in the Properties window.

To change the size of an object using the mouse, follow these steps:

1. **Click on the object that you want to resize.**

   Handles appear around the edges of your chosen object.

2. **Move the mouse to the edge of the object until the mouse pointer turns into a double-headed arrow.**

3. **Hold down the mouse button and drag the mouse. When the object is in the shape you want, release the mouse button.**

To change the size of a form using the Properties window, follow these steps:

1. **Click on the object you want to resize.**

2. **Open the Properties window.**

   To do so, press F4, choose <u>V</u>iew⇨Properties Window, click on the Properties Window icon in the Solution Explorer window, or right-click on a form and choose P<u>r</u>operties. The Properties window appears.

3. **Click on the plus sign that appears to the left of the Size property (in the Layout category).**

   Visual Basic .NET displays the Width and Height properties

4. **Type the new values you want for the Width and Height properties.**

Use the mouse method when the exact size of your object isn't crucial. Change the Height and Width properties manually when you want absolute precision or when you feel like being picky about details that nobody else cares about.

Instead of changing the Width and Height properties, you can type numbers directly into the Size property, which displays the values of the Width and Height properties as Width, Height. So if the Width property of your object is 97 and the Height property is 23, the Size property would display those two values as 97, 23.

Moving objects on the screen

Objects can appear anywhere on a form. Visual Basic .NET provides two ways to define the position of an object on the form:

- ✔ Use the mouse.
- ✔ Change the X and Y properties, under the Layout category, in the Properties window.

To change the position of an object using the mouse, follow these steps:

1. **Click on the object you want to move so that black handles appear around the object.**

2. **Move the mouse over the object (not over one of the object's handles). Then hold down the left mouse button and move the mouse to where you want the object to appear.**

3. **Release the mouse button.**

Use the mouse whenever you want to move an object quickly without regard to exact placement on the screen. For more precise measurements when moving an object, use the Properties window and type in values for the X and Y properties.

The X property measures the distance from the left edge of the form to the left edge of the object. The Y property measures the distance from the top of the form to the top of the object.

To change the position of an object using the Properties window, follow these steps:

1. **Click on the object you want to move.**

   Visual Basic .NET highlights your chosen object by displaying handles around the object's edges.

2. **Open the Properties window.**

   To do so, press F4, choose View⇨Properties Window, click on the Properties Window icon in the Solution Explorer window, or right-click on a form and choose Properties. The Properties window appears.

3. **Click on the plus sign that appears to the left of the Location property in the Layout category.**

   Visual Basic .NET displays the X and Y properties.

4. **Type the new values you want for the X and Y properties.**

Instead of changing the X and Y properties, you can type numbers directly into the Location property, which displays the values of the X and Y properties as X, Y. So if the X property of your object is 45 and the Y property is 2, the Location property would display those two values as 45, 2.

Docking your objects within a form

In case you want your objects to fill an entire form or to appear across the top, bottom, right, or left side of a form (no matter how large or small, the user may resize the form), you can dock your objects along one side of your form.

To dock objects, follow these steps:

1. **Click on the object that you want to dock along one side of your form.**

   Handles appear around the edges of your chosen object.

2. **Open the Properties window.**

   To do so, press F4, choose View⇨Properties Window, click on the Properties Window icon in the Solution Explorer window, or right-click on a form and choose Properties. The Properties window appears.

3. **Click on the Dock property (in the Layout category) of the Properties window.**

   A downward-pointing arrow appears.

4. **Click on the downward-pointing arrow.**

   A graphical menu pops up, showing gray rectangles that represent the position you can dock your chosen object, as shown in Figure 5-4.

Figure 5-4:
The docking menu is where you can choose where to dock an object on a form.

5. **Click on a gray button that represents the docking option you want, such as the top or left side of the form.**

   Visual Basic .NET immediately shows you what your docked object looks like on the form.

   If you click on the None button, you can undock a previously docked object.

Anchoring your objects

When you dock an object, that object automatically resizes itself to fill one side of the form, such as the bottom or right side. In case you don't want your objects to fill one entire edge of a form, you might try anchoring your objects instead.

Anchoring tells your objects to stick close to one or more edges of a form no matter how large or small the user may resize that form. To anchor an object, follow these steps:

1. **Click on the object that you want to anchor.**

   Handles appear around the edges of your chosen object.

2. **Open the Properties window.**

   To do so, press F4, choose View➪Properties Window, click on the Properties Window icon in the Solution Explorer window, or right-click on an object and choose Properties. The Properties window appears.

3. **Click on the Anchor property (in the Layout category) of the Properties window**.

   A downward-pointing arrow appears.

4. **Click on the downward-pointing arrow.**

   A graphical menu pops up, showing dotted line rectangles that represent the four edges (Top, Bottom, Right, and Left) that you can anchor your chosen object to, as shown in Figure 5-5.

Figure 5-5: The anchor menu is where you can choose which edges to anchor an object on a form.

5. **Click on one or more of the anchoring positions (such as Top and Left).**

   The next time you run your program, your chosen object maintains its exact distance from the edges of the form that you anchored the object to. So, if you anchored the object to the Top and Left edges of a form, that object never moves from the top or left edges of that form no matter how large or small a user may resize that form (window).

Copying an existing object (to avoid drawing a new one)

After you draw an object that is the exact size you need, you may want to make a copy of the object rather than create a new one and go through the trouble of resizing it.

To copy an object, follow these steps:

1. **Click on the object you want to copy.**

   Handles appear around your chosen object.

2. **Press Ctrl+C, choose Edit➪Copy, or click on the Copy icon.**

3. **Press Ctrl+V, choose Edit➪Paste, or click on the Paste icon.**

   Visual Basic .NET pastes a copy directly over your chosen object.

4. **Move this copy of the object anywhere on your screen.**

   To learn how to move an object, see the previous section "Moving objects on the screen."

After copying an object, you still need to type a unique name for your newly created object. (Unless you don't mind the generic name that Visual Basic .NET gives your object such as Button3.)

Deleting objects off the face of the earth

Sometimes you draw an object and then decide that you don't need it after all. To delete an object, follow these steps:

1. **Click on the object you want to delete.**

2. **Press Delete or choose Edit➪Delete.**

If you press Ctrl+Z right after you delete an object, you can undelete the object you previously deleted.

Selecting more than one object to move, copy, or delete

Before you can move, copy, or delete any object, you have to select the object by clicking on it. However, if you want to move, copy, or delete more than one object at the same time, you have two choices:

✔ Use the mouse to select multiple objects.

✔ Click on multiple objects while holding down Ctrl or Shift.

To use the mouse to select multiple objects, follow these steps:

1. **Position the mouse at the upper-left corner of the group of objects you want to select. (But don't position the mouse directly over any of the objects you want to select.)**

   If you move the mouse pointer over an object, you'll wind up moving that object instead of selecting it.

2. **Hold down the left mouse button while you drag the mouse to the lower-right corner of the group of objects you want to select.**

   Visual Basic .NET displays a dotted line around all the objects you select.

3. **Release the mouse button.**

   Visual Basic .NET displays a gray rectangle around all the objects you selected.

To click on multiple objects while holding down Ctrl or Shift, follow these steps:

1. **Click on the first object that you want to select.**

   Visual Basic .NET displays black handles around the object.

2. **Point to the second object that you want to select.**

3. **Press Ctrl or Shift while you click on the second object.**

   Visual Basic .NET displays gray rectangles around this object and each of your previously selected objects.

4. **Repeat Steps 2 and 3 until you select all the objects you want.**

Defining the TabIndex property of your objects

Instead of using a mouse to select objects, Visual Basic .NET also gives users the option of choosing objects by using the Tab key on the keyboard. To determine the order of the objects that the Tab key highlights, most (but not all) objects have a special property called the *TabIndex.*

An object with a TabIndex property set to 0 appears highlighted as soon as your program runs. If the user presses Tab, the object with a TabIndex property of 1 is highlighted next, and so on.

The first object that you create has a TabIndex property of 0. The second object that you create has a TabIndex property of 1, and so on.

The TabIndex property determines the order in which Visual Basic .NET highlights your objects when the user presses the Tab, up-arrow, down-arrow, right-arrow, left-arrow, or Shift+Tab keys.

- ✔ The Tab, down-arrow, and right-arrow keys highlight the object with the next-highest TabIndex value.

- ✔ The Shift+Tab, up-arrow, and left-arrow keys highlight the object with the next-lowest TabIndex value. To highlight RadioButtons, you can use only the up, down, right, and left arrow keys, but not the Tab or Shift+Tab keys.

- ✔ The spacebar or Enter key selects a highlighted object. (Similar to clicking on the object with the mouse.)

Some objects, such as PictureBoxes, don't have a TabIndex property, so you can't highlight them by pressing any keys.

To change the TabIndex property of an object, follow these steps:

1. Choose <u>V</u>iew➪Ta<u>b</u> Order.

Visual Basic .NET displays the TabIndex property values directly on the objects, as shown in Figure 5-6.

Figure 5-6: The TabIndex property value of each object defines the order they appear highlighted when the user presses the Tab key.

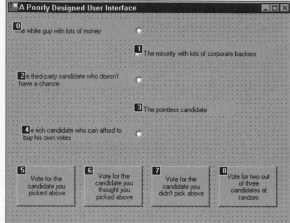

2. Click on the object that you want to appear highlighted first (with a TabIndex property value of 0).

Visual Basic .NET displays the number zero (0) on your chosen object.

3. Click on the object that you want to appear highlighted next (with a TabIndex property value one higher than the previous object that you clicked on).

4. Repeat Step 3 until all your objects have a TabIndex value in the order you want them to appear if the user clicks the Tab key.

5. Choose <u>V</u>iew➪Ta<u>b</u> Order.

Visual Basic .NET hides the TabIndex property values on your objects.

For some reason if you don't want the user to be able to highlight an object by pressing the Tab key, you can set that object's TabStop property (under the Behavior category) to False. The Tab Stop property only appears if you have turned the Tab Order off so the tab order numbers don't appear on the objects.

Dimming objects

If you don't want the user to choose a particular object (such as a button, a check box, or a picture box), you can dim that object, as shown in Figure 5-7. A dimmed object tells the user, "Sometimes you can click on this object but not right now. So there."

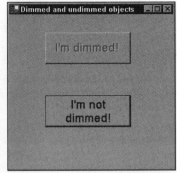

Figure 5-7:
A dimmed object and a nondimmed object.

To dim an object, follow these steps:

1. **Click on the object that you want to dim.**

2. **Open the Properties window.**

   To do so, press F4, choose View⇨Properties Window, click on the Properties Window icon in the Solution Explorer window, or right-click on a form and choose Properties. The Properties window appears.

3. **Click on the Enabled property (in the Behavior category) and set it to False.**

A dimmed object doesn't do anything, so if you want to undim it while your program is running, you need to use BASIC code.

To give you a sneak preview of the incredible power of BASIC code, here's how BASIC undims and dims a button. To undim a button, set the button's Enabled property to True. The following example undims a button named btnExit:

```
btnExit.Enabled = True
```

To dim a button using BASIC code, set the button's Enabled property to False. The following example dims a command button named btnExit:

```
btnExit.Enabled = False
```

You can dim and undim buttons using BASIC code while your program is running. That way, you can dim and undim buttons in response to whatever the user is doing (typing, moving the mouse, pounding helplessly on the keyboard, and so on).

Making objects invisible

Rather than dimming an object (which essentially taunts the user because the object is there but unavailable), you can make objects disappear completely.

To make an object disappear, follow these steps:

1. **Click on the object you want to disappear.**

2. **Open the Properties window.**

    To do so, press F4, choose View➪Properties Window, click on the Properties Window icon in the Solution Explorer window, or right-click on a form and choose Properties. The Properties window appears.

3. **Click on the Visible property in the Behavior category and set it to False.**

You can also make an object disappear using BASIC code. To do so, set the object's Visible property to False. The following example makes a command button named btnNew disappear:

```
btnNew.Visible = False
```

Like dimmed objects, invisible objects are useless unless you can make them visible once in a while. To make an object appear again, you have to use BASIC code to set the object's Visible property to True. The following example makes a command button named btnNew appear:

```
btnNew.Visible = True
```

See How to Change Text on an Object for Yourself

To see how you can use the awesome power of BASIC code to change the Text property of a button, draw one button on a form and change the properties of the button and form as shown in Table 5-3.

Table 5-3	Properties to Change for CAPTION.VBP	
Object	*Property*	*Setting*
Form	Text	The Incredible Changing Text
Button1	Name	btnChangeMe
	Text	Change Text

Double-click on the btnChangeMe button and type the following event-handling procedure:

```
Protected Sub btnChangeMe_Click(ByVal sender As_
        System.Object, ByVal e As System.EventArgs)
  btnChangeMe.Text = "It works!"
End Sub
```

When you run this program, just click on the button labeled Change Text. Visual Basic .NET immediately displays It works! on the button. To stop this wonderfully complex program from running, click on the Close box of the form.

Chapter 6

Designing Forms

· ·

· ·

*T*he main part of a user interface is a window, which Visual Basic .NET calls a form. Most Visual Basic .NET programs use at least one form, but more complicated programs use two or more forms.

For example, a typical program may use one form to display a list of buttons to click. If the user clicks on a certain button, a second form appears, displaying information such as names, addresses, and telephone numbers of people you're planning to fire.

Creating a Form

When you create a Windows Application project, Visual Basic .NET automatically creates one form for you to start drawing your user interface. Unless you're creating a very simple program, you'll probably need additional forms for your program.

To create a form, follow these steps:

1. **Choose Project⇨Add Windows Form (or click on the downward-pointing arrow to the right of the Add New Item icon on the toolbar and choose Add Windows Form).**

   An Add New Item dialog box appears.

2. **Type a name for your form in the Name text box.**

   When you name a form, you don't have to type the .VB file extension; it adds this extension to your file automatically.

3. **Click Open.**

   Visual Basic .NET displays your new form, ready for you to use.

Get into the habit of periodically saving your work by pressing Ctrl+Shift+S or choosing File⇨Save All. If your computer fails or the power goes out, you will lose only the changes that you've made since you last saved your work.

Naming your forms

Visual Basic .NET automatically names your forms with a generic name such as Form3.vb. To give your form a unique name all its own, follow these steps:

1. **Open the Solution Explorer.**

   To do so, press Ctrl+Atl+L, choose View⇨Solution Explorer, or click on the Solutions Explorer icon on the toolbar.

2. **Click on the form that you want to name.**

   You can right-click on a form, choose Rename, and then type a new name for your form. If you do this, you can skip Steps 3 and 4 below.

3. **Open the Properties window.**

   To do so, press F4, choose View⇨Properties Window, click on the Properties Window icon in the Solution Explorer window, or right-click on a form and choose Properties. The Properties window appears.

4. **Double-click on the Name property (in the Design category) and type a new name.**

Visual Basic .NET always adds the .VB file extension as part of your form's name such as frmMain.vb.

Viewing different forms

Because your Visual Basic .NET program will likely consist of two or more forms, you may want to view all your forms, one at a time. To display a form, follow these steps:

1. **Open the Solution Explorer.**

   To do so, press Ctrl+Atl+L, choose View⇨Solution Explorer, or click on the Solutions Explorer icon on the toolbar.

2. **Double-click on the form you want to view.**

   Visual Basic .NET displays your chosen form.

Visual Basic .NET can only display one form on the screen at a time. However, if you have previously chosen other forms to view, Visual Basic .NET displays tabs that contain the form's name and the word *(Design)* next to it, as shown in Figure 6-1. To view your form, click on the Design tab. To view any BASIC code that makes your form work, click on the Code tab.

Figure 6-1:
You can quickly switch between different forms by clicking on the Design tab of each form.

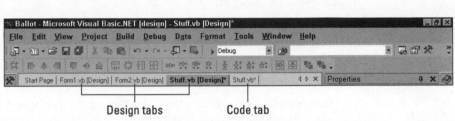

Design tabs   Code tab

Changing the Look of a Form

After you've created a form and sprinkled any user interface objects on it (such as buttons or check boxes), you may want to take some time to customize the appearance of your forms so they don't look like boring gray rectangles hovering in the middle of the screen.

Colors can make your program look more attractive or really obnoxious, so make sure the users of your program approve of the colors you've chosen or else they might not want to use your program at all.

Coloring your forms

By default, Visual Basic .NET gives all your forms a gray background. While there's nothing wrong with gray forms, you may want to add some color to your forms so your programs look just a little more attractive than the side of a battleship.

To change the background of a form, follow these steps:

1. Open the Solution Explorer.

To do so, press Ctrl+Atl+L, choose View➪Solution Explorer, or click on the Solutions Explorer icon on the toolbar.

2. **Double-click on the form that you want to modify.**

   Visual Basic .NET displays handles around your chosen form.

3. **Open the Properties window.**

   To do so, press F4, choose View⇨Properties Window, click on the Properties Window icon in the Solution Explorer window, or right-click on a form and choose Properties. The Properties window appears.

4. **Click on the BackColor property (in the Appearance category).**

   A downward-pointing arrow appears.

5. **Click on the downward-pointing arrow.**

   A dialog box appears, as shown in Figure 6-2, offering three choices for background colors:

   - Custom: Displays various gradations of colors

   - Web: Displays colors designed for Web pages (although you can use them in your programs too)

   - System: Displays colors used by your Windows desktop, such as menu bars

Figure 6-2:
Choosing a
background
color for
your form.

6. **Click on the Custom, Web, or System tab and choose a color that you want.**

   Visual Basic .NET changes the background of your chosen form.

Putting a background image on a form

Besides filling the background of your form with color, you can also add a graphic image on a form as well, such as a company logo, a mountain, or your boss's face.

To put a graphic image on the background of a form, follow these steps:

1. **Open the Solution Explorer.**

   To do so, press Ctrl+Atl+L, choose View⇨Solution Explorer, or click on the Solutions Explorer icon on the toolbar.

2. **Double-click on the form that you want to modify.**

   Visual Basic .NET displays handles around your chosen form.

3. **Open the Properties window.**

   To do so, press F4, choose View⇨Properties Window, click on the Properties Window icon in the Solution Explorer window, or right-click on a form and choose Properties. The Properties window appears.

4. **Click on the BackgroundImage property (in the Appearance category).**

   A button with three dots appears.

5. **Click on the button with three dots.**

   An Open dialog box appears.

6. **Click on the graphic image you want to use and click Open.**

   You may have to switch drives or folders to find the graphic file you want to use. If your form is larger than the image you chose, Visual Basic .NET tiles that image so multiple copies fill up the entire background of your form.

To remove a background image, right-click on the button with the three dots on it in Step 5 and choose Reset.

Drawing borders around forms

Besides helping to make your forms look pretty, borders also give nations something to argue about. Visual Basic .NET offers the following seven choices, as shown in Figure 6-3:

- ✔ **None:** Doesn't display a border or title bar on your form, but any objects your form contains can still be seen. A user cannot move, resize, or minimize this type of form.

- ✔ **FixedSingle:** Displays a Control box, title bar, and Close box. Users can move, minimize, and maximize, but not resize, this type of form.

- ✔ **Fixed3D:** Exactly like the FixedSingle border style except that the form appears with a 3D effect around the edges. Users can move, minimize, and maximize, but not resize, this type of form.

- **FixedDialog:** Displays a Control box, title bar, and Close box. Users can move, minimize, and maximize, but not resize, this type of form.

- **Sizable:** The default style for all forms, this style displays a Control box, a title bar, Minimize and Maximize buttons, and the Close box. Users can move, resize, and minimize or maximize this form.

- **Fixed ToolWindow:** Displays a title bar and Close box. Users can move this form but cannot resize, minimize, or maximize this style of form.

- **Sizable ToolWindow:** Displays a title bar and Close box. Users can move (by dragging the title bar) and resize (by dragging the edge or corner) this form.

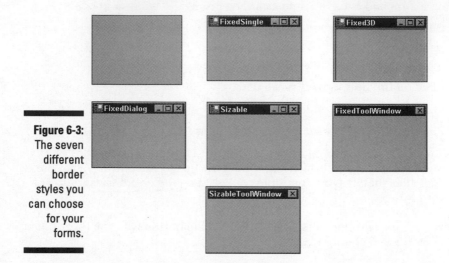

Figure 6-3:
The seven different border styles you can choose for your forms.

In addition to changing the way your forms look, each border style also affects whether the user can move or resize the form.

To change the borders around a form, follow these steps:

1. **Open the Solution Explorer.**

   To do so, press Ctrl+Atl+L, choose View➪Solution Explorer, or click on the Solutions Explorer icon on the toolbar.

2. **Double-click on the form that you want to modify.**

   Visual Basic .NET displays handles around your chosen form.

3. **Open the Properties window.**

   To do so, press F4, choose View➪Properties Window, click on the Properties Window icon in the Solution Explorer window, or right-click on a form and choose Properties. The Properties window appears.

4. **Click on the FormBorderStyle property (in the Appearance category).**

   A downward-pointing arrow appears.

5. **Choose a border style (such as Fixed3D)**

   Visual Basic .NET changes your chosen form's borders.

Minimizing and maximizing forms

Forms can appear minimized (so only the title bar appears), maximized (covering the entire screen), or normal (covering just part of the screen), as shown in Figure 6-4.

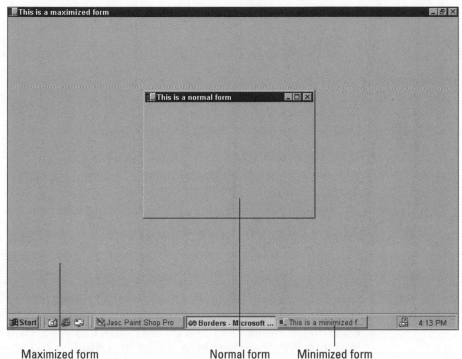

Figure 6-4: A maximized, normal, and minimized form.

Maximized form   Normal form   Minimized form

To make your form appear as normal, minimized, or maximized when your program runs, follow these steps:

1. **Open the Solution Explorer.**

   To do so, press Ctrl+Atl+L, choose View⇨Solution Explorer, or click on the Solutions Explorer icon on the toolbar.

2. **Double-click on the form that you want to modify.**

   Visual Basic .NET displays handles around your chosen form.

3. **Open the Properties window.**

   To do so, press F4, choose View➪Properties Window, click on the Properties Window icon in the Solution Explorer window, or right-click on a form and choose Properties. The Properties window appears.

4. **Click on the WindowState property (in the Layout category).**

   A downward-pointing arrow appears.

5. **Click on the downward-pointing arrow and choose an option (such as Normal or Minimized).**

Most forms display Minimize and Maximize buttons so the user can minimize or maximize your form at any time. Of course, you can always hide these buttons if you don't want users to minimize or maximize your forms.

If you define a BorderStyle of None, Fixed Single, Fixed ToolWindow, or Sizable ToolWindow, the Minimize and Maximize buttons won't appear on your form.

To hide or display Minimize and Maximize buttons on a form, follow these steps:

1. **Open the Solution Explorer.**

   To do so, press Ctrl+Atl+L, choose View➪Solution Explorer, or click on the Solutions Explorer icon on the toolbar.

2. **Double-click on the form that you want to modify.**

   Visual Basic .NET displays handles around your chosen form.

3. **Open the Properties window.**

   To do so, press F4, choose View➪Properties Window, click on the Properties Window icon in the Solution Explorer window, or right-click on a form and choose Properties. The Properties window appears.

4. **Click on the MinimizeBox (or the MaximizeBox) property (in the Windows Style category) in the Properties window and choose True or False.**

If you're going to allow users to resize or maximize your forms, make sure you anchor the user interface objects (radio buttons, check boxes, and so on) that appear on that form; otherwise, resizing your form might make your user interface look weird or even hide some objects altogether. To find out about anchoring objects, see the "Anchoring your objects" section in Chapter 5.

Positioning a form on the screen

To make sure your program looks the way you want, you can specify the location on the screen where your forms appear. If you don't specify where your forms appear, they may appear on top of each other or at the top of the screen when you'd really rather have them appear in the center of the screen.

If you have set the WindowState property of your form to Minimized or Maximized, the location of your form on the screen is irrelevant because a maximized form covers the entire screen and a minimized form just appears in the Windows taskbar.

To define the location of your form on the screen, you need to choose one of five values for the StartPosition property under the Layout category:

- ✔ **Manual:** Allows you to manually define the Location property (in the Layout category) to define the specific location of the form.
- ✔ **CenterScreen:** Centers your form on the screen.
- ✔ **WindowsDefaultLocation:** Allows your program to determine the best location for your form, (which may not always be what you think is the best location for your form).
- ✔ **WindowsDefaultBounds:** Allows your program to determine the best location and size for your form, (which may not always be what you think is the best location or size).
- ✔ **CenterParent:** Centers your form inside another form.

To define the location where you form appears on the screen, follow these steps:

1. **Open the Solution Explorer.**

   To do so, press Ctrl+Atl+L, choose <u>V</u>iew⇨Solution Ex<u>p</u>lorer, or click on the Solutions Explorer icon on the toolbar.

2. **Double-click on the form that you want to modify.**

   Visual Basic .NET displays handles around your chosen form.

3. **Open the Properties window.**

   To do so, press F4, choose <u>V</u>iew⇨Properties Window, click on the Properties Window icon in the Solution Explorer window, or right-click on a form and choose P<u>r</u>operties. The Properties window appears.

4. **Click on the StartPosition property (in the Layout category).**

A downward-pointing arrow appears.

5. **Click on the downward-pointing arrow and choose an option, such as CenterScreen.**

You can also use BASIC code to define the location of your form while your program is running. To do this, you need to use BASIC code such as:

```
ActiveForm.Location = New Point (X, Y)
```

ActiveForm tells Visual Basic .NET to move the currently active form (window). The X and Y numbers determine how far from the left edge of the screen the form should appear (X) and how far from the top of the screen the form should appear (Y).

Removing (and adding) forms

Occasionally, you may decide you don't want a particular form as part of your Visual Basic .NET program after all. To remove a form from your Visual Basic .NET program, follow these steps:

1. **Open the Solution Explorer.**

To do so, press Ctrl+Atl+L, choose <u>V</u>iew⇨Solution Ex<u>p</u>lorer, or click on the Solutions Explorer icon on the toolbar.

2. **Click on the form that you want to remove.**

3. **Choose <u>P</u>roject⇨Exclude From Project (or right-click on the form and choose Exclude From Project).**

Visual Basic .NET removes the form from the Solution Explorer window.

If you remove a form that you've previously saved, the form still exists on your hard disk; it just isn't part of your Visual Basic .NET project anymore. To physically remove all traces of a form out of existence, use the Windows Explorer to physically delete the form file off your hard disk.

In case you want to add an existing form (such as one that you previously excluded), choose <u>P</u>roject⇨Add E<u>x</u>isting Item, or press Shift+Alt+A and click on the form that you want to include.

Test your newfound knowledge

1. What is a form?

   a. Visual Basic .NET's technical term for a window.

   b. A series of physical movements often associated with dancing, tai chi, or the martial arts.

   c. Something useless that you have to fill out just to get a job.

   d. The carcass of a tree, sliced into thin sheets and coated with black ink to form characters.

2. If your program contains two or more forms, how can you view each form?

   a. You can't. That's what makes programming so complicated and confusing.

   b. You have to buy a separate computer to display each form on the screen.

   c. Click on the Design tab on each form that you want to view. If a form's Design tab isn't visible, open the Solution Explorer window and double-click on the form you want to see.

   d. You have to peek at each form through a pair of binoculars while you're hiding in the bushes underneath the window.

Choosing Which Form Visual Basic .NET Displays First

When your program runs, the first form your program displays is generally the first form you created when you initially created your program. To make another form appear first, follow these steps:

1. **Open the Solution Explorer.**

   To do so, press Ctrl+Atl+L, choose View➪Solution Explorer, or click on the Solutions Explorer icon on the toolbar.

2. **Right-click on the project name.**

   A pull-down menu appears.

3. **Click Properties.**

   The Property Pages dialog box appears, as shown in Figure 6-5.

4. **Click on the downward-pointing arrow of the Startup Object list box to display a list of all the forms for your project.**

5. **Choose the form you want to display first and click OK.**

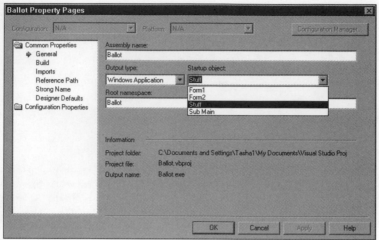

Figure 6-5:
The
Property
Pages
dialog box
allows you
to choose a
different
form as your
start-up
form.

Opening, Hiding, and Closing Forms

Having multiple forms as part of your Visual Basic .NET program may be nice, but when your Visual Basic .NET program runs, it normally displays one form. To make the other forms of your program appear (or disappear), you have to use BASIC code to tell your program, "Okay, now put this particular form on the screen and hide this other form out of sight."

Opening, hiding, and closing forms requires using BASIC commands, which you'll discover more about in Part IV of the book. For now, just browse through the rest of this chapter and don't get too bogged down in the specific details on what the BASIC code does.

Opening a form

Before you can open (or close) a form, you need to know the specific name of the form you want to open or close. The Solution Explorer window lists the names of all the forms that make up your Visual Basic .NET program, such as a form named frmMain.vb.

After you know the name of the form that you want to display, you need to use BASIC command to open the form, such as the following:

```
Dim oForm As FormName
oForm = New FormName()
oForm.Show()
oForm = Nothing
```

In case the above four lines of BASIC code look confusing, here's a quick explanation on what they do:

1. The first line tells Visual Basic .NET, "Define an object named oForm, which will represent the form that you want to open, which is called FormName." So, if you wanted to open a form named frmMain, you would type:

```
Dim oForm As frmMain
```

(The oForm name is arbitrary and can be any name you choose. The "o" is just shorthand for saying this is an object.)

2. The second line tells Visual Basic .NET, "Create a new object named oForm, which represents the form represented by the name FormName." (The main difference between the first and second lines is that the first line just told Visual Basic .NET to get ready to create an object to represent your form while the second line actually creates that object to represent your form. If this sounds confusing, don't worry about it for now.)

3. The third line tells Visual Basic .NET, "Show the form represented by the object oForm."

4. The fourth line tells Visual Basic .NET, "Set the object named oForm to nothing to free up the memory that it was taking up."

It's important to set the object to Nothing to free up memory because if you open up too many forms without releasing the memory they use, the computer could run out of memory and cause your program to freeze or crash.

Hiding (and showing) a form

If you want to temporarily make a form disappear, you can use the magic Hide command, such as:

```
FormName.Hide()
```

After you've hidden a form, you'll eventually want to make it visible again by using the Show command, such as:

```
FormName.Show()
```

Closing a form

Hiding a form just tucks it out of sight, but the form is still loaded in the computer's memory. To clear a form out of memory, you need to use the Close command, such as:

```
FormName.Close()
```

To make your program end, you have to shut down all your forms. At least one form of your program needs to have an exit command such as an Exit button or a File⇨Exit command available from a pull-down menu. The BASIC code to close the last form of your program looks like this:

```
Me.Close()
```

If you look at the BASIC code that Visual Basic .NET automatically creates for each form, you'll see a command that looks like this:

```
Form1 = Me
```

This command just tells Visual Basic .NET, "The word Me represents the current form. So instead of having to type the form's complete name, such as frmMainWindow, you can just type Me instead."

Chapter 7

Boxes and Buttons for Making Choices

In This Chapter

▶ Making buttons

▶ Creating check boxes and radio buttons

▶ Typing text on your objects

*T*o work properly, most programs need data from the user. For example, a program may ask the user, "What is your marital status?" Rather than force the user to type in this information, the program simply displays a list of acceptable options such as Married, Single, or Bitterly Divorced. When programs want the user to choose only one of many possible choices, these choices often appear as two or more radio buttons.

Although nearly every program needs to give users choices, this chapter explains how to create and use buttons, check boxes, and radio buttons on your Visual Basic .NET user interfaces.

Pushing Your Buttons

Pushing a button is a simple task that anyone can do. Even children can push buttons, which gives them the power to throw a hot dog in a microwave oven and shout with glee when the meat explodes before their eyes.

Because buttons are so familiar and easy to use, programs often display buttons on the screen that you can push with a mouse. Instead of forcing you to wade through various menus to find the right command, buttons conveniently display your options right before your eyes. All you have to do is figure out which button you want to click.

Essentially, a button is nothing more than an area on the screen that the user can click with the mouse. Most buttons display descriptive text that shows the user what command the button represents such as OK, Cancel, Open, or Exit.

To create a button, follow these steps:

1. **Choose View⇨Toolbox or press Ctrl+Alt+X. (Skip this step if the Toolbox is already visible.)**

   The Toolbox appears. You may need to click on the Windows Forms button to find the Button icon.

2. **Click on the Button object.**

   The mouse pointer turns into a crosshair shape.

   If you double-click on the Button icon in the Toolbox, Visual Basic .NET automatically draws a button on your form. You may need to move or resize this button.

3. **Move the mouse over the form where you want to draw your button, hold down the left mouse button, and drag the mouse. Then release the left mouse button.**

   Visual Basic .NET draws your button on the form.

After you create a button, you still have to write BASIC code to make the button do something when the user clicks on it. Part IV explains more about writing BASIC code.

Creating Check Boxes and Radio Buttons

Check boxes get their name from those silly questionnaires that ask, "Check all that apply," as in:

Why do you want to work here? (Check all that apply.)

- ❏　I need the money.
- ❏　I want to participate in employee theft.
- ❏　I want a place where I can steal more office supplies.
- ❏　I need a safe place to hide from the police.

Radio buttons get their name from those old AM car radios where you had to push a button to choose a station. Just as you can listen to only one radio station at a time, radio buttons only let you choose one option at a time. The following is an example of radio buttons.

What is your sex? (Choose only one.)

○   Male

○   Female

○   Ex-male (surgically a female)

○   Ex-female (surgically a male)

Creating a check box or radio button

To create a check box or radio button, follow these steps:

1. **Choose View➝Toolbox or press Ctrl+Alt+X. (Skip this step if the Toolbox is already visible.)**

   The Toolbox appears. You may need to click on the Win Forms button to find the Button icon.

2. **Click on the CheckBox or RadioButton object.**

   The mouse pointer turns into a crosshair shape.

   If you double-click on the CheckBox or RadioButton icon in the Toolbox, Visual Basic .NET automatically draws a check box or radio button on your form. You may need to move or resize this check box or radio button later.

3. **Move the mouse over the form where you want to draw your check box or radio button, hold down the left mouse button, and drag the mouse. Then release the left mouse button.**

   Visual Basic .NET draws your check box or radio button on the form.

Unlike ordinary buttons, check boxes and radio buttons don't need BASIC code to make them work. Instead, you need to write BASIC code to determine which check box or radio button the user chose. Chapter 16 explains how to do this, but to give you a sneak preview, the property that determines if a check box or radio button has been chosen is the Checked property, which appears in the Appearance category. If the check box or radio button is chosen, its Checked property is True. If it hasn't been chosen, its Checked property is False.

Aligning your check boxes and buttons

Check boxes and radio buttons normally appear with the check box or radio button to the left of descriptive text, such as:

❑   Check here if you are fed up with making choices

For variety, Visual Basic .NET can also display your check box or radio button in a total of nine different locations, as shown in Figure 7-1.

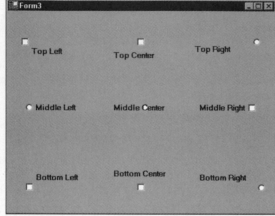

Figure 7-1: The nine different ways to align a check box or radio button with its accompanying text.

To change the alignment of text with a check box or radio button, follow these steps:

1. **Click on the check box or radio button that you want to align.**

2. **Open the Properties window.**

   To do so, press F4, choose View⇨Properties Window, click on the Properties Window icon in the Solution Explorer window, or right-click on a form and choose Properties. The Properties window appears.

3. **Click on the CheckAlign property (in the Appearance category).**

   A pop-up menu appears showing gray boxes that represent one of nine possible locations you can choose to align your check box or radio button (see Figure 7-2).

4. **Click on one of the gray boxes in the pop-up menu to choose a position.**

   Visual Basic .NET displays your check box or radio button in your chosen location.

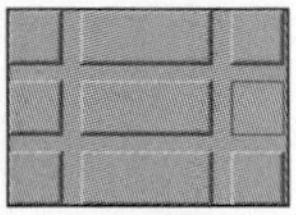

Figure 7-2:
You can
align your
check
boxes or
radio
buttons by
changing
the
CheckAlign
property.

To display a check box or radio button in certain positions, such as TopCenter, you may need to resize your check box or radio button.

As an alternative to changing the CheckAlign property (which defines the location of the check box or radio button), you may want to change the TextAlign property (in the Appearance category), which defines the location of the text of a check box or radio button.

Grouping check boxes and radio buttons

Check boxes and radio buttons rarely appear by themselves. Instead, two or more check boxes or radio buttons often huddle together like frightened farm animals. To isolate groups of check boxes and radio buttons, you can draw a GroupBox, which draws a border around a group of check boxes or radio buttons. After you draw a GroupBox, you can draw check boxes or radio buttons inside that GroupBox.

Versions of Visual Basic didn't have a GroupBox. Instead, they used something similar called a Frame. If you're already a Visual Basic programmer, make sure you remember this subtle difference.

If you have two or more radio buttons on a form, users can select only one radio button at a time. But if you isolate two groups of radio buttons into two separate GroupBoxes, users can choose two radio buttons; one radio button from within each GroupBox (as shown in Figure 7-3).

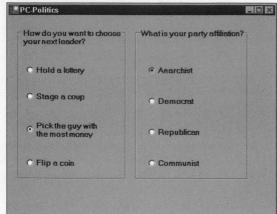

Figure 7-3:
A GroupBox can isolate separate groups of radio buttons.

To draw a GroupBox, follow these steps:

1. **Choose <u>V</u>iew⇨Toolbo<u>x</u> or press Ctrl+Alt+X. (Skip this step if the Toolbox is already visible.)**

   The Toolbox appears. You may need to click on the Windows Forms button to find the Button icon.

2. **Click on the GroupBox object.**

   The mouse pointer turns into a crosshair shape.

   If you double-click on the GroupBox icon in the Toolbox, Visual Basic .NET automatically draws a GroupBox on your form. You may need to move or resize this GroupBox later.

3. **Move the mouse over the form where you want to draw your GroupBox, hold down the left mouse button, and drag the mouse. Then release the left mouse button.**

   Visual Basic .NET draws your GroupBox on the form. At this point you can start drawing check boxes or radio buttons inside your GroupBox.

To highlight your GroupBox, you may want to change the BackColor property (in the Appearance category) to choose a background color that appears only inside your GroupBox.

If you click on a GroupBox so handles appear, you can double-click on the CheckBox or RadioButton icon on the Toolbox to make Visual Basic .NET automatically draw your check boxes or radio buttons inside your chosen GroupBox.

Test your newfound knowledge

1. What is the main difference between a check box and a radio button?

   a. You can choose one or more check boxes but only one radio button.

   b. Radio buttons tune in to your favorite radio station, but check boxes are places where you save canceled checks.

   c. I don't know. Aren't you supposed to be the teacher with all the answers?

   d. Everything is one, man. Like, the answer is all in your point of view.

2. What property determines the words that appear on a button, check box, radio button, or GroupBox?

   a. This is a communist society. All properties belong to the government.

   b. I think it's the property that you land on right after you pass Go and collect $200 in the Monopoly board game made by Parker Brothers.

   c. Properties are a capitalistic invention designed to assign arbitrary ownership to a part of nature that everyone should be able to enjoy for free.

   d. The Text property.

After you draw a check box or radio button inside a GroupBox, that check box or radio button remains trapped inside that GroupBox. When you move the GroupBox, all check boxes and radio buttons inside move along with the GroupBox.

Displaying Text on a Button, Check Box, Radio Button, or GroupBox

After you create a button, check box, radio button, or GroupBox, you need to type a descriptive text to appear on the screen, such as OK, Cancel, Yes, No, or Blame It On Your Parents. To display text on an object, you need to change the Text property.

To change the Text property, follow these steps:

1. **Click on the button, check box, radio button, or GroupBox that you want to modify.**

   Visual Basic .NET displays handles around your chosen button, check box, radio button, or GroupBox.

2. **Open the Properties window.**

   To do so, press F4, choose <u>V</u>iew⇨Properties Window, click on the Properties Window icon in the Solution Explorer window, or right-click on a form and choose P<u>r</u>operties. The Properties window appears.

3. **Double-click on the Text property (in the Appearance category).**

   Visual Basic .NET highlights the current text stored in the Text property.

4. **Type the text that you want to appear on your button, check box, GroupBox, or radio button.**

You may also want to click on the Font property (in the Appearance category) to change the font or display the text as bold or italicized.

Chapter 8

Text Boxes and Labels for Typing and Showing Words

In This Chapter

▶ Making labels and text boxes

▶ Customizing a text box for fun and profit

Despite the growing acceptance of icons and graphical user interfaces, not all choices can be offered through buttons, check boxes, or radio buttons. Sometimes your program may need to display a word, sentence, paragraph, or entire novel on the screen. And sometimes the user may want to type in a good word or two as well.

If you just want to display text to the user, you can use a Label object on your user interface. If you want to display text to the user and allow users to type text into your program, use a TextBox object.

Text boxes have two purposes in life:

- ✔ To show text on the screen
- ✔ To let the user type text into the program

Text boxes are among the most flexible programming objects because you can display instructions in a text box and the user can type a reply using ordinary words. If you use enough text boxes in your programs, you may help increase literacy among our population today.

Creating a Label or Text Box

In real life, you see labels all the time, such as the label MEN or WOMEN on a restroom door, FIRE EXTINGUISHER over a fire extinguisher in a public building, or POWER next to your monitor's on-and-off button. Labels simply call your attention to something you may otherwise overlook.

Although a text box can also display text, it's used more often to allow users to type text into your program such as their name, a password, or their phone number. Text boxes and labels are often used together where a label describes what type of information you should type into the text box (such as "Type the name of your worthless boss here:").

Both text boxes and labels can display text on-screen. The main difference is that the user can modify the text inside a text box but can't modify text inside a label.

To create a label or text box, follow these steps:

1. **Choose <u>V</u>iew⇨Toolbo<u>x</u> or press Ctrl+Alt+X. (Skip this step if the Toolbox is already visible.)**

   The Toolbox appears. You may need to click on the Windows Forms button to find the Label or TextBox icon.

2. **Click on the Label or TextBox icon.**

   The mouse pointer turns into a crosshair shape.

   If you double-click on the Label or TextBox icon in the Toolbox, Visual Basic .NET automatically draws a label on your form. You may need to move or resize this label or text box later.

3. **Move the mouse over the form where you want to draw your label or text box, hold down the left mouse button, and drag the mouse. Then release the left mouse button.**

   Visual Basic .NET draws your label or text box on the form.

4. **Open the Properties window.**

   To do so, press F4, choose <u>V</u>iew⇨Properties Window, click on the Properties Window icon in the Solution Explorer window, or right-click on a form and choose P<u>r</u>operties. The Properties window appears.

5. **Double-click on the Text property (in the Appearance category) and type the text that you want to appear inside your label or text box.**

   For text boxes, you may want to delete all text in the Text property so the text box appears blank, ready for users to type their own text into the text box.

To make your text look extra special, you may want to modify the Font property (in the Appearance category) as well.

You don't need to write BASIC code to make your labels or text boxes work. However, you will need to use BASIC code to retrieve data stored in the Text property of a text box. That way your program knows what the user typed in. Chapter 16 gives more details about retrieving data from text boxes.

Changing fonts displayed in a label or text box

To make your text look extra special, you may want to pick a different font, font size, or styles (such as bold or italics). To choose a different font, follow these steps:

1. **Click on the label or text box whose text you want to change.**

2. **Open the Properties window.**

   To do so, press F4, choose <u>V</u>iew⇨Properties Window, click on the Properties Window icon in the Solution Explorer window, or right-click on a form and choose P<u>r</u>operties. The Properties window appears.

3. **Click on the Font property (in the Appearance category).**

   A button with three dots on it appears.

4. **Click on the button with the three dots.**

   A Font dialog box appears.

5. **Click on the font, font style, size, and any effects you want (such as Strikeout) and click OK when you're finished.**

Labels and text boxes can display only one font, one size, and one type style (such as bold or italics) at a time. So, if you want to display multiple fonts in a text box, give up on that thought right now because you can't.

Coloring text in a label or text box

If you loved the idea of writing in different colors with crayons when you were a kid, you're going to love the idea of coloring text using Visual Basic .NET.

Normally, Visual Basic .NET displays text in black against a white (in a text box) or gray (in a label) background. For more creativity, you can change both the foreground and background colors of your text.

The color that fills the inside of a label or text box *(background color)* is defined by the BackColor property. The color of the text itself *(foreground color)* is defined by the ForeColor property. Both the BackColor and ForeColor properties can be found under the Appearance category of the Properties window.

To change the background or foreground color of a text box, follow these steps:

1. **Click on the label or text box whose background or foreground color you want to modify.**

2. **Open the Properties window.**

   To do so, press F4, choose View➪Properties Window, click on the Properties Window icon in the Solution Explorer window, or right-click on a form and choose Properties. The Properties window appears.

3. **Click on the BackColor or ForeColor property (in the Appearance category).**

   A downward-pointing arrow appears.

4. **Click on the downward-pointing arrow.**

   A dialog box appears displaying three tabs: Custom, Web, and System.

5. **Click on a tab (such as Web) and click on the color you want to use.**

   Visual Basic .NET shows you the effect of your chosen color on your label or text box.

By changing the color of your text boxes, you can highlight certain information and make it easier for the user to see (or ignore). Just remember that too many colors can be distracting and that some people may be colorblind, which means they won't experience the full effect of your program if they can't see the text displayed in certain colors. So use colors sparingly.

Adding pretty borders

Normally, labels don't display any visible borders and just display text on a form like a disembodied head floating in midair. Text boxes, however, do show a simple border. Of course, to give you maximum freedom of choice, you can change the borders of labels and text boxes.

To modify the border around a label or text box, follow these steps:

1. **Click on the label or text box whose border you want to change.**

2. **Open the Properties window.**

   To do so, press F4, choose View➪Properties Window, click on the Properties Window icon in the Solution Explorer window, or right-click on a form and choose Properties. The Properties window appears.

3. **Click on the BorderStyle property (in the Appearance category) and choose one of the following:**

   - None (the default border for labels)

   - FixedSingle

   - Fixed3D (the default border for text boxes)

Aligning text within a label or text box

To change the way your labels and text boxes display text, you might want to change the alignment of text. Visual Basic .NET can align text to the left, center, or right.

Users may not be able to tell how your labels or text boxes are aligning text unless your labels and text boxes display a border around their edges or unless you have other labels or text boxes nearby for comparison.

To align text in a label or text box, follow these steps:

1. **Click on the label or text box containing the text that you want to align.**

2. **Open the Properties window.**

   To do so, press F4, choose View➪Properties Window, click on the Properties Window icon in the Solution Explorer window, or right-click on a form and choose Properties. The Properties window appears.

3. **Click on the TextAlign property (in the Appearance category) and choose an option.**

   The options for aligning text in a text box are

   - Left

   - Right

   - Center

   The options for aligning text in a label are

   - Top Left (the default alignment)

   - Top Center

   - Top Right

   - Middle Left

   - Middle Center

   - Middle Right

   - Bottom Left

   - Bottom Center

   - Bottom Right

Customizing a Text Box

By default, text boxes are pretty stupid at handling text. If you type too much text into a text box, the text cheerfully scrolls out of sight. If users need to move the cursor inside a text box, they can use the following keys:

- **Delete:** Erases the character to the right of the cursor
- **Backspace:** Erases the character to the left of the cursor
- **Left arrow:** Moves the cursor one character to the left
- **Right arrow:** Moves the cursor one character to the right
- **Ctrl+Left arrow:** Moves the cursor one word to the left
- **Ctrl+Right arrow:** Moves the cursor one word to the right
- **Home (or Ctrl+Home):** Moves the cursor to the beginning of the line
- **End (or Ctrl+End):** Moves the cursor to the end of the line
- **Shift+any movement key (such as Home or Right arrow):** Highlights text

Depending on what you need, you can customize a text box to display word-wrapping like a word processor, accept passwords (by hiding text behind characters such as an asterisk), or limit the maximum amount of text allowed in a text box in the first place.

Word-wrapping text boxes

Rather than force users to type text and watch it scroll off to one side of a text box, you can make your text boxes do word-wrapping. That way users can see two or more lines of text in your text box.

To turn on word-wrapping for a text box, follow these steps:

1. **Click on the text box where you want to display word-wrapping.**

2. **Open the Properties window.**

   To do so, press F4, choose <u>V</u>iew⇨Properties Window, click on the Properties Window icon in the Solution Explorer window, or right-click on a form and choose P<u>r</u>operties. The Properties window appears.

3. **Click on the Multiline property (in the Behavior category).**

   A downward-pointing arrow appears.

4. **Click on the downward-pointing arrow and choose True.**

Until you change the Multiline property in the Behavior category to True, you won't be able to increase the height of your text box.

5. **Click on the text box that you chose in Step 1 and resize the height of that text box.**

   As an alternative, click in the Height property (in the Layout category) and type a new value for your text box's height.

6. **Make sure the WordWrap property (in the Behavior category) is set to True.**

   The WordWrap property is set to True by default when you create a text box, but if you have changed this to False, you need to set its value back to True. The next time you run your program, your text box will display text on multiple lines and wrap the words within the confines of the text box.

You may want to set the ScrollBars property (in the Appearance category) to Vertical. That way if someone types a large chunk of text in your text box, he can use the vertical scroll bar to view that text.

Making a password text box

In case you work for the CIA, FBI, NSA, DIA, IRS, or any organization that spends lots of money, buries itself in secrecy, and hides behind a three-letter acronym, you may be interested in the ability of Visual Basic .NET to create special password text boxes.

Rather than display ordinary text, *password text boxes* mask any text you type into a text box with a single character, such as an asterisk (*). Figure 8-1 shows how the password "Top Secret" appears as only asterisks in the "CIA Software" text box.

Figure 8-1:
When a user types text into a password text box, the characters get masked by a character such as an asterisk.

To create a password text box, you need to define the character for the text box to display when someone types in text. To do this, you need to follow these steps:

1. **Click on the text box that you want to turn into a password text box.**

2. **Open the Properties window.**

   To do so, press F4, choose View➪Properties Window, click on the Properties Window icon in the Solution Explorer window, or right-click on a form and choose Properties. The Properties window appears.

3. **Click on the Multiline property (in the Behavior category).**

   A downward-pointing arrow appears.

4. **Click on the downward-pointing arrow and choose False.**

   If you don't set the MultiLine property of a password text box to False, the password text box won't mask any typed characters. This is the Visual Basic .NET way of saying that passwords can't be so long that they require two or more lines to write.

5. **Double-click on the PassChar property (in the Behavior category) and type a single character (such as an asterisk *) that you want to appear when the user types into your text box.**

   The masking character can only be a single character. The most common character used to mask passwords is the asterisk (*).

Limiting the length of text

To prevent people from getting too wordy, you can set the maximum length of text for a text box. This way, people can't type rambling essays about what they did last summer in your text boxes.

To define the maximum length of characters that a text box can accept, follow these steps:

1. **Click on the text box whose maximum character length you want to define.**

2. **Open the Properties window.**

   To do so, press F4, choose View➪Properties Window, click on the Properties Window icon in the Solution Explorer window, or right-click on a form and choose Properties. The Properties window appears.

Test your newfound knowledge

1. Give two uses for text boxes.

   a. To store letters from your Scrabble game and to contain words that may win you a million dollars on Wheel of Fortune.

   b. To display text on-screen and to let users type text into a program.

   c. To store all the computer books that you buy but never read and to make cardboard forts that your children can hide in.

   d. To use as a litter box and to give your cat something to read.

2. If a text box has the PasswordChar property set to * (asterisk) and the MaxLength property set to 10, what happens?

   a. I have to flip back through the pages of this book to find the answer, so wait while I do that.

   b. I'm not sure, but whatever happens must be important because this question is listed here.

   c. This defines the secret password that is needed to unleash the latest computer virus.

   d. The text box accepts a maximum of 10 characters and displays an asterisk (*) in place of an actual typed character.

3. **Double-click on the MaxLength property (in the Behavior category) and type any number greater than zero.**

   A value of zero effectively means that there is no limit to the number of characters a user can type in a text box.

   The MaxLength property defines the maximum number of characters a user can type into a text box. However, a text box will always display all the text that you type into the Text property for that particular text box.

Chapter 9

Showing Choices with List and Combo Boxes

In This Chapter

▶ Creating list boxes and combo boxes

▶ Sorting items in a list box or combo box

▶ Making listed items look pretty

Check boxes and radio buttons can display multiple choices for the user to pick from, but the problem is that each check box or radio button takes up space on a form. The more check boxes or radio buttons displayed, the more confusing the choices may be.

So to provide another way to display choices to users, you can use list boxes or combo boxes. Both list boxes and combo boxes can show more choices to the user while taking up much less room than multiple check boxes or radio buttons. In addition, a combo box also offers users the chance to type in data just like a text box does.

Making a List Box and a Combo Box

List boxes display long lists of options from which users can choose. If users want to choose something that isn't on the list, too bad. They can't.

Combo boxes also display long lists of options for the user to choose. The difference is that combo boxes also let the user type in a choice if the selection the user wants cannot be found on the list. Figure 9-1 shows an example of a list box and a combo box. Notice that the combo box displays items only if you click on the down arrow while the list box always displays items.

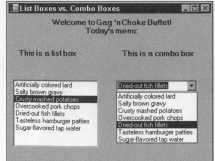

Figure 9-1:
What a list
box and a
combo box
look like.

Creating list boxes and combo boxes

List boxes are like fast-food menus. You can choose only what's on the menu because the folks working there don't know how to handle special requests. Combo boxes are like fancy restaurants where you have a choice of ordering off the menu or saying, "I know this is a vegetarian restaurant, but I want the cook to grill me a steak anyway."

To create a list box or combo, follow these steps:

1. **Choose <u>V</u>iew⇨<u>Toolbox</u> or press Ctrl+Alt+X. (Skip this step if the Toolbox is already visible.)**

   The Toolbox appears. You may need to click on the Windows Forms button to find the ListBox or ComboBox icon.

   If you double-click on the ListBox or ComboBox icon in the Toolbox, Visual Basic .NET draws your list box or combo box for you automatically.

2. **Click on the ListBox or ComboBox icon.**

   The mouse pointer turns into a crosshair shape.

   If you want to create a list box that displays check boxes next to each item, as shown in Figure 9-2, click on the CheckedListBox icon on the Toolbox.

Figure 9-2:
Comparing
an ordinary
list box with
a checked
list box.

3. **Move the mouse to the place on the form where you want to draw the list box or combo box.**

4. **Hold down the left mouse button and move the mouse to draw the list box or combo box.**

Visual Basic .NET draws your list box or combo box with a dull caption such as ListBox3 or ComboBox1.

Choosing a combo box style

For added fun and amusement, combo boxes can be one of three different styles, as shown in Figure 9-3:

- ✔ **Simple:** Displays a list of items that always appear on the screen.

  Unlike the other two combo box styles that never vary in height, you must adjust the height of a Simple combo box style so users can see the list of items stored underneath.

- ✔ **DropDown:** Initially displays the contents of the Text property. If the user clicks on the downward-pointing arrow of the combo box, a drop-down list appears.

- ✔ **DropDownList:** Initially displays a blank box, regardless of the value of the Text property. If the user clicks on the downward-pointing arrow of the combo box, a drop-down list appears.

Unlike the Simple or DropDown combo boxes, users cannot type anything into a DropDownList combo box.

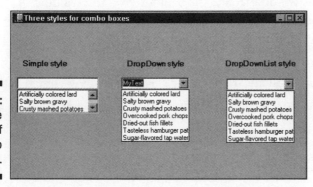

Figure 9-3:
The three styles of combo boxes.

Test your newfound knowledge

1. What is the major difference between a list box and a combo box?

   a. A combo box gives you a choice of typing an item or choosing one from a displayed list. A list box forces you to choose an item from a displayed list.

   b. A list box is spelled L-I-S-T, but a combo box is spelled C-O-M-B-O.

   c. Combo boxes are cooler than list boxes because they tend to be more confusing to the average user.

   d. No difference. In fact, two out of three French chefs think that they both taste exactly like butter.

2. How can you display items in a list box or combo box?

   a. Draw them on the screen with a permanent marking pen.

   b. Through secret pagan rituals and incantations that border close to heresy.

   c. Hook the list box or combo box up to a Web cam.

   d. You can display items in a list box and a combo box?

To define the style for a combo box, follow these steps:

1. **Click on the combo box that you want to change.**

   (This assumes that you've already created the combo box.)

2. **Open the Properties window.**

   To do so, press F4, choose View⇨Properties Window, click on the Properties Window icon in the Solution Explorer window, or right-click on a form and choose Properties. The Properties window appears.

3. **Click on the DropDownStyle property (in the Appearance category).**

   A downward-pointing arrow appears.

4. **Click on the downward-pointing arrow to display your list of choices.**

   (Hey, what do you know? The Style Property is an example of a drop-down list box!)

5. **Click on the combo box style you want, such as Simple or DropDownList.**

   Visual Basic .NET displays your combo box in your chosen style.

Filling List Boxes and Combo Boxes with Stuff

After you create your list box or combo box, you have to fill up your box with items. (Otherwise, the list box and combo box don't display anything.) Visual Basic .NET gives you two ways to add items to a list box or combo box:

✔ Use the Items property (in the Data category) of the Properties window.

✔ Use BASIC code.

To add items to a list box or a combo box using the Items property, follow these steps:

1. **Click on the list box or combo box that you want to add items to.**

2. **Open the Properties window.**

   To do so, press F4, choose View⇨Properties Window, click on the Properties Window icon in the Solution Explorer window, or right-click on a form and choose Properties. The Properties window appears.

3. **Click on the Items property (in the Data category).**

   A button with three dots appears.

4. **Click on the button with three dots.**

   A String Collection Editor dialog box appears, as shown in Figure 9-4.

Figure 9-4:
To add items to a list box or combo box, you can type them into the String Collection Editor dialog box.

5. **Type each item that you want to appear in the list box or combo box and press Enter after each item.**

6. **Repeat Step 5 for each item you want to add in your list box or combo box.**

7. **Click OK.**

In case you want to change the list of items that appear in a list box or combo box while your program is running, you have to use BASIC code. If you want to add an item so that it appears at the bottom of all available choices in your list box or combo box, you can use the following magical BASIC command:

```
BoxName.Items.Add ("Add me")
```

The above BASIC code does the following:

1. `BoxName` tells Visual Basic .NET to look for a list box or combo box named `BoxName`. (Obviously you need to change this name to identify the specific list box or combo box that you want to add an item to.)

2. `Items.Add` tells Visual Basic .NET to get ready to add an item to the list box or combo box identified by `BoxName`.

3. `("Add me")` tells Visual Basic .NET to add the string `"Add me"` to the bottom of the list box or combo box identified by `BoxName`. (In a real program, you would type your own text inside the quotation marks.)

Normally, `Items.Add` adds your text to the bottom of the items already stored in the list box or combo box. If you have changed the Sorted property (in the Behavior category) to True, however, Visual Basic .NET sorts your newly added item alphabetically. See the following section, "Sorting items in a list box or combo box" for more information about sorting.

In case you want to specify the exact position to display a newly added item in a list box or combo box, you can use `Insert` instead of the `Add`, such as:

```
BoxName.Items.Insert (X, "Add me")
```

The above BASIC code does the following:

1. `BoxName` tells Visual Basic .NET to look for a list box or combo box named `BoxName`. (Obviously you need to change this name to identify the specific list box or combo box that you want to add an item to.)

2. `Items.Insert` tells Visual Basic .NET to get ready to insert an item into a specific location in the list box or combo box identified by `BoxName`. This specific location will be identified by a number.

3. `(X, "Add me")` tells Visual Basic .NET to add the string `"Add me"` to the position in the list represented by the number X. The first item in a

list box or combo box is at location zero (0), the second item is at location one (1), and so on. So if you wanted to insert the text "Add me" to the second position in a list box or combo box, you would type **(1, "Add me")** because the number 1 represents the second position in the list.

Sorting items in a list box or combo box

The order that you add items to a list box or combo box is the order in which the items appear. For a little variety, you may want Visual Basic .NET to sort the items in a list box or combo box alphabetically.

When Visual Basic .NET sorts a list alphabetically, the list is sorted without regard to whether items are capitalized or not. For example, Visual Basic .NET considers "Your Momma" and "YOUR MOMMA" to be identical when it comes to list and combo boxes.

To sort items in a list box or combo box alphabetically, follow these steps:

1. **Click on the list box or combo box in which you want to display items alphabetically.**

2. **Open the Properties window.**

   To do so, press F4, choose View⇨Properties Window, click on the Properties Window icon in the Solution Explorer window, or right-click on a form and choose Properties. The Properties window appears.

3. **Click on the Sorted property (in the Behavior category).**

   A downward-pointing arrow appears.

4. **Click on the downward-pointing arrow and choose True (or False if you want to turn off sorting).**

   When the Sorted property is set to True, your list box or combo box automatically sorts your list of items alphabetically.

Visual Basic .NET always sorts items with the A's on top and the Z's at the bottom. (If you have numbers in your list box or combo box, Visual Basic .NET sorts the numbers from 0 to 9. If you have a mixture of numbers and letters, Visual Basic .NET sorts the numbered items at the top of the list or combo box and the character items underneath the sorted numbered items.) You cannot sort items in descending order, with the Z's on top and the A's at the bottom (unless, of course, you flip your monitor upside down).

If alphabetic sorting isn't what you want, you can manually sort items by typing them in the order you want them to appear in the String Collection Editor dialog box, or by using the Items.Insert BASIC command to specify the exact numerical location for each item.

Removing items from a list box or combo box

Adding items and sorting them may make your lists look nice, but wiping out an item to satisfy that destructive urge that everyone experiences once in a while is more fun.

Visual Basic .NET gives you two ways to remove an item from a list:

✔ Use the `Items.RemoveAt` BASIC command to specify which item to remove.

✔ Use the `Items.Clear` BASIC command to wipe out an entire list at once.

To use the `Items.Remove` BASIC command, you have to know the location of the item that you want to remove. For example, to remove the third item from a list box named lstToDo, use the following BASIC statement:

```
lstToDo.Items.RemoveAt (2)
```

The first item in a list is at location zero (0), the second is at location one (1), and the third is at location two (2).

If you want to remove the currently selected item, you can use this statement:

```
ComboBox1.Items.RemoveAt (ComboBox1.SelectedItem)
```

To use the `Items.Clear` BASIC command to wipe out an entire list in a single blow, you need the name of the list box or combo box that contains the list you want to kill. To wipe out the entire contents of a combo box named cboHideIn, use the following BASIC statement:

```
cboHideIn.Items.Clear()
```

Before using `Clear`, make sure that you really want to wipe out an entire list.

Making Listed Items Look Pretty

To spice up your lists and make them look a little less like boring shopping lists, change the font, type style, and size of your list's items.

Fonts are different ways to display text. Normally, Visual Basic .NET uses the MS Sans Serif font, but you can use any font stored in the memory of your computer. (MS Sans Serif is similar to the Helvetica font, and the Visual Basic .NET MS Serif font is similar to the Times Roman font.)

To change the font of items that appear in a list box or combo box, follow these steps:

1. **Click on the list box or combo box that you want to modify.**

2. **Open the Properties window.**

   To do so, press F4, choose View⇨Properties Window, click on the Properties Window icon in the Solution Explorer window, or right-click on a form and choose Properties. The Properties window appears.

3. **Click on the Font property (in the Appearance category) in the Properties window.**

   A button with three dots appears.

4. **Click on the button with three dots on it.**

   Visual Basic .NET displays a Font dialog box.

5. **Click on the font, font style, size, and any effects you want (such as strikeout) and click OK.**

   Visual Basic .NET immediately changes the text in your list box or combo box.

Be careful when you use fonts. Novices often get carried away and use so many bizarre fonts that all semblance of normality is lost. Unless you have a really good reason to use different fonts, let Visual Basic .NET use its default font of MS Sans Serif.

The more attractive you make your list boxes and combo boxes, the more likely the user is going to notice the boxes (if not use them). Just remember that you want to make your program easy to use, not a work of art. If you want to get creative, take up finger-painting. If you want to create useful programs and make millions of dollars, make your programs easy, fun, and simple to use.

Chapter 10

Fine-Tuning the Appearance of Your User Interface

After you've sprinkled a few user interface objects (such as buttons, text boxes, or radio buttons) on a form, Visual Basic .NET provides several ways to tidy up your user interface that include:

✔ Making your objects the same size

✔ Aligning objects

✔ Arranging the spacing of your objects

✔ Locking objects in place

Resizing Your Objects

If you've drawn multiple objects that need to be the same size, such as groups of check boxes or radio buttons, you can have Visual Basic .NET automatically resize your objects.

To automatically resize multiple objects, follow these steps:

1. **Click on the first object (such as a radio button) that you want to resize.**

2. **Hold down the Ctrl key and click on one or more additional objects (such as a check box) that you want to resize.**

   Visual Basic .NET highlights each of your chosen objects.

3. **Click on the object that you want to use as the standard for resizing all the objects you chose in Step 1 and 2.**

   If you want all the objects to appear the same size as a specific button, click on that specific button in Step 2. Visual Basic .NET highlights the last object you chose with white handles. This is Visual Basic .NET's way of saying, "I'm going to keep this last object at its original size but change the size of all the other objects."

4. **Choose Format⇨Make Same Size, and choose one of the following:**

   - Width: Changes the width of your objects
   - Size to Grid: Squeezes all your objects to precisely line up to the grid displayed on the form
   - Height: Changes the height of your objects
   - Both: Changes both the width and height of your objects

   After you choose one of the preceding options, Visual Basic .NET cheerfully resizes your chosen objects.

If you suddenly don't like the way Visual Basic .NET resized your objects, press Ctrl+Z or click on the Undo icon on the Standard toolbar.

Neatly Aligning Objects

Multiple objects may look awkward when viewed next to each other. So you may want to align multiple objects with one another in the following ways as shown in Figure 10-1:

- ✔ **Lefts:** Aligns objects along their left edges
- ✔ **Centers:** Aligns objects vertically along their center
- ✔ **Rights:** Aligns objects along their right edges
- ✔ **Tops:** Aligns objects along their top edges
- ✔ **Middles:** Aligns objects horizontally along their center
- ✔ **Bottoms:** Aligns objects along their bottom edges
- ✔ **To Grid:** Aligns objects to the grid displayed on the form

You can modify the grid size that appears on a form by clicking on the form (not on any objects that may appear on that form), opening the Properties window, and then changing the GridSize Width and Height properties in the Design category. A higher number displays grid dots farther apart while a lower number displays grid dots spaced closer together.

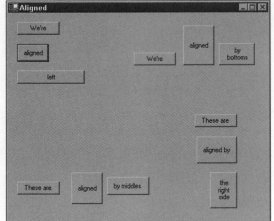

Figure 10-1:
Several
different
ways to
align
objects.

To align multiple objects, follow these steps:

1. **Hold down the Ctrl key and click on one or more objects (such as a radio button) that you want to align.**

   Visual Basic .NET highlights each of your chosen objects.

2. **Click on the object that you want to use as the standard for aligning your objects.**

   The last object you choose will remain fixed. All the objects you chose in Step 1 will align themselves to the last object you picked.

3. **Choose Format⇨Align and choose an option such as Lefts or Middles.**

   Visual Basic .NET aligns all your chosen objects.

You can always press Ctrl+Z or click on the Undo icon on the Standard toolbar right away to undo the way Visual Basic .NET aligned your objects.

Putting Space Between Your Objects

Another way to align your objects is to adjust the horizontal and vertical spacing between your objects.

To change the spacing between your objects, follow these steps:

1. **Hold down the Ctrl key and click on one or more objects (such as a radio button) that you want to align by defining the horizontal or vertical spacing.**

   Visual Basic .NET highlights each of your chosen objects.

2. **Click on the object that you want to use as the standard for spacing your other objects.**

   The last object you choose will remain fixed in its current position while all the objects you chose in Step 1 will move.

3. **Choose Format⇨Horizontal Spacing/Vertical Spacing and choose one of the following:**

   - Make Equal: Moves all objects so the horizontal or vertical spacing between them are all equal.

   - Increase: Moves the objects away from the object you chose in Step 2.

   - Decrease: Moves the objects closer to the object you chose in Step 2.

   - Remove: Shoves all your selected objects so they touch.

If Visual Basic .NET made the spacing between your objects look too weird, you can fix this problem by pressing Ctrl+Z or clicking on the Undo icon on the Standard toolbar right away to undo the way Visual Basic .NET aligned your objects.

Test your newfound knowledge

1. Why is aligning your objects so important?

   a. So that they can form a barrier that prevents stupid people from getting too close to you.

   b. To help you create uglier and messier user interfaces.

   c. To help you create neater and precisely designed user interfaces.

   d. Wait a minute, I meant to choose answer c.

2. When you choose to align or resize your objects, which object does Visual Basic .NET NOT change in any way?

   a. The last object that you clicked on before choosing an alignment or resize command.

   b. The object that's stuck between your coworker's front teeth.

   c. The object that someone drew on the wall in the public restroom.

   d. Visual Basic .NET changes everything. That's what makes programming so cool.

Centering Your Objects

To make your user interface look aesthetically pleasing, you may want to center one or more objects on a form. Rather than force you to do this manually, Visual Basic .NET can center objects on a form automatically, either vertically or horizontally.

To center an object, follow these steps:

1. **Click on one or more objects that you want to center on a form.**

   You can choose multiple objects by holding down the Ctrl key and clicking on each object that you want to center.

2. **Choose Format➪Center in Form and then choose either Horizontally or Vertically.**

   Visual Basic .NET centers all your chosen objects.

Locking Down Your Objects

Locking is like gluing your objects on a specific location on a form so no one else can accidentally or purposely move that object later. Locking your objects can be especially useful if two or more programmers are working on the same program. That way one programmer can keep a second programmer from messing up the user interface.

Locking objects just keeps you from moving them, but you can still delete them or edit their properties at any time.

Locking (and unlocking) all the objects on a form

To lock the position and size of all objects that appear on a form, follow these steps:

1. **Click on any object (such as a text box) on your form.**

2. **Choose Format➪Lock Controls.**

   Visual Basic .NET locks all the objects on your chosen form.

After you've chosen the Lock Controls command, if you click on an object, Visual Basic .NET highlights it with a white border to show you visually that the object is locked and you can't move or resize it, as shown in Figure 10-2.

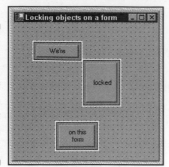

Figure 10-2:
Locked
objects on a
form appear
with a white
border
when you
select them.

To unlock all the objects on a form, click on any object on a form and choose Format⇨Lock Controls again.

Locking (and unlocking) individual objects

Rather than lock every object on a form, you may just want to lock one or two objects so you can keep moving or resizing the other objects around. To lock an individual object, follow these steps:

1. **Click on the object (such as a text box) that you want to lock.**

2. **Open the Properties window.**

   To do so, press F4, choose View⇨Properties Window, click on the Properties Window icon in the Solution Explorer window, or right-click on a form and choose Properties. The Properties window appears.

3. **Click on the Locked property (in the Design category).**

   A downward-pointing arrow appears.

4. **Click on the downward-pointing arrow and choose True.**

   Visual Basic .NET now displays your chosen object with a white border around it to show you that it's locked in place.

To unlock an individual object, repeat Steps 1 through 4 except choose False in Step 4.

Part III
Making Menus

The 5th Wave   By Rich Tennant

"You ever get the feeling this project could just up and die at any moment?"

In this part . . .

*P*ull-down menus are a fancy way to organize all the
options available in your program. That way, if users
want to do something with your program, they just have
to choose the right pull-down menu and pick the appropri-
ate command.

This part of the book shows you how to make pull-down
menus in your own programs. Believe it or not, making
your own menus is actually simple. (The hard part is
making your program actually work the way you want it
to, which is something that even eludes the grasp of
Microsoft's own legion of programmers.)

Chapter 11

Creating and Editing Pull-Down Menus

· ·

In This Chapter

▶ Creating menus and menu titles

▶ Naming your menus

▶ Prettying up your menus

· ·

*P*ull-down menus organize groups of related commands in one place. That way you don't have to clutter up your user interface with group boxes, panels, or tab controls to organize related options together.

The Basic Elements of a Menu Bar

The most common menu titles found on most programs include File, Edit, Window, and Help.

The File menu, as shown in Figure 11-1, typically contains commands directly related to file operations, such as opening, closing, saving, and printing files, as well as quitting the program so that you can go to the kitchen and get something to eat.

The Edit menu typically contains commands related to editing (duh), such as Undo (and Redo), Cut, Copy, Paste, Clear, and Select All.

The Windows menu typically contains commands related to opening, closing, arranging, and switching among different windows.

The Windows menu only appears in programs that allow you to open up multiple windows, such as a word processor. If a program doesn't need to open multiple windows, then the Windows menu won't be needed.

Menu title   Menu commands

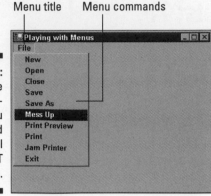

Figure 11-1:
An example
of a pull-
down menu
as displayed
in a Visual
Basic .NET
program.

The Help menu contains commands for getting help from the program. Typical help commands include a table of contents to the help system, an alphabetical index, propaganda about product support, and an About command that displays useless information the programmers think you want to see.

Usually the File and Edit menu titles appear side by side and any menu titles unique to your particular program appear sandwiched between the Edit and the Window menu titles. For example, many word-processing programs have a Tools menu title that displays commands for grammar checking, hyphenation, macro creation, and other commands that 99 percent of the working population of the world is never going to use.

If your menu titles are unique to your particular program (in other words, they're not the standard Edit or Window menu titles found on other programs), try to make your menu titles descriptive — that way users will have a better idea about where to find a specific command.

Making Menus for Your User Interface

To create pull-down menus, follow these steps:

1. **Click on the form that you want your pull-down menus to appear on.**

2. **Double-click on the MainMenu icon in the Toolbox.**

   Visual Basic .NET displays a blank menu on your form and displays a MainMenu1 icon in a separate window near the bottom of the screen, as shown in Figure 11-2.

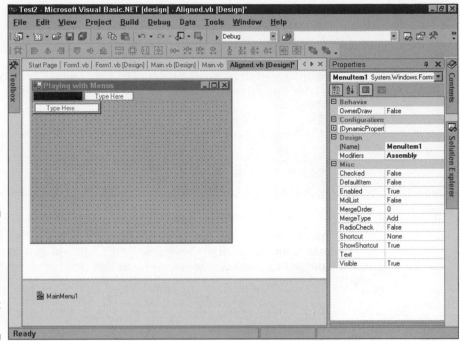

Figure 11-2:
What a
pull-down
menu looks
like when
you first
create it.

3. **Click in the box on your form that displays the words** `"Type Here"` **and type your menu title, such as File or Format.**

   Visual Basic .NET displays your text as a menu title or menu command and automatically creates an additional "Type Here" box for creating new menu titles or menu commands.

   To create a hot key for your menus, type the ampersand character (&) in front of the letter that you want to appear underlined in your menu. For example, to display a typical File menu, you would type **&File** in the "Type Here" box.

4. **Repeat Step 3 for each menu title or menu command that you want to add.**

If you click on your pull-down menus, nothing happens because you haven't written any BASIC code to tell your program what to do when the menu commands are selected.

Adding and deleting menu titles and commands

After you've created your pull-down menus, you may want to add or delete menu titles later. To add another menu title or command to a form, follow these steps:

1. **Open the form that contains the pull-down menus that you want to edit.**

2. **Click on the pull-down menu.**

   If you click on a menu title, Visual Basic .NET displays a pull-down menu.

3. **Do one of the following:**

   • To add a new menu title, click on an existing menu title. When you add a new menu title, Visual Basic .NET will add it to the left of the existing menu title that you chose in this step.

   • To add a new menu command, click on an existing menu command. When you add a new menu command, Visual Basic .NET will add it above the existing menu command you chose in this step.

4. **Press Insert.**

   Visual Basic .NET inserts your new menu title or command on your pull-down menus.

To delete a menu title or command, follow these steps:

1. **Open the form that contains the pull-down menus that you want to edit.**

2. **Click on the pull-down menu.**

   If you click on a menu title, Visual Basic .NET displays a pull-down menu.

3. **Press Delete.**

   If your chosen item has any additional menu commands attached to it, a dialog box appears, asking if you really want to delete your chosen item.

4. **Click Yes.**

When you delete a menu title or menu command, any BASIC code you've written for that particular menu command still exists, so you'll have to delete this code as well.

Moving menu titles and commands around

Instead of adding or deleting parts of your pull-down menus, you may need to rearrange their position instead. To move a menu title or command, follow these steps:

1. **Open the form that contains the pull-down menus that you want to edit.**

2. **Do one of the following:**

   - Click on the menu title that you want to move. When you move a menu title, you automatically move any menu commands attached to that menu title.

   - Click on the menu title that contains the command that you want to move. Then click on that menu command.

   Visual Basic .NET highlights your chosen menu title or command.

3. **Hold down the left mouse button and drag the mouse to the new location where you want to move the menu title or command.**

   Visual Basic .NET displays the new location of your menu title or command.

   You can move a menu title so it becomes a command underneath another menu title and vice versa.

4. **Release the left mouse button when you're happy with the new location of your menu title or command.**

Naming Menus

Every menu title and menu command needs a name so you can identify it later. Names cannot include spaces, punctuation, or words that the editors at Hungry Minds deem offensive and, hence, may harm sales of this book.

When naming your menu titles and commands, you may want to use the mnu prefix such as:

- ✔ mnuFile
- ✔ mnuWindow
- ✔ mnuFileOpen

Visual Basic .NET doesn't care whether you use uppercase or lowercase consistently. If you really want to, you can use the following names for menus:

- MNufiLEmNuwINDow
- MNUfileOPEN

Of course, such names are not only hard to read, but the scattered casing also makes you look illiterate. So for consistency (and to protect your image), the best method is to adopt a consistent naming style whenever you use Visual Basic .NET.

To identify menu commands that appear under certain menu titles, include the menu title as part of a menu command's name. For example, if the menu title File is named mnuFile, menu commands (such as the Open, Save, and Exit commands) that appear in the File menu should have names like mnuFileOpen, mnuFileSave, and mnuFileExit.

To name your menu titles and commands, follow these steps:

1. **Open the form that contains the pull-down menus that you want to edit.**

2. **Do one of the following:**

   - Click on the menu title that you want to name.

   - Click on the menu title that contains the command that you want to name. Then click on that menu command.

   Visual Basic .NET highlights your chosen menu title or command.

3. **Open the Properties window.**

   To do so, press F4, choose View⊅Properties Window, click on the Properties Window icon in the Solution Explorer window, or right-click on a form and choose Properties. The Properties window appears.

4. **Double-click in the Name property (in the Design category).**

   Visual Basic .NET highlights the current Name property.

5. **Type the name you want for your menu title or command.**

Making Menus Pretty

To make your menus easier to use, you can separate menu commands with separator bars, display check marks next to currently used menu commands, add shortcut keys so users don't have to use your pull-down menus at all, and dim or remove menu items altogether.

Putting separator bars in menus

Separator bars are lines in a pull-down menu that divide groups of commands, as shown in Figure 11-3. Generally, separator bars group related items so that users can find the command they want.

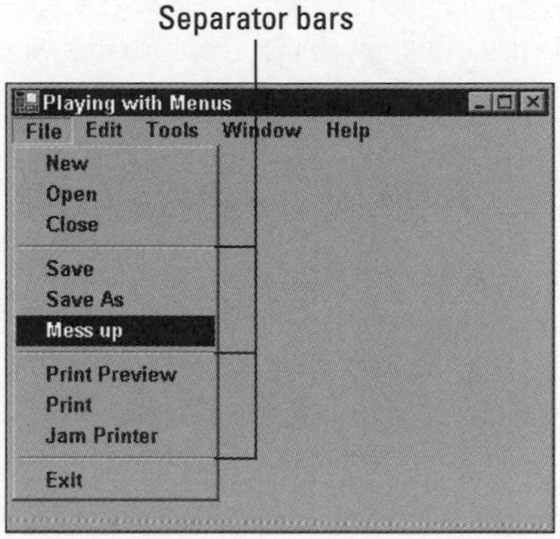

Separator bars

Figure 11-3:
Separator
bars can
help you
organize
related
commands
together.

To create a separator bar, follow these steps:

1. **Open the form that contains the pull-down menus that you want to edit.**

2. **Click on the pull-down menu where you want to add separator bars.**

   Visual Basic .NET displays your chosen pull-down menu.

3. **Click on the menu command that you want to appear directly below your separator bar.**

4. **Press Insert.**

   Visual Basic .NET displays an empty box directly above the menu command you chose in Step 3.

5. **Click in this empty box and type a dash (-).**

   Visual Basic .NET displays a dash in the menu command. The next time you run your program, that dash magically appears in your pull-down menu as a separator bar.

Test your newfound knowledge

1. Why are pull-down menus so useful?

   a. They hide commands so that users can't find them.

   b. They make programs easier to use by organizing related commands in easy-to-find menus.

   c. Pull-down menus are useful for confusing people while giving them the illusion that it's their fault for not knowing how to use your program in the first place.

   d. If pull-down menus are so useful, how come people still need to buy 400-page books to teach them how to use these stupid programs?

2. How can you create and edit pull-down menus in a Visual Basic .NET program?

   a. Double-click on the MainMenu icon in the Toolbox.

   b. Copy someone else's program and hope that they don't notice.

   c. To create pull-down menus, you need to earn a four-year degree studying C++ and Java.

   d. Visual Basic .NET can create pull-down menus?

Assigning shortcut keys

For commonly used commands, you can assign commands to *shortcut keys*, such as Ctrl+S to choose the Save command or Ctrl+X to choose the Cut command. Shortcut keys let the user give a command without wading through multiple pull-down menus. Figure 11-4 shows some shortcut keys.

Figure 11-4:
Shortcut keys allow users to choose commonly used commands by pressing unique keystrokes.

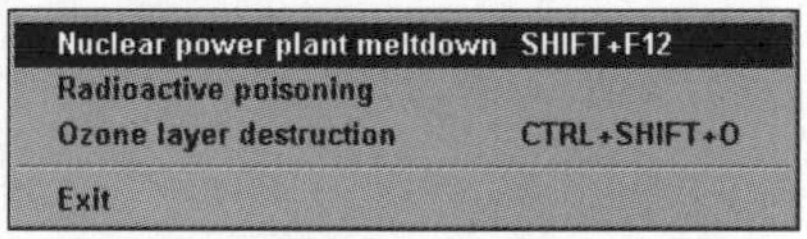

Nuclear power plant meltdown	SHIFT+F12
Radioactive poisoning	
Ozone layer destruction	CTRL+SHIFT+O
Exit	

Shortcut keys appear on menus next to the commands they represent. In this way, users can quickly discover the shortcut keys for all your menu commands.

To assign shortcut keys to menu commands, follow these steps:

1. **Open the form that contains the pull-down menus that you want to edit.**

2. **Click on the pull-down menu where you want to add shortcut keys to a command.**

   Visual Basic .NET displays your chosen pull-down menu.

3. **Click on the menu command where you want to add a shortcut key.**

4. **Open the Properties window.**

   To do so, press F4, choose View⇨Properties Window, click on the Properties Window icon in the Solution Explorer window, or right-click on a form and choose Properties. The Properties window appears.

5. **Click on the Shortcut property (in the Misc category).**

   A downward-pointing arrow appears.

6. **Click on the downward-pointing arrow.**

   A pop-up list of available shortcut keys appears, as shown in Figure 11-5.

Figure 11-5:
Choosing a
shortcut key
for your
menu
command.

7. **Click on the shortcut key that you want to use for your menu command.**

Ideally, you want to choose keystroke combinations that are easy to remember, such as Ctrl+S for the Save command or Ctrl+X for the Cut command.

Visual Basic .NET won't let you assign the same shortcut keys to different commands. If you try to, it scolds you with an Error dialog box.

When you run your program, the shortcut keys appear on your pull-down menu. Until you write BASIC code to tell your menus how to act, nothing will happen if you press a menu command's shortcut key.

If you change the ShowShortcut property (in Misc category to False), your shortcut won't appear on the menu.

Putting check marks next to menu commands

Check marks, which appear next to items on a menu, visually show that the items already have been selected.

Check marks can appear next to commands that appear in a pull-down menu. Visual Basic .NET won't let you display a check mark next to a pull-down menu title.

Visual Basic .NET can display two types of check marks: an ordinary check mark and a radio check mark, which looks like a round circle.

To add a check mark to a menu command, follow these steps:

1. **Open the form that contains the pull-down menus that you want to edit.**

2. **Click on the pull-down menu where you want to add a check mark.**

   Visual Basic .NET displays your chosen pull-down menu.

3. **Click on the menu command where you want to display a check mark.**

4. **Open the Properties window.**

   To do so, press F4, choose View➪Properties Window, click on the Properties Window icon in the Solution Explorer window, or right-click on a form and choose Properties. The Properties window appears.

5. **Click on the Checked property (in the Misc category).**

   A downward-pointing arrow appears. The Checked property displays a check mark. The RadioCheck property displays a round dot.

6. **Click on the downward-pointing arrow and choose True.**

   The next time you run your Visual Basic .NET program, a check mark appears next to your chosen menu command.

To add a radio check mark to a menu command, follow these steps:

1. **Open the form that contains the pull-down menus that you want to edit.**

2. **Click on the pull-down menu where you want to add a check mark.**

   Visual Basic .NET displays your chosen pull-down menu.

3. **Click on the menu command where you want to display a check mark.**

4. **Open the Properties window.**

   To do so, press F4, choose <u>V</u>iew⇨Properties Window, click on the Properties Window icon in the Solution Explorer window, or right-click on a form and choose P<u>r</u>operties. The Properties window appears.

5. **Click on the Checked property (in the Misc category).**

   A downward-pointing arrow appears.

6. **Click on the downward-pointing arrow and choose True.**

7. **Click on the RadioCheck property (in the Misc category).**

   A downward-pointing arrow appears.

8. **Click on the downward-pointing arrow and choose True.**

   The next time you run your Visual Basic .NET program, a radio check mark appears next to your chosen menu command.

If you put check marks next to your menu commands, you may eventually want to remove those check marks. To do this, you have to use (gasp!) BASIC code.

To remove a check mark that's next to a menu command, just set the command's Checked (or RadioCheck) property to False. The following example removes a check mark from a menu command named mnuFont12:

```
mnuFont12.Checked = False
```

To add a check mark using BASIC code, just set the menu command's Checked (or RadioCheck) property to True. The following example adds a radio check mark next to a menu command named mnuFontHelvetica:

```
MnuFontHelvetica.Checked = True
mnuFontHelvetica.RadioCheck = True
```

To display a radio check mark, you must set both the Checked and the RadioCheck property to True. If you just want to display a normal check mark, you only need to set the Checked property to True.

Dimming menu commands

Sometimes using certain commands doesn't make sense. For example, until you select a block of text, having the Cut or Copy commands as options is pointless. To prevent users from choosing menu commands that aren't available, you can dim the commands. That way, the commands still appear in the menus, but the user can't choose them at that particular time.

To dim a menu item, follow these steps:

1. **Open the form that contains the pull-down menus that you want to edit.**

2. **Click on the pull-down menu where you want to dim a menu command.**

   Visual Basic .NET displays your chosen pull-down menu.

3. **Click on the menu command that you want to dim.**

4. **Open the Properties window.**

   To do so, press F4, choose View⇨Properties Window, click on the Properties Window icon in the Solution Explorer window, or right-click on a form and choose Properties. The Properties window appears.

5. **Click on the Enabled property (in the Misc category).**

   A downward-pointing arrow appears.

6. **Click on the downward-pointing arrow and choose False.**

   The next time you run your Visual Basic .NET program, your chosen menu command appears dimmed.

If you dim a menu command, eventually you're going to want to undim the command. To do so, you have to use BASIC code. To undim a menu command, set the command's Enabled property to True. The following example undims a menu command named mnuEditCut:

```
mnuEditCut.Enabled = True
```

To dim a menu command while your program is running, use BASIC code. Just set the menu command's property to False. The following example dims a menu command named mnuEditCopy:

```
mnuEditCopy.Enabled = False
```

Making menu commands invisible

Rather than dim a menu command, you can make the command disappear completely from sight. For example, some programs remove all menu titles except File and Help from the menu bar until the user opens or creates a file. (After all, displaying an Edit menu when you have nothing to edit is pointless.)

To remove a menu item, follow these steps:

1. **Open the form that contains the pull-down menus that you want to edit.**

2. **Click on the pull-down menu where you want to dim a menu command.**

   Visual Basic .NET displays your chosen pull-down menu.

3. **Click on the menu command that you want to dim.**

4. **Open the Properties window.**

   To do so, press F4, choose View⇨Properties Window, click on the Properties Window icon in the Solution Explorer window, or right-click on a form and choose Properties. The Properties window appears.

5. **Click on the Visible property (in the Misc category).**

   A downward-pointing arrow appears.

6. **Click on the downward-pointing arrow and choose False.**

   The next time you run your Visual Basic .NET program, your chosen menu command appears dimmed.

After you make a menu command invisible, eventually you're going to have to make the command visible. To do so, you have to use BASIC code. To make a menu command visible, set the command's Visible property to True. The following example makes a menu title named mnuEdit visible:

```
mnuEdit.Visible = True
```

To make a menu command invisible while your program is running, use BASIC code and set the menu item's property to False. The following example makes a menu title named mnuTools disappear:

```
mnuTools.Visible = False
```

Just remember that pull-down menus are meant to make your program easier to use and look professional. That's the real reason programmers spend so much time creating a user interface — so that users aren't going to blame the programmers when the program fails catastrophically.

Chapter 12

Submenus, Growing Menus, and Pop-Up Menus

A pull-down menu can hold only so many commands on the screen. So what happens if you write a killer application that requires more commands than can possibly appear on a pull-down menu? The solution is to use submenus (or redesign your program).

Creating Submenus

Submenus often bury a command several layers deep within a series of pull-down menus. For example, many programs have a Format menu title. Under this Format menu may be commands such as TypeStyle, Font, and Size. Choosing Font often displays a submenu listing all the possible fonts available, as shown in Figure 12-1.

Visual Basic .NET lets you create up to four levels of submenus (see Figure 12-1). Although this number of submenus can be handy, most programs use only one level of submenus to avoid burying commands so deeply that no one can find them again.

Whenever a menu item displays an arrowhead symbol, that means a submenu exists for that item. When you create submenus, Visual Basic .NET displays this arrowhead symbol automatically.

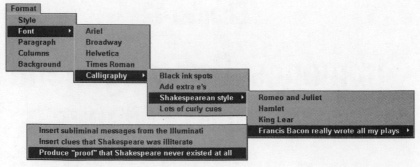

Figure 12-1:
You can
bury
commands
in multiple
submenus.

To create submenus, follow these steps:

1. **Open the form that contains the pull-down menu where you want to add a submenu.**

2. **Click on the pull-down menu.**

   Visual Basic .NET displays your chosen pull-down menu.

3. **Click on the menu command where you want a submenu to appear.**

   Visual Basic .NET displays a "Type Here" box to the right of your chosen menu command.

4. **Click in the "Type Here" box and type the first command on your submenu.**

   Visual Basic .NET displays a "Type Here" box to the right and under-neath your newly created submenu command.

5. **Repeat Step 4 for each command you want to add to your submenu.**

   If you click on the "Type Here" box that appears to the right of your command, you can create another submenu.

The more submenus your program displays, the harder it will be for users to find the command they want and the harder your program will be to use.

Rather than using multiple levels of submenus, most of the really cool programs use dialog boxes. (See Chapter 13 to find out all about dialog boxes.) A *dialog box* lets users make multiple choices all at once instead of making choices one at a time through many submenu levels. While submenus are fine for choosing a few options, dialog boxes are better for choosing a lot of options.

Changing Menu Commands While Your Program Is Running

In certain cases, you may want to change a menu command while the program is running. The most common menu command that changes in most programs is the Undo command in the Edit menu. After choosing the Undo command, it disappears and a Redo command appears in its place.

To change a menu command while your program is running, you have to use BASIC code. Just find the name of the menu item that you want to change and set the item's Text property to a new word or phrase. The following example changes the mnuEditUndo caption to Redo:

```
mnuEditUndo.Text = "Redo"
```

The following example changes the mnuEditUndo caption back to Undo:

```
mnuEditUndo.Text = "Undo"
```

Designing Dynamically Growing Menus

In many programs, the File menu displays a list of the last four or five files you worked on (see Figure 12-2). If you ever open two or more windows in the same program, you may notice that the Window menu also lists the names of the files currently open.

Not all programs can or need to open two or more windows at a time. Programs that can open two or more windows (such as a word processor or spreadsheet) are known as Multiple Document Interface (MDI) programs. Programs that can only display a single window at a time are called Single Document Interface (SDI) programs.

Such menus are called *dynamically growing menus,* which are useful for keeping track of certain files or windows while your program is running. Visual Basic .NET provides two ways to create a dynamically growing menu:

 ✔ At design time, while you're creating your pull-down menus

 ✔ At run time, while your program is running

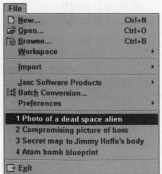

Figure 12-2:
A
dynamically
growing File
menu as
seen in
Paint Shop
Pro.

Making a dynamically growing menu at design time

If you know in advance that you want to create a dynamically growing menu, you can plan ahead by creating a fixed number of empty spaces in a pull-down menu that you can later fill using BASIC code to add (or subtract) items to make the items visible (or invisible).

To create a dynamically growing menu, follow these steps:

1. **Open the form that contains the pull-down menu where you want to add a submenu.**

2. **Click on the pull-down menu.**

   Visual Basic .NET displays a "Type Here" box at the bottom of your chosen pull-down menu.

3. **Click in the "Type Here" box at the bottom of the pull-down menu, type any letter, and then push the Backspace key to erase that character.**

   This creates an empty place in your pull-down menu.

4. **Open the Properties window.**

   To do so, press F4, choose View⇨Properties Window, click on the Properties Window icon in the Solution Explorer window, or right-click on a form and choose Properties. The Properties window appears.

5. **Click in the Visible property (in the Misc category).**

   A downward-pointing arrow appears.

6. **Click on the downward-pointing arrow and choose False.**

   This makes your newly created menu command invisible.

7. Double-click in the Name property (in the Design category) and type a name for your submenu.

Make this name memorable because you will need to use this name to write BASIC code to display an item on your pull-down menu.

The preceding steps create blank spaces in a pull-down menu, but to actually add items to this menu, you have to use BASIC code.

Suppose you created a blank space, named mnuFileOne, in a pull-down menu. The following BASIC code snippet shows how to display an item in that blank space to give the illusion of a dynamically growing menu:

```
mnuFileOne.Visible = True
mnuFileOne.Text = "1 C:\My Documents\Flame.txt"
```

1. The first line tells Visual Basic .NET, "Make the menu command, identified in the pull-down menu as mnuFileOne, visible so that it appears."

2. The second line tells Visual Basic .NET, "Display the text "1 C:\My Documents\Flame.txt" in the menu command named mnuFileOne."

The above two steps, filling text in a blank space in a pull-down menu and making that blank space visible, gives users the illusion that your menus can grow as the program runs.

Test your newfound knowledge

1. Explain why you may want your menu commands to change while your program is running.

   a. To confuse your users so that they think they're doing something wrong.

   b. To move important commands every five minutes to keep users on their toes.

   c. To toggle menu commands like Undo and Redo.

   d. Because you aren't considered a real programmer unless you use every possible feature of a programming language to make your program more complicated to use.

2. Why would you want to use submenus?

   a. To create programs that tell the computer how to make submarine sandwiches.

   b. To display related commands together without having to create a separate pull-down menu.

   c. For writing programs designed to be used in submarines.

   d. To hide important commands from the user.

Making a dynamically growing menu at run time

The problem with creating a dynamically growing menu at design time is that you may not know how many new items you want to add to a particular menu. So for more flexibility (and complexity), you can create a dynamically growing menu at run time by using BASIC code.

You'll discover more about writing BASIC code in Part IV of the book. So you may just want to browse through this section and return to it later when you can better understand how BASIC code works.

To create a dynamically growing menu using BASIC code, follow these steps:

1. **Open the code editor for the form that contains the pull-down menu where you want to add a dynamically growing menu.**

2. **Add a pull-down menu to your form and give it a distinctive name such as mnuFirstMenu.**

   See Chapter 11 for more information about adding pull-down menus to a form.

3. **Type the following in your code.**

   The following code is called a *method* by Visual Basic .NET. Essentially a method is a miniature program within a larger program. Typically methods solve one specific task.

```
Public Sub AddMenuItem(ByVal NewStuff As String)
        Dim myMenuItemNew As New MenuItem()
        myMenuItemNew.Text = NewStuff
        mnuFileMenu.MenuItems.Add(myMenuItemNew)
End Sub
```

4. **Add the following code somewhere in your program to call the above method and actually add a new item to your menu:**

```
AddMenuItem ("My new menu item")
```

To help you better understand how the following method works, here's a step by step description:

```
Public Sub AddMenuItem(ByVal NewStuff As String)
        Dim myMenuItemNew As New MenuItem()
        myMenuItemNew.Text = NewStuff
        mnuFileMenu.MenuItems.Add(myMenuItemNew)
End Sub
```

1. The first line tells Visual Basic .NET, "This is a method named `AddMenuItem` (you can substitute any name here if you want) that accepts a string that gets stored in a variable called `NewStuff`."

2. The second line tells Visual Basic .NET, "Create a variable called `myMenuItemNew` (you can substitute any name here) that represents an object called `MenuItem`."

3. The third line tells Visual Basic .NET, "Set the value of `NewStuff` to the Text property of the object represented by `myMenuItemNew`."

4. The fourth line tells Visual Basic .NET, "Add a new menu item, represented by the variable `myMenuItemNew`, and stuff it in a pull-down menu named `mnuFileMenu`."

5. The fifth line tells Visual Basic .NET, "This is the end of the list of instructions to follow."

In the preceding example, the italicized names can be any names you care to use. So instead of calling the method `AddMenuItem`, you could call it anything you want, such as `GrowMenu`. The important thing isn't the specific name you use. It's whether you use the name consistently.

Making Pop-up Menus

Besides offering pull-down menus, many programs also offer pop-up (or in the words of Visual Basic .NET) *context menus*. Context menus pop up on the screen whenever the user clicks the right mouse button. You have two ways to create a context menu:

- ✔ Type commands to appear in the context menu.
- ✔ Copy commands from an existing pull-down menu to appear in the context menu.

Typing commands into a context menu

To type commands into a context menu, follow these steps:

1. **Open the form on which you want your context menu to appear.**

2. **Double-click on the ContextMenu icon in the Toolbox.**

The ContextMenu icon appears in the Windows Forms category of the Toolbox. You may need to press the down-arrow key or scroll down using your mouse wheel to find the ContextMenu icon, which normally is hidden out of sight in the Toolbox.

Visual Basic .NET displays a ContextMenu icon in a window underneath your form, as shown in Figure 12-3, and displays a "Context Menu" box at the top of your form.

3. **Click on the "Context Menu" box at the top of your form.**

   A "Type Here" box appears directly below the "Context Menu" box.

4. **Click in the "Type Here" box and type each command you want to appear in your context menu.**

5. **Repeat Step 4 for each new command you want to add to your context menu.**

After you've created a context menu, you can always edit it later by clicking on the ContextMenu icon in the window that appears underneath your form. Visual Basic .NET then displays your context menu at the top of the form where you can add, delete, or move items around. See Chapter 11 for more information about editing menus.

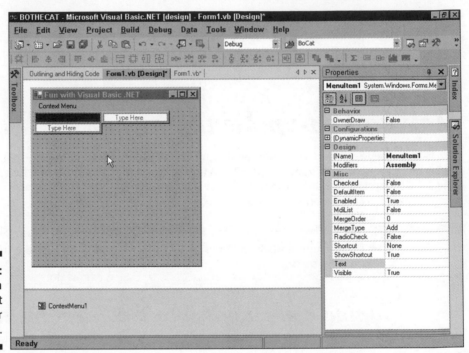

Figure 12-3:
Creating a context menu for your form.

Making your context menu pop up

After you've created a context menu and given it a (hopefully) descriptive name, the next step is to tell your form to pop up your context menu whenever the user clicks the right mouse button.

To make a context menu pop up, follow these steps:

1. **Click on the form that contains your context menu.**

2. **Open the Properties window.**

   To do so, press F4, choose View⇨Properties Window, click on the Properties Window icon in the Solution Explorer window, or right-click on a form and choose Properties. The Properties window appears.

3. **Click in the ContextMenu property (in the Behavior category).**

   A downward-pointing arrow appears.

4. **Click on the downward-pointing arrow.**

   Visual Basic .NET displays the names of all the context menus stored on that particular form.

5. **Click on the name of the context menu that you want to appear whenever the user clicks the right mouse button.**

   At this point, you're finished. Whenever the user clicks the right mouse button on the form, your context menu pops up on the screen.

Copying commands into a context menu

After you create a context menu and get it to pop up on the screen whenever the user clicks the right mouse button, the final step is to write BASIC code to make your context menu actually do something.

Because context menus often contain the same commands stored in a pull-down menu, you may just want to copy existing commands from your pull-down menus to your context menus. To copy commands, follow these steps:

1. **Open the form that contains the pull-down menu that you want to copy.**

2. **Click on the pull-down menu title (such as File) that contains the command that you want to copy (such as Print).**

   You may first need to click on the pull-down menu icon that appears in the window beneath your form. Visual Basic .NET displays all the commands in your chosen pull-down menu.

3. **Right-click on the menu command that you want to copy.**

   A pop-up menu appears.

4. **Choose Copy.**

5. **Click on the icon in the window that appears beneath your form, which represents the context menu that you want to copy your command to.**

   Visual Basic .NET displays your chosen context menu on the form.

6. **Right-click on a "Type here" box that appears on your context menu.**

   A pop-up menu appears.

7. **Choose Paste.**

   Visual Basic .NET copies your command to your chosen location on the context menu.

After copying a command to a context menu, you still need to write BASIC code to make your context menu command work, even if the command you copied already had BASIC code written for it.

Chapter 13

Showing Dialog Boxes

• •

• •

*P*ull-down menus certainly make life easier for users (provided, of course, that the users know how to use the menus). In addition to pull-down menus, nearly every program also uses dialog boxes.

Dialog boxes are those tiny windows that pop up on the screen. Most of the time, the computer uses dialog boxes to let the user know what it is doing, such as "Now printing page 4 of 67" or "Windows 98 just crashed again and here's an application error number that you won't understand anyway."

However, dialog boxes also let the computer ask questions of users, such as "Cancel printing?" or "Do you really want to exit Windows?" A fancy dialog box may be crammed full of options so that the user can make multiple choices all at one time. Just as most Windows-based programs use similar pull-down menus (File, Edit, Help), these programs also use similar dialog boxes.

Creating a Simple Dialog Box

A dialog box displays a brief message on the screen along with one or more command buttons. Dialog boxes typically contain the following four parts:

✔ A title bar

✔ A message

✔ An eye-catching icon

✔ One or more buttons

The title bar identifies the purpose of the dialog box, such as About This Program. The message contains text that appears in the dialog box, such as "Would you like to start work on your new project?" The icon provides visual information about the dialog box's importance. The number of buttons typically varies from one to three.

The simplest dialog box is one that displays a message on the screen and provides an OK command button so that the user can make the dialog box go away. To create a simple dialog box, you just need to use the MsgBox command and define the text you want to appear in the title bar and the text to appear inside your dialog box.

The following BASIC code creates the simple dialog box displayed in Figure 13-1:

```
MsgBox ("Ready to try Linux yet?", ," Windows just crashed_
         again")
```

This simple dialog box does nothing more than appear on the screen and then disappear when the user clicks on OK.

Figure 13-1:
What a simple dialog box looks like.

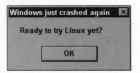

Adding icons to a dialog box

Icons can help grab a user's attention to your dialog box. Visual Basic .NET uses four icons (see Figure 13-2).

Figure 13-2:
The four types of icons you can include in a simple dialog box.

 Critical

 Exclamation

 Information

 Question

✔ **Critical:** (A red circle with an X inside.) Alerts the user to an extremely important question, such as "If you continue, you are going to erase all the files on your hard disk. Are you sure that you want to do this?"

✔ **Exclamation:** (An exclamation mark.) Emphasizes warnings that the user needs to know about, such as "You are about to replace all 79 pages of your document with a period!"

✔ **Information:** (The letter "i" inside a cartoon voice balloon.) Makes otherwise drab and boring messages look interesting, such as "Printing all 3,049 pages of your document may take a long time. Click on OK if you want to go through with this."

✔ **Question:** (A question mark inside a cartoon voice balloon.) Highlights less-threatening questions, such as "Do you really want to keep using Microsoft Windows?"

To add an icon to a dialog box, you first need to add the following line to the top of your BASIC code:

```
Imports.Microsoft.VisualBasic.MsgBoxStyle
```

The preceding line needs to be the very first line in your code or else Visual Basic .NET will get confused and not work properly.

After adding the preceding line to your BASIC code, you can type the words Critical, Exclamation, Information, or Question in between the dialog box message and the title bar text, as follows:

```
MsgBox ("Ready to try Linux yet?", Critical, "Windows_
         Crashed Again")
```

This code creates the dialog box shown in Figure 13-3.

Figure 13-3:
Displaying
a Critical
icon in a
dialog box.

If you omit adding the `Imports.Microsoft.VisualBasic.MsgBoxStyle` line in your BASIC code, instead of typing Critical, you would have to type `Microsoft.VisualBasic.MsgBoxStyle.Critical` such as:

```
MsgBox ("Ready to try Linux yet?",_
        Microsoft.VisualBasic.MsgBoxStyle.Critical,_
        "Windows just crashed Again")
```

Normally, Visual Basic .NET lets you display only one of four possible icons in a dialog box. If this seems limiting and downright boring, you can create your own dialog box from scratch. To do this, create a separate form, set the form's BorderStyle property to Fixed Dialog, and draw buttons and a picture box directly on this form. You can then draw a picture box on the form and load any type of icon you want.

Just remember that creating a dialog box by using a separate form requires you to draw the buttons, label, and picture box, and to write BASIC code to make the whole dialog box work. If you just want to create a dialog box quickly and easily, use the MsgBox command instead.

Defining the number and type of command buttons in a dialog box

Dialog boxes can contain from one to three buttons. A numerical value represents each command button. Table 13-1 lists the six command button combinations.

Table 13-1	Command Button Combinations Available in Visual Basic .NET	
Displays	*Value*	*Visual Basic .NET Constant*
OK button	0	OKOnly
OK and Cancel buttons	1	OKCancel
Abort, Retry, and Ignore buttons	2	AbortRetryIgnore
Yes, No, and Cancel buttons	3	YesNoCancel
Yes and No buttons	4	YesNo
Retry and Cancel buttons	5	RetryCancel

To define a button combination, choose the combination you want (such as OK and Cancel buttons) and type the constant value of that combination in between the dialog box's message text and title bar text, such as

```
MsgBox ("File not found", OKCancel, "Cryptic Error Message")
```

Before you can use any of the command button combinations listed in Table 13-1, the following line needs to appear as the first line in your code:

```
Imports.Microsoft.VisualBasic.MsgBoxStyle
```

If you omit the preceding line, you'll have to include the `Microsoft.VisualBasic.MsgBoxStyle` code in your **MsgBox** command, such as:

```
MsgBox ("File not found",_
        Microsoft.VisualBasic.MsgBoxStyle.OKCancel,_
        "Cryptic Error Message")
```

You can combine both icons and button combinations together by separating them with the magical Or command. So if you wanted to display an Information icon along with a YesNo button combination, you would use the following, as shown in Figure 13-4:

```
MsgBox ("File not found", YesNo Or Information, "Cryptic_
        Error Message")
```

Figure 13-4:
Combining
button
combina-
tions with
icons.

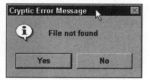

Which command button did the user select in a dialog box?

If a dialog box just displays an OK button, clicking on that OK command button makes that dialog box go away. However, dialog boxes with two or more command buttons give users a choice. When dealing with multiple buttons on a dialog box, you have to write BASIC code to figure out

✔ Which button the user chose

✔ What your program should do depending on which button the user chose

The seven possible buttons a user can choose are represented by the numerical values in Table 13-2.

Table 13-2	Command Buttons a User Can Choose	
Button Selected	*Numerical Value*	*Visual Basic .NET Constant*
OK	1	OK
Cancel	2	Cancel
Abort	3	Abort
Retry	4	Retry
Ignore	5	Ignore
Yes	6	Yes
No	7	No

To make your program determine which button a user chose, you have to set a variable equal to the MsgBox BASIC code, as shown in the following line:

```
Dim intReply As Integer
intReply = MsgBox("File not found", OKCancel, "Cryptic_
          Message")
```

This code displays a dialog box with the OK and Cancel buttons. If the user clicks on OK, the value of intReply is OK (1). If the user clicks on Cancel, the value of intReply is Cancel (2).

Commonly Used Dialog Boxes

While a simple dialog box may be sufficient occasionally, you may want to use a more complicated, yet more common, dialog box such as a File Save or Print dialog box. To help you create these dialog boxes, Visual Basic .NET provides the following predesigned dialog box objects in the Toolbox:

- ✔ OpenFileDialog
- ✔ SaveFileDialog
- ✔ ColorDialog
- ✔ FontDialog
- ✔ PrintDialog
- ✔ PageSetupDialog

Test your newfound knowledge

1. Why do you want to display an icon in a dialog box?

    a. In case an illiterate computer user wants to use your program.

    b. To catch the eye of the user and provide a visual cue. For example, a Critical icon can warn users that something terrible is about to happen if they don't do something immediately.

    c. To see if the user is smart enough to realize that the dialog box has nothing important to say.

    d. To frighten users with icons they don't understand so they feel even more intimidated when using your program.

2. To use the predefined Open, Save As, Color, Font, or Print dialog box, what must you do first?

    a. Buy the Visual Basic .NET manuals that used to come with the program for free.

    b. Create a new form, draw three command buttons, two check boxes, one list box, and a partridge in a pear tree.

    c. Save your file and exit Visual Basic .NET.

    d. Double-click on the appropriate icon (such as the PrintDialog icon) in the Toolbox to add the dialog box to your form.

If you can't see these objects in the Toolbox, click on any icon in the Toolbox (such as TextBox) and then press the down-arrow key or scroll down using your mouse wheel. Visual Basic .NET hides these dialog box icons near the bottom of the Toolbox under the Windows Forms category.

Displaying the OpenFile dialog box

The *OpenFile dialog box* allows users to choose a file to open. The user also has the choice of displaying only specific file types, such as those matching the *.TXT or *.EXE criteria.

To create an OpenFile dialog box, follow these steps:

1. **Open a form.**

2. **Double-click on the OpenFileDialog icon in the Toolbox. (You may need to scroll down to find the OpenFileDialog icon buried in the Windows Forms category of the Toolbox, as shown in Figure 13-5.)**

    Visual Basic .NET displays an OpenFileDialog icon (such as OpenFileDialog1) in a window underneath your form.

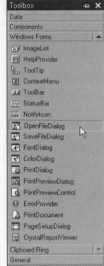

Figure 13-5:
The
OpenFile
Dialog icon
buried in the
Toolbox.

After you've added the OpenFile dialog box to your form, you still need to write a BASIC command to display that OpenFile dialog box. The BASIC command to do this is

```
OpenFileDialog1.ShowDialog()
```

OpenFileDialog1 is the generic name that Visual Basic .NET gives an OpenFile dialog box. If you changed the name of your OpenFile dialog box after you created it, you must substitute that name in place of OpenFileDialog1 in the preceding example.

If you want to define the list of files that the OpenFile dialog box displays, you have to use something technical called a filter. A *filter* tells Visual Basic .NET what types of files to display, such as all those with the TXT or BAT file extension.

A filter consists of two parts: the label that appears in the list box and the filter itself. Table 13-3 lists some examples of labels and filters. For added clarity, labels usually include the filter they use.

Text files, for example, usually have the file extension TXT, but sometimes they have the file extension ASC. So the label "Text Files (*.TXT)" lets you know that the dialog box shows only text files with the TXT file extension (and not text files with the ASC file extension).

Table 13-3	Labels and Filters
Label	*Filter*
All Files (*.*)	*.*
Text Files (*.TXT)	*.TXT
Batch Files (*.BAT)	*.BAT
Executable Files (*.EXE)	*.EXE

To define your labels and filters, follow these steps:

1. **Open the form that contains the OpenFile dialog box.**

2. **Click on the OpenFileDialog icon in the window that appears underneath the form.**

3. **Open the Properties window.**

   To do so, press F4, choose View⇨Properties Window, click on the Properties Window icon in the Solution Explorer window, or right-click on a form and choose Properties. The Properties window appears.

4. **Double-click in the Filter property (in the Misc category) and type the filter you want to use.**

   A filter consists of a short description of the file followed by the filter, such as:

   ```
   Text files (*.txt)| *.txt
   ```

   In the preceding example, the portion of text to the left of the vertical line symbol appears in the Files of type list box. The portion of text to the right of the vertical line symbol is the actual filter for displaying files with certain file extensions.

   You can type the vertical line symbol by pressing Shift and the key that has the \ symbol on it.

   You can also create multiple filters such as:

   ```
   Text files (*.txt)| .txt | All files (*.*) | *.*
   ```

   Just separate each additional filter with another vertical line symbol.

If you choose to create multiple filters, you need to tell Visual Basic .NET which filter to display when the OpenFile dialog box appears. To define the filter to use, you have to change the FilterIndex property and set its value to a number such as 1, 2, 3, and so on.

When you have multiple filters, the first filter is defined as FilterIndex 1, the second is FilterIndex 2, and so on. So in the preceding example, if you wanted to display Text files (*.TXT) in the OpenFile dialog box, you would set the FilterIndex property to 1.

To determine which filter to use, follow these steps:

1. **Open the form that contains the OpenFile dialog box.**

2. **Click on the OpenFileDialog icon in the window that appears underneath the form.**

3. **Open the Properties window.**

   To do so, press F4, choose <u>V</u>iew⇨Properties Window, click on the Properties Window icon in the Solution Explorer window, or right-click on a form and choose P<u>r</u>operties. The Properties window appears.

4. **Double-click in the FilterIndex property (in the Misc category) and type a number that represents the filter you want to use.**

   The next time you run your program, your OpenFile dialog box displays your chosen filter.

Which file did the user choose from an OpenFile dialog box?

After you display an OpenFile dialog box, the next big question is to find out which file the user chose. When the user clicks on a file displayed by the OpenFile dialog box, Visual Basic .NET stores the file name in the Filename property of the OpenFile dialog box. So if you want to retrieve the file name that the user clicked on, you need to set a variable to store the file name property, such as

```
Dim strWhatFile As String
strWhatFile = OpenFileDialog1.filename
```

The Filename property contains both the file name and the directory that the file is stored in, such as C:\MyDocuments\Secrets\ Resume.txt. If the user clicks on the Cancel command button in the OpenFile dialog box, the file name property is set to " " (no text).

Displaying a SaveFile dialog box

A SaveFile dialog box is nearly identical to the OpenFile dialog box. However, the text of the title bar isn't the same. (The OpenFile dialog box's title bar says "Open" and the SaveFile dialog box's title bar says "Save As.")

To create a SaveFile dialog box, follow these steps:

1. **Open a form.**

2. **Double-click on the SaveFileDialog icon in the Toolbox. (You may need to scroll down to find the SaveFileDialog icon buried in the Windows Forms category of the Toolbox.)**

   Visual Basic .NET displays a SaveFileDialog icon (such as SaveFileDialog1) in a window underneath your form.

After adding the SaveFile dialog box to your form, you next have to use the following BASIC command to display the SaveFile dialog box:

```
SaveFileDialog1.ShowDialog()
```

Like the OpenFile dialog box, the SaveFile dialog box can also use filters so you can selectively choose the type of files you want it to display. To use filters, you need to change the Filter property of the SaveFile dialog box. Just follow the steps in the previous section, "Displaying the OpenFile dialog box."

Which file did the user choose from a Save As dialog box?

Like the OpenFile dialog box, the SaveFile dialog box stores the file name in the Filename property of the SaveFile dialog box. To retrieve the file name that the user typed in the SaveFile dialog box, you need to set a variable to store the file name property, such as

```
Dim strWhatFile As String
strWhatFile = SaveFileDialog1.Filename
```

The SaveFile dialog box doesn't actually save files on its own. To save a file, you have to write additional BASIC code that tells your computer to physically save a file onto a disk.

Displaying a Color dialog box

The Color dialog box lets users choose colors or mix their own, as shown in Figure 13-6.

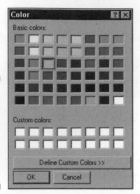

Figure 13-6:
The Color
dialog box
allows users
to pick a
color to use.

To create a Color dialog box, follow these steps:

1. **Open a form.**

2. **Double-click on the ColorDialog icon in the Toolbox. (You may need to scroll down to find the ColorDialog icon buried in the Windows Forms category of the Toolbox.)**

   Visual Basic .NET displays a ColorDialog icon (such as ColorDialog1) in a window underneath your form.

After adding a Color dialog box to a form, you have to use the following BASIC command to display your Color dialog box:

```
ColorDialog1.ShowDialog()
```

Which color did the user choose from the Color dialog box?

The Color dialog box stores the color the user chose in the Color property of the Color dialog box. After you retrieve the value in the Color property from the Color dialog box, you can assign this color to the BackColor or ForeColor property of another object (such as a button), as the following code demonstrates:

```
Button1.BackColor = ColorDialog1.Color
```

Displaying a Font dialog box

The Font dialog box, shown in Figure 13-7, lets users choose different fonts, font styles, and point sizes. Each time the user chooses an option, this dialog box displays a sample so that the user can see whether the font, font style, or point size looks okay.

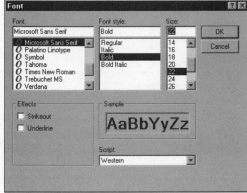

Figure 13-7:
The Font dialog box allows users to pick a font to use.

To create a Font dialog box, follow these steps:

1. **Open a form.**

2. **Double-click on the FontDialog icon in the Toolbox. (You may need to scroll down to find the FontDialog icon buried in the Windows Forms category of the Toolbox.)**

   Visual Basic .NET displays a FontDialog icon (such as FontDialog1) in a window underneath your form.

After adding a Font dialog box to your form, you can display the Font dialog box using this BASIC command:

```
FontDialog1.ShowDialog()
```

Which options did the user choose from the Font dialog box?

When the Font dialog box appears, users can choose a font, font size, and any additional effects such as bold or italics. Whatever the user chooses gets stored in the Font property in the Misc category of the Font dialog box. If you click on the plus sign that appears to the left of the Font property in the

Properties window, Visual Basic .NET shows all the specific properties that hold the information that the user selected from the Font dialog box, as listed in Table 13-4.

Table 13-4	Properties That Store Values from the Font Dialog Box
Property	**What Information It Contains**
Name	Name of the font chosen (such as Microsoft Sans Serif), stored as a string
Size	An integer representing the font size, such as 8 or 12
Bold	True or False value
Italic	True or False value
Strikeout	True or False value
Underline	True or False value

To retrieve values chosen from the Font dialog box, you need to use BASIC code such as:

```
Dim strWhatFont As String
strWhatFont = FontDialog1.Font.Name
```

When retrieving data from a Font dialog box, make sure you include the name of the Font dialog box (such as FontDialog1), the Font property, followed by the property that contains the data you want to retrieve such as Name or Bold.

Displaying a Print dialog box

A Print dialog box, shown in Figure 13-8, lets users choose the printer, the print range, and the print quantity.

To create a Print dialog box, follow these steps:

1. **Open a form.**

2. **Double-click on the PrintDialog icon in the Toolbox. (You may need to scroll down to find the PrintDialog icon buried in the Windows Forms category of the Toolbox.)**

   Visual Basic .NET displays a PrintDialog icon (such as PrintDialog1) in a window underneath your form.

3. **Double-click on the PrintDocument icon in the Toolbox. (You may need to scroll down to find the PrintDocument icon buried in the Windows Forms category of the Toolbox.)**

   Visual Basic .NET displays a PrintDocument icon (such as PrintDocument1) in a window underneath your form. (*Note:* If you change the Name property of the PrintDocument object, you will need to choose this name later in Step 7.)

4. **Double-click on the PrintDialog icon in the Toolbox.**

   Visual Basic .NET displays a PrintDialog icon (such as PrintDialog1) in a window underneath your form.

5. **Open the Properties window.**

   To do so, press F4, choose View⇨Properties Window, click on the Properties Window icon in the Solution Explorer window, or right-click on a form and choose Properties. The Properties window appears.

6. **Click in the Document property (in the Misc category) of the Properties window.**

   A downward-pointing arrow appears.

7. **Click on the downward-pointing arrow and choose the name of PrintDocument object that you want to use (such as PrintDocument1).**

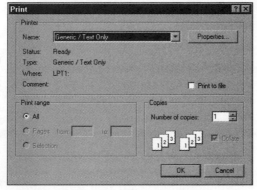

Figure 13-8: The Print dialog box allows users to choose pages to print.

The PrintDocument object contains the DocumentName property in the Misc category, which tells the Print dialog box which document to print.

After you have added a PrintDocument and a PrintDialog object to your form, you can finally display a Print dialog box by using the following BASIC command:

```
PrintDialog1.ShowDialog()
```

The Print dialog box doesn't actually print anything. You still need to write BASIC code to make your program print out something.

Displaying a PageSetup dialog box

A PageSetup dialog box, shown in Figure 13-9, lets users define margins and paper size for printing your file.

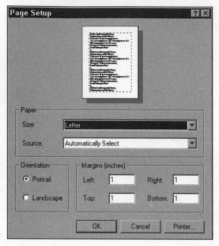

Figure 13-9:
The Page Setup dialog box allows users to choose margins and paper size for printing a file.

To create a PageSetup dialog box, follow these steps:

1. **Open a form.**

2. **Double-click on the PrintDocument icon in the Toolbox. (You may need to scroll down to find the PrintDocument icon buried in the Windows Forms category of the Toolbox.)**

   Visual Basic .NET displays a PrintDocument icon (such as PrintDocument1) in a window underneath your form. (*Note:* If you change the Name property of the PrintDocument object, you will need to choose this name later in Step 6.)

3. **Double-click on the PageSetupDialog icon in the Toolbox.**

   Visual Basic .NET displays a PageSetupDialog icon (such as PageSetupDialog1) in a window underneath your form.

4. **Open the Properties window.**

   To do so, press F4, choose View⇨Properties Window, click on the Properties Window icon in the Solution Explorer window, or right-click on a form and choose Properties. The Properties window appears.

5. **Click in the Document property (in the Misc category) of the Properties window.**

   A downward-pointing arrow appears.

6. **Click on the downward-pointing arrow and choose the name of PrintDocument object that you want to use (such as PrintDocument1).**

The PrintDocument object contains the DocumentName property in the Misc category, which tells the PageSetup dialog box which document will use the defined page settings. You will have to use BASIC code to define the name of the document and also write BASIC commands to modify the actual settings before printing.

After you have added both a PrintDocument and a PageSetup dialog box object to your form, you can finally display a Print dialog box by using the following BASIC command:

```
PageSetupDialog1.ShowDialog()
```

Part IV
The Basics of Writing Code

The 5th Wave   By Rich Tennant

"You know how cats love to play with strings? Well, Mittens would rather write them."

In this part . . .

Hurray! Here's the first chapter where you actually find out how to write your own BASIC code to make your computer do something worthwhile. Until now, you may have only drawn the parts that make up a user interface (with an occasional BASIC command thrown in). But everyone knows that looks aren't everything (unless you're a centerfold, looking to marry a multimillionaire who will die within a year). What matters is not only that your user interface looks good, but that your user interface also responds to the user.

Although the thought of writing BASIC code may seem intimidating, it's not. BASIC code is nothing more than a set of step-by-step instructions that tell the computer exactly what to do. So get ready to start *coding* (a programmers' term for writing computer commands). You'll find that programming can really be fun, easy, and almost as addictive as drawing your user interface or playing a computer game.

Chapter 14

Writing Event-Handling Procedures

*W*henever the user takes any action, such as clicking the mouse, pressing a key, passing out on the keyboard, or putting a bullet through the monitor, the action is called an *event*. The moment an event occurs, Visual Basic .NET looks for BASIC code to tell the program what to do. The BASIC code that responds to a specific event is called an *event-handling procedure* or just as *event handler*.

A single Visual Basic .NET program can consist of several thousand event-handling procedures. If you have that many, however, you have a tremendously complicated program or you're an incredibly incompetent programmer.

With so many possible events and so many possible event-handling procedures in a single program, how does Visual Basic .NET know which event-handling procedure to use?

The answer is easy. When an event occurs, this event is usually directed at some part of your program's user interface. For example, most users click the mouse button only when the mouse is pointing at an object, such as a button, check box, or menu command on the screen.

Every object can have one or more event-handling procedures, and each event-handling procedure responds to one specific event, such as clicking the mouse or pressing a key.

Working with the Code Editor

The code editor is where you can type honest to goodness BASIC code to make your Visual Basic .NET programs do something worthwhile. To view the code editor, follow these steps:

1. **Choose View⇨Solution Explorer, or press Ctrl+Alt+L.**

   The Solution Explorer window appears.

2. **Click on a form and choose View⇨Code, press F7, or click on the View Code icon in the Solution Explorer window.**

   Visual Basic .NET displays the code editor for your chosen form.

When you start storing BASIC code in files other than forms, you would click on that file name in Step 2.

After you open the code editor for a form, you can switch back to it quickly by clicking on the Code tab that appears next to the (Design) tab directly above your form.

Expanding and collapsing BASIC code

In a perfect world, your BASIC code should fit on a single screen so anyone can examine and modify it without having to scroll up or down. By making your programs short, they should be easier to read, understand, and ultimately, to modify.

Unfortunately, BASIC code rarely fits on a single screen, which means you (or another programmer) will be forced to scroll endlessly up and down just to see all the BASIC code that makes a program work. But to help simplify this task, Visual Basic .NET offers you the chance to expand or collapse chunks of BASIC code.

Visual Basic .NET automatically knows how to collapse (or expand) entire procedures. In case you want to choose which chunks of code to collapse, you can highlight the code, choose Edit⇨Outlining⇨Hide Selection.

To collapse a chunk of BASIC code, just click on the minus sign that appears to the left of the BASIC code chunk that you want to collapse. Visual Basic .NET collapses this code and displays three dots to show you that there's more BASIC code hidden from sight, so don't think that you're seeing the entire program.

To expand a chunk of BASIC code, click on the plus sign that appears to the left of the code you want to expand. Figure 14-1 shows the code editor with some code expanded and some collapsed.

Collapsed code

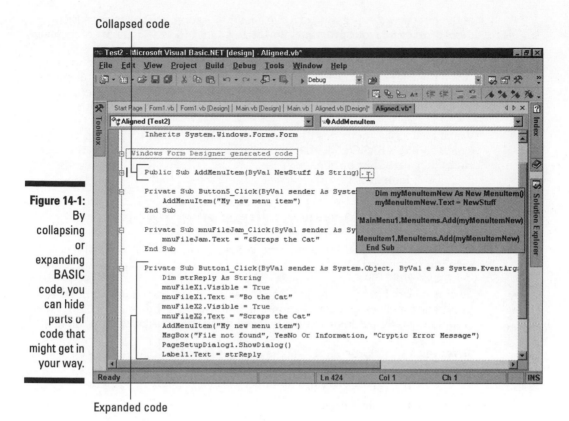

Figure 14-1:
By
collapsing
or
expanding
BASIC
code, you
can hide
parts of
code that
might get in
your way.

Expanded code

Types of Events

Events can be classified into three categories:

- **Keyboard events:** Occur when the user presses a certain key, such as Tab, or a certain keystroke combination, such as Ctrl+P.

- **Mouse events:** Occur when the user moves the mouse, clicks or double-clicks on the mouse button, or drags the mouse across the screen.

- **Program events:** Occur when a Visual Basic .NET program does something on its own, such as loading a form or changing the contents of a text box. Whereas keyboard and mouse events occur when the user does something, program events occur when BASIC code does something.

Although Visual Basic .NET can respond to a multitude of events, you generally want your user interface to respond only to a few events, such as the clicking of the mouse or the pressing of a certain key. As soon as Visual Basic .NET detects an event, your program immediately looks to see what part of the user interface needs to respond.

When the user clicks the mouse, for example, Visual Basic .NET first identifies the event. ("Okay, that was a mouse click.") Next, it looks to see where the user clicked the mouse. ("The user clicked the mouse on the OK button.")

Visual Basic .NET then finds that particular button's event-handling procedure, which contains BASIC code that tells your program what to do when the user clicks that particular button.

Creating event-handling procedures

One object can respond to one or more events. For example, a button can respond to the user clicking on the mouse button or pressing the Enter key.

Two or more objects can respond to the same event. For example, both a button and a check box can respond to a mouse click, but they (usually) have completely different instructions that tell Visual Basic .NET what to do next.

To write an event procedure, you have to perform the following tasks:

1. Identify the part of your user interface that is going to respond.
2. Open the code editor.
3. Identify the event to which Visual Basic .NET is to respond.
4. Write BASIC code to process the event.

Make sure that all the objects of your user interface have names before creating any event procedures. If you create an event-handling procedure for an object and later change that object's name, you will have to rewrite your event-handling procedures.

The following three parts of a user interface can have events associated with them:

- Forms
- Objects (buttons, check boxes, list boxes, and so on)
- Pull-down menus

To create an event-handling procedure for an object such as a form, button, pull-down menu, check box, and so on, follow these steps:

1. **Open the form that contains the object that you want to create an event-handling procedure for, such as a button or a check box.**

    If you double-click on an object (such as a button or even the form itself), Visual Basic .NET displays the code editor right away and creates the most common event-handling procedure for your chosen object.

2. **Open the code editor by pressing F7 or choosing View⇨Code.**

    Visual Basic .NET displays the code editor on the screen. (Refer to Figure 14-1.)

3. **Click in the Class Name list box.**

    A list of different objects appears, such as Label1 or Button2.

    You should change the Name property of an object before creating an event-handling procedure for it. That way, the name can be descriptive of the object's purpose in your program rather than a generic name.

4. **Click in the Method Name list box.**

    A list of different events for your chosen object appears, such as Click or MouseHover.

5. **Click on the event you want your object to respond to (such as Click).**

    Visual Basic .NET creates an empty event-handling procedure. At this point you can start writing BASIC code to make your event-handling procedure actually do something, such as change the properties of another object on your form.

To create an event-handling procedure for a pull-down menu command, follow these steps:

1. **Click on the pull-down menu title containing the menu command you want.**

2. **Double-click on the menu command for which you want to create an event-handling procedure.**

    Visual Basic .NET creates an empty event-handling procedure.

Getting to know the parts of event-handling procedures

When you create an event procedure for the first time, Visual Basic .NET displays an empty event-handling procedure in the code editor. All empty event procedures consist of two lines, such as

```
Private Sub Button1_Click(ByVal sender As System.Object,_
          ByVal e As System.EventArgs) Handles Button1.Click

End Sub
```

The first line of any event-handling procedure contains five parts:

- **Private Sub:** Identifies the procedure as a subroutine.
- **The object's name:** In this example, the object is a button named Button1.
- **An underscore.**
- **The event name:** In this example, the event is a mouse click.
- **A pair of parentheses, containing any data that the subroutine may need to work.**
- **The Handles keyword:** Associates the event (in this case Button1.Click) with the event-handling procedure.

Don't worry about the technical details of the preceding event-handling procedure. The important point is to get a rough understanding of how to identify the different parts of an event-handling procedure.

The preceding event-handling procedure says to the computer, "Here are the instructions to follow whenever the user clicks the mouse on a button named Button1. Now leave me alone."

Because this example contains no instructions to follow, this event procedure does absolutely nothing, much like many coworkers you may know.

Any time you change the name of an object, make sure that you change the name of all event procedures connected to the newly named object as well. Otherwise, Visual Basic .NET doesn't know which event procedures belong to which objects on your user interface.

Splitting the code editor in half

After you start to write lots of event-handling procedures, the code editor may not be able to display all your event handling procedures at the same time. One way to solve this problem is to collapse certain parts of your BASIC code to tuck them out of sight temporarily. (See the previous section "Expanding and collapsing BASIC code.")

A second way to help you view your BASIC code is to split the code editor in half. That way you can view the top part of your BASIC code and the bottom part at the same time.

You can divide the code editor only in half (not in thirds, quarters, and so on).

To split the code editor in half, follow these steps:

1. **Choose Window⇨Split.**

   Visual Basic .NET divides the code editor in half.

2. **Move the mouse over the Split bar, hold down the left mouse button, and drag the mouse down to adjust the size of the top and bottom of the code editor.**

   When the Split bar divides the code editor the way you want, let go of the mouse button (see Figure 14-2).

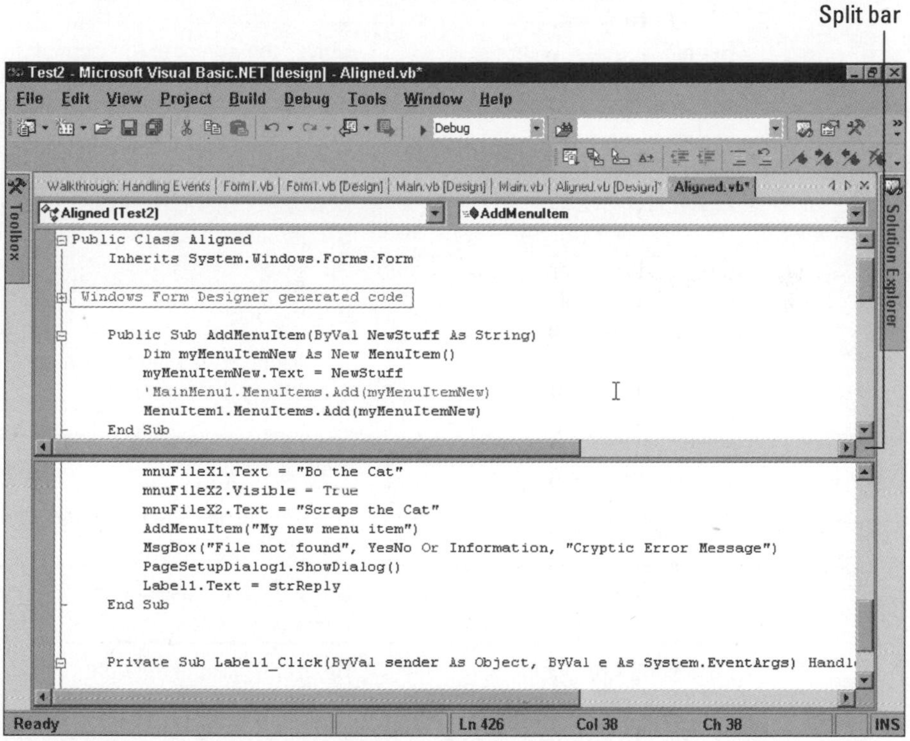

Split bar

Figure 14-2:
By splitting
the code
editor in
half, you
can see
different
parts of your
BASIC
code.

To display the code editor as a single window again, choose Window⇨ Remove Split.

Using the Code Editor

The code editor works like a simple word processor. Table 14-1 lists the different keystroke commands you can use to edit your event procedures.

Table 14-1	Common Editing Keys
Keystroke	*What Happens*
Delete	Deletes the character to the right of the cursor
Backspace	Deletes the character to the left of the cursor
Home	Moves the cursor to the front of the line that the cursor is on
End	Moves the cursor to the end of the line that the cursor is on
Ctrl+Home	Moves the cursor to the first line of your BASIC code
Ctrl+End	Moves the cursor to the last line of your BASIC code
Ctrl+Down arrow	Scrolls the code editor down one line without moving the cursor
Ctrl+Up arrow	Scrolls the code editor up one line without moving the cursor
Ctrl+Page Down	Goes to the last line in the code editor (not the last line in your code)
Ctrl+Page Up	Goes to the top of the code editor (not the top of your code)
Ctrl+Right arrow	Goes one word to the right
Ctrl+Left arrow	Goes one word to the left
Page Down	Displays the next page down in the code editor
Page Up	Displays the next page up in the code editor
Insert	Toggles the Insert mode on or off
Ctrl+X	Cuts a selected block of text

Keystroke	What Happens
Ctrl+C	Copies a selected block of text
Ctrl+V	Pastes a previously cut or copied block of text
Ctrl+Z	Undoes the last thing you did (typed a letter, erased a sentence, and so on)
Ctrl+F	Finds a word that you specify
F1	Displays the Visual Basic .NET help system
F6	Switches between code editor panes (if the code editor is split)
Ctrl+H	Searches for a word and replaces it with something else
Ctrl+P	Displays the Print dialog box

To help you write BASIC code, the code editor also automatically highlights BASIC-reserved keywords in color. This way you can see which commands are BASIC-reserved keywords and which are commands you've created on your own.

Any time you make a mistake in the code editor, press Ctrl+Z to reverse the last action you did, such as if you accidentally deleted a line.

Viewing Different Event Procedures

A typical Visual Basic .NET program consists of several event-handling procedures stored in each form file. Rather than scroll through the code editor, looking for the one event-handling procedure you want to find, you can use the Class Name and Method Name list boxes at the top of the code editor.

The Method Name list box lists all the objects available on your form such as buttons, pull-down menu commands, and check boxes. The Method Name lists all the different events that your objects can respond to.

To find an event-handling procedure by using the Class Name and Method Name list boxes, follow these steps:

1. **Click in the Class Name list box.**

   Visual Basic .NET displays a list of available objects, as shown in Figure 14-3. So if you're looking for an object named btnClickMe, look for it in this list.

Figure 14-3:
The typical contents of the Class Name list box.

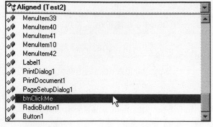

2. **Click on an object name (such as btnClickMe if that's the name of the object you want to find).**

3. **Click in the Method Name list box.**

   Visual Basic .NET displays a list of available events your chosen object can respond to, as shown in Figure 14-4. When you see an event displayed in bold, that means Visual Basic .NET has already created an event-handling procedure for that event.

Figure 14-4:
The typical list of events available in the Method Name list box.

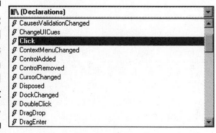

4. **Click on an event.**

   Visual Basic .NET displays your chosen event-handling procedure.

If you click on an event that appears in bold, Visual Basic .NET displays an existing event-handling procedure for your chosen object. If you click on an event that appears in normal type (not bold), Visual Basic .NET creates and displays an empty event-handling procedure.

Table 14-2 lists some (but not all) of the possible events to which objects can respond.

Table 14-2	Common Events
Event	*Occurs When . . .*
Click	The user clicks the mouse button once on the object.
DoubleClick	The user clicks the mouse button twice in rapid succession on an object.
DragDrop	The user holds down the mouse button on an object, moves the mouse, and releases the mouse button.
DragOver	The user holds down the mouse button on an object and moves the mouse.
GotFocus	An object becomes highlighted when the user presses Tab or clicks on an object, or if a form loads.
KeyDown	The user presses a key.
KeyPress	The user presses and releases an *ANSI key,* such as a keyboard character, Ctrl key combination, Enter, or backspace key. (Basically, an ANSI key can be any letter, number, or oddball keystroke combination that you press.)
KeyUp	The user releases a key.
LostFocus	An object is no longer highlighted because the user pressed Tab or clicked on another object, or if a form has unloaded.
MouseDown	The user presses a mouse button.
MouseHover	The user moves the mouse over the object.
MouseUp	The user releases a mouse button.

The combination of the object name and the event name defines the name for an event-handling procedure. Because object names must always be unique, no two-event procedures on the same form can have the same name.

A single object can have multiple event-handling procedures to make your program do something different depending on the event that occurs, such as if the user clicks on an object or moves the mouse over that same object. In most cases, most objects only need a few event-handling procedures to make them useful.

Writing an Event-Handling Procedure

To make your user interface work, you need to create event-handling procedures and fill them with BASIC code. An event-handling procedure can contain three types of BASIC code that do one or more of the following:

- ✔ Retrieve a value that the user stored in a user interface object. (Accept outside data.)
- ✔ Calculate a result based on data retrieved from user interface object property. (Calculate a result.)
- ✔ Change the properties of a user interface object. (Display a result back to the user.)

Retrieving data from the user

Retrieving data from your user interface involves creating a variable (which is explained in Chapter 15), retrieving a value stored in a user interface object (such as retrieving a number that the user typed into a text box, which is covered in Chapter 16), and then storing that value into a variable so another part of your program can use it to calculate a new result.

Calculating a result from the data

Calculating a result means using arithmetic (covered in Chapter 17) or string-manipulation commands (covered in Chapter 18) to create a new result.

Any BASIC code that calculates a result should be stored in a module (explained in Chapter 27) or class file (explained in Chapter 31). That way, if your program doesn't work right, you can quickly isolate the location of the problem. If your program is calculating a result incorrectly, the problem (bug) must be in the BASIC code stored in your module or class files. If your program calculates the right result but somehow displays the wrong data, the problem (bug) must be in one of your event-handling procedures.

Displaying a result to the user

Displaying data to the user involves storing a new value in a user interface object's property, such as changing the Text property of a text box to show a number or message. Thus, your program's user interface serves two purposes: allows the user to type or give data to your program and allows your program to display information back to the user.

The event-handling procedure that every program needs

The simplest and most important event-handling procedure that every program needs is one that stops your program. The following event-handling procedure tells Visual Basic .NET to stop running your program the moment the user clicks on a button named Button1:

```
Private Sub Button1_Click(ByVal sender As System.Object,_
          ByVal e As System.EventArgs) Handles Button1.Click
   Me.Close()
End Sub
```

If you don't include an event-handling procedure to stop your program, the only way a user can stop your program is by rebooting the computer or turning the whole system off. Because this isn't the best way to exit a program, always make sure that your program contains at least one or more ways for the user to exit your program at any given moment.

Test your newfound knowledge

1. What is an event, and what are the three types of events?

   a. An event is something that you must get tickets for, such as a concert, a sports event, or the circus.

   b. Events are things that happen to your computer, such as having a drink spilled on the keyboard, having all your files erased by mistake, and having the dog eat a floppy disk.

   c. Events occur when the user presses a key or mouse button or when the program changes appearance. The three types are keyboard, mouse, and program events.

   d. An event is a holiday or celebration that lets you take the day off from work. The three types of events are legal holidays, reunions, and funerals for nonexistent relatives.

2. What do the Class Name and Method Name list boxes do in the code editor?

   a. They list all the possible reasons why you need to write your program in C++ or Java rather than in Visual Basic .NET.

   b. The Class Name list box lets you choose an object for which you can write an event procedure. The Method Name list box lets you choose all the possible events to which an object can respond.

   c. The Class Name list box contains a list of all the blunt objects you can use to hit your computer. The Method Name list box lists all the events that you can attend instead of staring at your computer screen.

   d. Neither list box does anything worth remembering, so don't bother to ask me this question again.

Chapter 15

Using Variables

After you know what you want your program to do, you can start writing BASIC code. So what happens when a user types a name, an address, or a telephone number into a program? Obviously, the program must read this information from the user interface and then do something with that information. When computers need to store information temporarily, they use something called *variables*.

Reading Data

Any information that a program gets from outside the computer is *data*. Nearly all but the simplest programs receive data, do something to the data, and spit the data out again.

A word processor receives data as characters, which it formats to look pretty and then prints neatly on paper while a nuclear-missile guidance system receives data as numbers that may represent target coordinates. The missile system uses this data to guide a warhead to a target.

The whole purpose of a program is to turn computers into electronic sausage grinders. Stick information in one end and out comes the information, in a different form, on the other end. All programs manipulate the following:

✔ Numbers

✔ Strings

Numbers can be positive or negative, whole numbers or fractions, or just about any other type of number you can think of (including telephone numbers to hot dates, numbers that form a combination to a safe containing wads of money, and imaginary numbers that no one except mathematicians truly understand).

Strings are characters strung together. A *character* is anything you can type from the keyboard, including letters, punctuation marks, and (don't get confused now) numbers.

Technically, computers only understand numbers. When a computer manipulates a string, it uses numbers to represent each character.

Depending on how the program decides to treat them, numbers can be considered as numbers or as a string. For example, most programs treat your telephone number or street address as a string but treat your age or weight as a number.

A single letter is considered a string. An entire sentence is also a string. You can even consider the first chapter of *War and Peace* a string. Strings can be any collection of letters, spaces, and numbers grouped together.

Understanding Values and Variables

When you type a number or a string into a program, your program needs to retrieve or manipulate this data later. So your program says, "Okay, where did I put this information? Oh, that's right, I stored the information in a place (variable) called PhoneNumber." The computer obediently rushes to the `PhoneNumber` variable and yanks out whatever number or word the computer stored there.

Variables can hold a wide variety of data (which is why they're called *variables,* a more scientific-sounding name than *junk, stuff,* or *garbage*). The information stored in a variable is called a *value* because a value represents either a string or a number.

Using variables

Two types of variables exist:

- Those you make up
- Those already defined as the properties of every object on a form

Every time you draw an object to make your user interface, Visual Basic .NET automatically creates a whole bunch of variables (called *properties*) set with default values. To look at the values of an object's properties, you have to use the Properties window. (Press F4 or choose View⇨Properties Window.)

Property values can represent numbers (such as defining the width and height of an object), True or False (such as defining whether an object is visible), or strings (such as text that appears on a button). Properties simply define the appearance of an object on the screen.

Variables are names that can represent any type of value. Properties are special names for variables that affect the appearance or behavior of an object.

To create a variable on your own, you have to declare that variable first, which essentially tells the computer, "I'm going to make up a variable name and tell you what kind of data it can hold."

Declaring variables

To declare a variable, you need to define two items:

- ✔ The name of your variable
- ✔ The type of data your variable can hold

In the world of Visual Basic .NET, creating a variable means following this example:

```
Dim VariableName As DataType
```

There are three reasons why Visual Basic .NET forces you to define data types for all your variables:

- ✔ So that you can easily see the type of data each variable can hold
- ✔ To prevent variables from accidentally storing the wrong type of data and causing an error
- ✔ To use memory more efficiently because some data types (such as double) require more memory to use than other data types (such as byte)

It's a good idea to name your variable something descriptive such as PersonAge or PhoneNumber. Visual Basic .NET doesn't care if you choose variable names like XCPEIQ or Stuff, but trying to decipher what these variables represent can make your program more difficult to understand and modify later on.

The type of data that your variable can hold can be either a number or a string. So if you wanted to create a variable name called Enemy2Eliminate, you would use this command:

```
Dim Enemy2Eliminate As String
```

If you want your variable to hold a number, you have to define the type of number. Table 15-1 lists the available data types you can choose and how much memory (listed under the Storage Size heading) that each data type requires.

Table 15-1	The Visual Basic .NET Data Types	
Data Type	**Storage Size**	**Accepts Numbers That Range From . . .**
Boolean	2 bytes	True (1) or False (0)
Byte	1 byte	0 to 255
Char	2 bytes	0 to 65535
Date	8 bytes	Dates between January 1, 0001 and December 31, 9999
Decimal	16 bytes	+/-79,228,162,514,264,337,593,543,950,335 with no decimal point; +/-7.9228162514264337593543950335 with 28 places to the right of the decimal; smallest non-zero number is +/-0.0000000000000000000000000001
Double	8 bytes	-1.79769313486231E+308 to -4.94065645841247E-324 (negative numbers) and 4.94065645841247E-324 to 1.79769313486232E308 (positive numbers)
Integer	4 bytes	-2,147,483,648 to 2,147,483,647
Long	8 bytes	-9,223,372,036,854,775,808 to 9,223,372,036,854,775,807
Short	2 bytes	-32,768 to 32,767
Single	4 bytes	-3.402823E+38 to -1.401298E-45 (negative numbers) and 1.401298E-45 to 3.402823E38 (positive numbers)
String	Varies	0 to approximately 2 billion Unicode characters

Unicode characters represent a standard for assigning unique numbers to specific characters such as letters, numbers, symbols, and foreign language characters. To find out more about the Unicode standard, visit www.unicode.org.

So if you wanted to create a variable named `PersonAge`, you could choose one of the following:

```
Dim PersonAge As Integer
```

or

```
Dim PersonAge As Byte
```

The difference between an Integer and a Byte data type is that a Byte data type can only hold numbers that range between 0 and 255 while an Integer data type can hold numbers that range between -2,147,483,648 to 2,147,483,647. Because a person's age will never go below 0 or above 255, you should use the Byte data type in this case since a Byte data type takes up 1 byte of memory while an Integer data type takes up 4 bytes.

Use the data type that uses the least amount of memory possible. That way your program will require less memory to run and will run more efficiently as a result.

If you try to cram a number that's larger (or smaller) than the largest (or smallest) number that a particular data type can hold, your program won't work. So if you try to cram the number 2000 into a variable declared as a Byte data type, Visual Basic .NET will scream and refuse to run your program.

You can also declare multiple variables at once, such as:

```
Dim VariableName1, VariableName2 As DataType
```

So if you wanted to define two variables named `StupidPeople` and `IQ` as integers, you would use the following basic code:

```
Dim StupidPeople, IQ as Integer
```

Visual Basic .NET actually gives you two ways to declare a variable:

```
Dim MyString As String
```

or

```
Dim MyString$
```

The first method can be verbose but clear. The second method uses something called *type declaration characters*. This makes declaring variables easier but makes your commands harder to read and understand at first glance.

If you want to be clear and don't mind typing a lot of extra words like "As String" or "As Integer," use the first method. If you want to save time and don't care to make your code readable, use the second method. Here's a short table listing all the type declaration characters you can use to declare variables as different data types:

Data Type	Character	Example	Equivalent To
Decimal	@	Dim Loot@	Dim Loot As Decimal
Double	#	Dim Average#	Dim Average As Double
Integer	%	Dim Age%	Dim Age As Integer
Long	&	Dim Huge&	Dim Huge As Long
Single	!	Dim Tiny!	Dim Tiny As Single
String	$	Dim Name$	Dim Name As String

Naming variables

You can name your variables anything you want, and you can store anything you want in them. However, naming a variable PhoneNumber and then stuffing somebody's address in that same variable will be confusing.

Give your variables names that represent the data you're going to store in them. For example, naming a variable PhoneNumber makes sense if you're going to store phone numbers in the variable.

When naming your variables, you must adhere to some unbreakable rules, which follow; otherwise, Visual Basic .NET throws a tantrum. All variables must

- Begin with a letter.
- Be a maximum of 255 characters in length (with an obvious minimum of one character in length).
- Contain only letters, numbers, and the underscore character (_); spaces and punctuation marks aren't allowed.
- Be any word (including four-letter ones) except a Visual Basic .NET reserved word, such as End or Sub.

If your variable names meet these criteria, all is going to be well. (Of course, that doesn't mean your program is going to work, but at least Visual Basic .NET is going to be happy.) The following are examples of Visual Basic .NET-approved variable names:

```
Phone
Here_is_Your_Name
Route66
```

Test your newfound knowledge

1. What do the following lines of code do?

   ```
   Dim intCats As Integer
   Dim dblMyMoney@
   ```

   a. Absolutely nothing because everyone knows that Microsoft would rather have you master their new C# programming language instead.

   b. Declares a variable named intCats, which can hold an Integer data type, and another variable named dblMyMoney, which can hold a Decimal data type.

   c. Displays cryptic hieroglyphics that an alien race left for us to discover when their flying saucer crashed in New Mexico.

   d. These BASIC commands don't do anything if you don't turn on your computer and load Visual Basic .NET. So there.

2. What is the purpose for declaring variables?

   a. So programmers from the South can feel right at home talking to the computer. "Why, I declare! That looks just like a little ol' integer to me!"

   b. So you can hide the fact that you really don't know what you're doing.

   c. To provide a convenient list of all the variables used and to define them as storing particular types of data, such as integers or strings.

   d. To flush them out of hiding and into the open, where the variables can be tagged, tracked, and destroyed in the name of progress.

The following are some variable names that Visual Basic .NET will refuse to accept:

123Surprise	(This name begins with a number.)
Just Work	(This name contains a space.)
Sub	(This name is a Visual Basic .NET reserved keyword.)

 To help you identify at a glance the type of data a variable contains, many programmers like to use a three-letter prefix in front of the variable name to help identify the data type, such as:

intStupidPeople	(This identifies an Integer data type variable.)
lngJohnSilver	(This identifies a Long data type variable.)
strOfCongressmanAffairs	(This identifies a String data type variable.)

Three-letter prefixes can look kind of messy, so this book occasionally omits them for clarity when the variable name isn't the focus of a code example.

Assigning numbers to variables

Now that you know how to create variables by naming them, how do you assign a value to a variable and get the value back out again? Easy — you use something mysterious called an equal sign (=).

To assign a value to a variable, you have to write a BASIC command, as in the following example:

```
VariableName = Value
```

Rather than telling the computer, "Hey, stupid. Assign the number 36 to a variable named Age," you can just write:

```
Age = 36
```

Variables can hold only one value at a time. If a variable already holds a value and you assign another one to the variable, the variable cheerfully tosses out the old value and accepts the new one. You can give two commands, as in the following example:

```
Age = 36
Age = 49
```

Visual Basic .NET first says, "Okay, let my variable named Age hold the number 36." Then Visual Basic .NET looks at the second line and says, "Okay, let my variable named Age hold the number 49, and forget that the number 36 ever existed."

Assigning strings to variables

Assigning strings to variables is similar to assigning numbers to variables. The only difference is that you have to surround a string with quotation marks so that Visual Basic .NET knows where the string begins and ends.

For example, you can assign a variable with a single-word string:

```
Name = "John"
```

Or you can assign a variable with a string consisting of two or more words:

```
Name = "John Doe"
```

or

```
Name = "John Smith Doe the Third and proud of it"
```

Not all strings consist of letters. Sometimes you may want to assign a variable with a phone number or social security number, as follows:

```
PhoneNumber = "555-1234"
SocialSecurity = "123-45-6789"
```

What happens if you don't include the quotation marks and just type the following?

```
PhoneNumber = 555-1234
SocialSecurity = 123-45-6789
```

Without the quotation marks, Visual Basic .NET thinks the hyphen is a subtraction symbol and that you want the program to calculate a new result. Instead of storing 555-1234 in the `PhoneNumber` variable, Visual Basic .NET stores the number –679. Instead of storing 123-45-6789 in the `SocialSecurity` variable, Visual Basic .NET stores –6711.

When you assign a variable with letters or numbers that you want treated as a string, put quotation marks around the letters or numbers.

Assigning variables to other variables

Besides assigning numbers or strings to a variable, you can also assign the value of one variable to another variable. To do this, you have to write a BASIC command like the following:

```
FirstVariableName = SecondVariableName
```

For example, you may want to copy the value stored in the `LowIQ` variable into the `Moron` variable, such as:

```
Dim LowIQ, Moron As Byte
LowIQ = 9
Moron = LowIQ
```

When Visual Basic .NET sees the preceding BASIC code, this is what happens:

1. The first line tells Visual Basic .NET, "Create two variables named `LowIQ` and `Moron`, and make both of them hold a value from 0 to 255 (a Byte data type)."

2. The second line tells Visual Basic .NET, "Take the number 9 and store it in the variable called `LowIQ`."

3. The third line tells Visual Basic .NET, "Take the value of the variable `LowIQ` and store it in the variable called `Moron`. Now that `LowIQ` holds the number 9, the `Moron` variable also holds the number 9."

Assigning an object's property to a variable (and vice versa)

If you want to display a message on the screen, you can modify the properties of a label or text box. By changing the properties of an object, you can display information back to the user.

Because the properties of an object are variables, you can assign values to an object's property in the same way. For example, suppose that you wanted to change the Height property of a button named Button1 to 43, here's how you do this:

```
Button1.Height = 43
```

This tells Visual Basic .NET, "Find the object named Button1 and change the Height property to 43."

If you wanted to display a message in a label or text box, you would assign the Text property of that label or text box to a string, such as:

```
TextBox1.Text = "This appears in the text box."
```

One property that BASIC code cannot change is the Name property of any object. The only way to change the Name property of an object is through the Properties window during design time.

Understanding the Scope of Your Variables

One major cause of bugs in a program is when one part of a program messes around with data that another part of the program uses. So to isolate data, Visual Basic .NET limits which parts of your program can use a particular variable, which in computer programming terms is called the *scope* of a variable.

The *scope* of a variable determines the accessibility of a variable within a Visual Basic .NET program. Visual Basic .NET lets you declare the scope of variables in four ways:

- ✔ Block
- ✔ Procedure
- ✔ Module
- ✔ Project

Block variables

A *block variable* has the most limited scope because the variable only exists within a block of code, such as an If-Then-End If block (covered in Chapter 22) or a For-Next loop (covered in Chapter 25). To create a block variable, you have to use the magical Dim command inside that block of code, such as:

```
If YourSalary < CEOSalary Then
  Dim Message As String
  Message = "How come I get paid less but do all the work?"
  TextBox1.Text = Message
End If
```

In the preceding example, Visual Basic .NET creates the variable named Message on the second line. Prior to that line, the variable Message doesn't exist as far as Visual Basic .NET is concerned. Then, as soon as Visual Basic .NET reaches the last line, End If, it conveniently forgets that the Message variable ever existed in the first place.

Even though block variables can only be used within the block where they are declared, they retain the last value assigned to them. So if your program repeats a block more than once, you may need to initialize the variable each time to make sure your program doesn't accidentally wind up using the last value of that block variable.

Procedure variables

A procedure is a miniature program that typically solves one task, such as an event-handling procedure that tells your program what to do the moment someone clicks on a particular button. So a procedure variable can be accessed anywhere inside that particular procedure. That way, if a variable starts screwing up and storing the wrong value, you can easily isolate that problem to that single procedure. (See Chapters 14 and 27 for more information about event-handling procedures and general procedures.)

To create a procedure variable, declare the variable at the beginning of the procedure, such as:

```
Private Sub Button1_Click(ByVal sender As System.Object,_
         ByVal e As System.EventArgs) Handles Button1.Click
  Dim Losers As Integer

End Sub
```

Now any code sandwiched in between the Dim Losers As Integer line and the final End Sub line have complete access to the Losers variable. However, as far as the rest of your program knows, the Losers variable doesn't exist.

Module variables

A *module variable* can be used by any BASIC code stored in the same file such as a form file or a module file (Chapter 27 explains more about module files). Like a form file, a module file typically contains one or more procedures.

Module variables can be changed by any procedure stored in the same file. So if your module variable is receiving incorrect data, trying to track down the source of that problem involves digging through your entire module file, line by line, which makes your program harder to debug and fix.

To create a module variable, you need to substitute the `Dim` command with the `Private` command and type the following at the top of a module file or immediately following the `Public Class` line in a form file:

```
Private VariableName As DataType
```

The keyword `Private` tells Visual Basic .NET that this variable can only be used by any BASIC code stored in the same file. When you start creating Visual Basic .NET programs that consist of two or more files, each file keeps its module variables isolated from any other files that make up your program.

Namespace variables

Namespace variables (sometimes called global variables in other programming languages) are variables that can be used by any part of your Visual Basic .NET program. But be careful! Most programmers avoid using namespace variables because if your program stores the wrong value in a namespace variable, you have to search your entire program to find the line that may be causing the problem.

By comparison, if your program messes up a module variable, you can isolate the problem in the file in which you declared the module variable. Likewise, if your program messes up a procedure or block variable, the only possible place the problem can occur is in the procedure or block in which you declared the procedure or block variable.

To declare a namespace variable, you need to substitute the `Dim` command with the `Public` command and type the following at the top of any file, such as a module or form file:

```
Public VariableName As DataType
```

Using Variables to Represent Objects

In the simplest form, variables represent a data type (a number or a string). However, variables can also represent objects as well. One of the more common objects that variables can represent is a form.

Part VII of the book explains more about objects and object-oriented programming so if the idea of objects isn't clear to you at this moment, don't worry about it.

Sometimes you may want to open another form while your program is running. In that case, you have to use the following BASIC code:

```
Dim FormVariable As FormName
FormVariable = New FormName()
FormVariable.Show()
```

1. The first line tells Visual Basic .NET, "Create a variable that represents the form that you want to display." So if you wanted to assign a variable named MyForm (you can choose any name you want) to represent a form named frmWindow (stored on your hard disk as the file frmWindow.vb), you would use this code:

   ```
   Dim MyForm As frmWindow
   ```

2. The second line tells Visual Basic .NET, "Create a new copy of the form, identified by FormName, that you want to display."

3. The third line tells Visual Basic .NET, "Show (or display) the object represented by the FormVariable variable name." In this case, the FormVariable name represents a form object, so Visual Basic .NET displays that form on the screen.

Chapter 16

Getting Data from the User

● ●

● ●

A user interface makes your program look nice and pretty. Unfortunately, a nice and pretty user interface can be as useless as an attractive person without any brains (think of some of the people you've dated). If you want your program to have more substance than an empty-headed fashion model, you have to make sure that your program can respond intelligently to the user.

To make your user interface responsive, your program must

✔ Get information from the user interface

✔ Calculate a result

✔ Display that result back on the user interface

For example, when the user chooses an item from a list box, the program has no idea which item the user chose. If you look at the screen, you may be tempted to say, "Hey, stupid computer. If I can see which item the user has chosen, why can't you?"

But what you see on the user interface isn't what the computer sees. From the computer's point of view, the computer still has no idea which item the user selected from the list box.

To tell the computer what action a user took, you have to write BASIC code. This BASIC code grabs information that's stored in an object's properties. The three most common properties that store data from the user interface are

✔ Text (String data type)

✔ Checked (Boolean data type)

✔ Value (Integer, Long, or Decimal data type)

Retrieving Strings from the Text Property

The Text property stores (what else?) text, as a String data type, that the user types in or chooses from a list box. The following user interface objects use the Text property to store String data types:

- Text box
- Combo box
- List box
- Checked list box
- Rich text box
- DomainUpDown

Text boxes, rich text boxes, and combo boxes allow users to type any text they want. (If the combo box has its Style property set to DropDownList, users can't type any text into that combo box.)

Because users can type anything (including four-letter words or obviously stupid replies), you may need to write additional BASIC code to filter out useless data that users may type into your program. Otherwise, if users type data that your program doesn't know how to handle, your program could freeze, crash, or just work erratically.

List boxes, checked list boxes, combo boxes, and DomainUpDown objects display a list of text choices that users can pick. By limiting the available choices that a user can pick, these types of objects force users to choose only valid data.

The magic BASIC code to retrieving data from the Text property of an object is just to assign a variable to the object name and its Text property, such as:

```
VariableName = ObjectName.Text
```

You need to declare your variable as a String data type and then substitute the actual name of your object in place of `ObjectName`. So if you wanted to retrieve data from the Text property of a text box named `txtMessage` and store this information in a variable called `strInfo`, you would use the following BASIC code:

```
Dim strInfo As String
strInfo = txtMessage.Text
```

You can also use text boxes if you need users to type in a number, such as their age or IQ. Just remember that when users type a number into a text box, Visual Basic .NET treats that number as a string. To convert a string into a number, you have to use a special BASIC command such as CInt or CSng. Chapter 18 explains how to convert strings into different numeric data types.

Checking the Checked Property

Two of the most common user interface objects are radio buttons and check boxes, which usually appear in groups of two or more. To determine which check box or radio button a user chose, your program needs to examine each radio button's and check box's Checked property.

The Checked property is a Boolean data type that can represent one of two choices:

- ✔ True (selected)
- ✔ False (unselected)

An unselected radio button or check box appears blank. A selected radio button or check box appears with a dot or a check mark.

Rather than assign a separate variable to represent the Checked property of each radio button or check box, you can just use that radio button or check box's Checked value directly in your BASIC code. So instead of writing BASIC code like this:

```
Dim Flag As Boolean
Flag = RadioButton1.Checked
If Flag = True Then
   TextBox1.Text = "Release biological weapons now!"
End If
```

You can simplify your code by doing the following:

```
If RadioButton1.Checked = True Then
   TextBox1.Text = "Release biological weapons now!"
End If
```

Or to simplify even further, you can drop the = True part and just write the following:

```
If RadioButton1.Checked Then
  TextBox1.Text = "Release biological weapons now!"
End If
```

You'll find out more about using Boolean values in If-Then statements in Chapter 22. For now, just browse the preceding BASIC code to get a rough idea about what it looks like.

Getting a Number from the Value Property

If users need to type widely varying numbers into your program, such as 0.093 one moment and 84,757 the next, you'll be better off using a text box. But in most cases, users will only need to select from a limited range of numbers, such as between 0 and 100.

When you want users to choose from a range of possible values, you can use one of the following user interface objects:

- ✔ NumericUpDown (Decimal data type)
- ✔ Horizontal/vertical Scroll bars (Integer data type)
- ✔ TrackBar (Integer data type)
- ✔ DateTimePicker (Long data type)

Instead of forcing the user to type in a number, the preceding objects allow users to scroll, slide, or click on a number, which Visual Basic .NET stores in the Value property.

The BASIC code to retrieving data from the Value property of an object is just to assign a variable to the object name and its Value property such as:

```
VariableName = ObjectName.Value
```

You need to declare your variable as the proper data type, depending on the object. Then you have to substitute the actual name of your object in place of `ObjectName`. So if you wanted to retrieve a number from the Value property of a TrackBar named `TrackBar1` and store this information in a variable called `intMyNumber`, you would use the following BASIC code:

```
Dim intMyNumber As Integer
intMyNumber = TrackBar1.Value
```

Selecting Multiple Items in a List Box or Combo Box

If you change the SelectionMode property of a list box or combo box to MultiSimple or MultiExtended, users can pick two or more items by holding down the Ctrl or Shift key while clicking on the list of items available. When users select two or more items, the Text property only contains the first item the user chose.

To retrieve multiple items from a list box or combo box, you need to retrieve data using the SelectedItems and the SelectedIndices properties.

The SelectedItems property contains the actual items that the user selected. The SelectedIndices property contains the indices of each selected item. For example, if the user chose the first and third item in a list box, the Selected Indices property would contain 0 (the first item) and 2 (the third item).

How many items did the user select?

To determine how many items the user selected, you have to use the following BASIC code:

```
Dim intMyVariable As Integer
intMyVariable = BoxName.SelectedItems.Count
```

In the preceding example, substitute any name for intMyVariable and replace BoxName with the actual name of your list box or combo box, such as ListBox1.

You can only count how many items a user selected if the list box or combo box SelectionMode property is set to MultiSingle or MultiExtended.

Retrieving the items the user selected

When you know how many items the user selected, you can use a loop (explained in Chapters 24 and 25) to retrieve the actual selected items, which Visual Basic .NET stores in the SelectedItems.Item property, such as:

```
BoxName.SelectedItems.Item(x)
```

In the preceding example, BoxName is the name of your actual list box or combo box and x represents the number of the selected items. So if a user selects three items from a list box named ListBox1, the first selected item would have a value of 0, such as:

```
ListBox1.SelectedItems.Item(0)
```

The second selected item would have a value of 1, such as:

```
ListBox1.SelectedItems.Item(1)
```

The third selected item would have a value of 2 and so on, as shown in Figure 16-1.

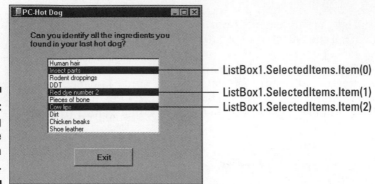

Figure 16-1:
Selecting multiple items from a list box.

When the user selects multiple items in a list box or combo box, Visual Basic .NET stores those selected items into a data type called a Collection (explained in Chapter 20). You need to convert the selected item from an Object data type to a String data type by using the `CStr` BASIC command.

One example of BASIC code that can retrieve multiple items selected in a list box or combo box is shown here:

```
Dim I As Integer
For I = 0 to (BoxName.SelectedItems.Count - 1)
  MsgBox (CStr(BoxName.SelectedItems.Item(I), , "This was_
          selected")
Next
```

1. The first line creates a variable named I that can hold Integer data types.

2. The second line creates a For-Next loop that counts from zero (0) to one less than the total number of items that the user selected. So if the user selected four items, the For-Next loop would count from 0 to 3, or four times. (If this is starting to confuse you, don't worry about it; you'll discover more about For-Next loops in Chapter 25.)

3. The third line displays a message dialog box using the `MsgBox` command. The title bar of this dialog box contains the string "`This was selected.`" When this code runs, the message dialog box pops up to display each selected item. So if the user selected three items, the dialog box pops up three times, each time displaying a different selected item.

4. The fourth line marks the end of the For-Next loop.

Test your newfound knowledge

1. What does the following BASIC command do?

   ```
   WhatIsIt =
   VScrollBar1.Value
   ```

   a. The command tries to identify UFOs named VScrollBar1.Value.

   b. The command questions the need for anything named `VScrollBar1.Value`.

   c. The command makes the computer ask, "What do you want me to do? Tell me and then leave me alone. I'm feeling bold today."

   d. The command yanks a number that's stored in the Value property of an object named `VScrollBar1`. Then it stuffs this number in a variable named `WhatIsIt`.

2. What are the two properties you need to use for retrieving multiple items selected in a list box or combo box?

   a. The BoxName.SelectedItems.Count and the BoxName.SelectedItems.Item, where BoxName is the actual name of the list box or combo box.

   b. Boardwalk and Park Place.

   c. When dealing with properties, it all depends on the location.

   d. Under a communist regime, the government owns all the property, so this question is invalid under communist rule.

Chapter 17

Math 101: Arithmetic, Logical, and Comparison Operators

. . . .

In This Chapter

▶ Adding, subtracting, multiplying, and dividing numbers

▶ Using the Not, And, Or, or Xor operators

▶ Comparing numbers and strings

▶ Understanding precedence

. . . .

After a program gets data from the user (either as a number or as a string), the next step is to calculate some sort of result with the data the program receives from the user.

To calculate a result, your program needs to get data from the user interface and then somehow change, modify, mutilate, or spindle that data. Changing anything involves an operation, so the special commands to work with data are called *operators*.

Visual Basic .NET provides the following three types of operators:

✔ Arithmetic

✔ Logical

✔ Comparison

Arithmetic and Concatenation Operators

Arithmetic operators essentially turn your $2,000 computer into a $4.95 pocket calculator. These operators let you add, subtract, multiply, and divide numbers or variables that represent numbers. Table 17-1 shows the most common arithmetic operators.

Table 17-1	Arithmetic Operators
Operator	**What the Operator Does**
+	Adds two numbers
−	Subtracts two numbers
*	Multiplies two numbers
/	Divides two numbers and returns a floating-point (decimal) number, such as 3.14, 16.2, or 392.2398
\	Divides two numbers and returns an integer, such as 8, 16, 302, or 25
Mod (or modulo)	Divides two numbers and returns only the remainder
^	Raises a number to an exponential power
&	Adds (concatenates) two strings

When using arithmetic operators, use compatible data types. If you must use arithmetic operators with different data types, you have to convert them to the same data type, such as converting an Integer data type to a Single data type (or vice versa). The section, "Converting data types," later in this chapter explains more about data type conversion.

Adding two numbers with the + operator

To add two numbers, use the addition operator (+), as shown in the following example:

```
Dim X, Y, Sum As Single
X = 10
Y = 15.4
Sum = X + Y
```

In this case, the value of Sum equals 10 + 15.4 or 25.4.

As a shortcut, you can also add two numbers together using the += operator, such as:

```
X += Y
```

This is equal to the following:

```
X = X + Y
```

Subtracting two numbers with the – operator

To subtract two numbers, use the subtraction operator (–), as shown in the following example:

```
Dim Income, Taxes, Real_Income As Integer
Income = 2000
Taxes = 2500
Real_Income = Income - Taxes
```

In this case, the value of Real_Income equals 2000 – 2500, or –500.

As a shortcut, you can also add two numbers together using the -= operator, such as:

```
X -= Y
```

This is equal to the following:

```
X = X - Y
```

Negating numbers with the – operator

The subtraction operator (–), used by itself, can turn a positive number into a negative number and vice versa. To negate a number, place the – operator in front of any number or variable, as shown in the following example:

```
Dim Amount, Balance As Integer
Amount = 250
Balance = - Amount
```

In the preceding example, the value of Balance is –250.

Multiplying two numbers with the * operator

To multiply two numbers, use the multiplication operator (*), as shown in the following example:

```
Dim Hours, Wages, Salary As Single
Hours = 25
Wages = 5.75
Salary = Hours * Wages
```

In this case, the value of Salary equals 25 * 5.75, or 143.75.

As a shortcut, you can also add two numbers together using the *= operator, such as:

```
X *= Y
```

This is equal to the following:

```
X = X * Y
```

Dividing two numbers with the / operator

To divide two numbers and calculate a floating-point (decimal) number, use the forward-slash division operator (/), as shown in the following example:

```
Dim GamesWon, TotalGames, WinningPercentage As Single
GamesWon = 104
TotalGames = 162
WinningPercentage = GamesWon / TotalGames
```

In the preceding example, the value of WinningPercentage equals 104 / 162, or 0.6419753.

As a shortcut, you can also add two numbers together using the /= operator, such as:

```
X /= Y
```

This is equal to the following:

```
X = X / Y
```

Dividing two numbers with the \ operator

To divide two numbers and calculate an integer, use the backslash division operator (\ ), as shown in the following example:

```
Dim CrateCapacity, Bottles_in_Crate, FullCrates As Integer
CrateCapacity = 72
Bottles_in_Crate = 1900
FullCrates = Bottles_in_Crate \ CrateCapacity
```

So how does Visual Basic .NET interpret these three BASIC commands? Glad you asked. Here's how:

1. The first command says "Create three variables named `CrateCapacity`, `Bottles_in_Crate`, and `FullCrates` and make them hold Integer data types."

2. The second command says "Assign the value of 72 to `CrateCapacity`."

3. The third command says, "Assign the value of 1900 to `Bottles_in_Crate`."

4. The fourth command says, "Make `FullCrates` equal to the value of `Bottles_in_Crate` divided by the value of `CrateCapacity`." In this case, the value of `FullCrates` equals 1900 \ 72, or 26.

Dividing two numbers often calculates a floating-point (decimal) number, so how does Visual Basic .NET handle rounding? Consider the following example:

```
Operand1 = 2.5
Operand2 = 1.5
Result = Operand1 \ Operand2
```

Before Visual Basic .NET performs a calculation using the \ operator, the operands are rounded to the nearest whole number. (If an operand is halfway between two whole numbers, such as 2.5 or 1.5, it's rounded up.) In this example, `Operand1` is rounded up to 3 and `Operand2` is rounded up to 2; therefore, `Result` = 3 \ 2, or 1.5. Because the \ operator must return an integer, the value of `Result` is rounded down to 1.

As a shortcut, you can also add two numbers together using the \= operator, such as:

```
X \= Y
```

This is equal to the following:

```
X = X \ Y
```

Dividing with the modulo (Mod) operator

To divide two numbers and calculate the remainder, use the modulo operator (`Mod`), as shown in the following example:

```
Dim CrateCapacity, Bottles_in_Crate, LooseBottles As Integer
CrateCapacity = 72
Bottles_in_Crate = 1900
LooseBottles = Bottles_in_Crate Mod CrateCapacity
```

For those curiosity seekers, this is how Visual Basic .NET interprets these commands:

1. The first command says "Create three variables named `CrateCapacity`, `Bottles_in_Crate`, and `LooseBottles` and make them hold Integer data types."

2. The second command says, "Assign the value of 72 to `CrateCapacity`."

3. The third command says, "Assign the value of 1900 to `Bottles_in_Crate`."

4. The fourth command says, "Make `LooseBottles` equal to the remainder of the value of `Bottles_in_Crate` divided by the value of `CrateCapacity`." In this case, the value of `LooseBottles` equals 1900 Mod 72, or 28.

Calculating an exponential with the ^ operator

An *exponential* is a fancy mathematical term that means to multiply the same number by itself a certain number of times. For example, multiplying the number 2 four times is represented by 2⁴, or 2 * 2 * 2 * 2.

Because you can't type 2⁴, and typing 2 * 2 * 2 * 2 is a bit cumbersome, Visual Basic .NET provides the caret operator (^), as shown in the following example:

```
2 ^ 4
```

As a shortcut, you can also add two numbers together using the ^= operator, such as:

```
X ^= Y
```

This is equal to the following:

```
X = X ^ Y
```

Adding (concatenating) two strings with the & operator

Adding or *concatenating* two strings means smashing them together. For this operation, use the ampersand operator (&), as shown in the following example:

```
Dim FirstName, LastName, FullName As String
FirstName = "John "
LastName = "Doe"
FullName = FirstName & LastName
```

When concatenating strings, always make room for a space between the two strings. Otherwise Visual Basic .NET just slams the two strings together as one word like "JohnDoe."

This is how Visual Basic .NET follows these three BASIC commands:

1. The first command says, "Create three variables named `FirstName`, `LastName`, and `FullName`, and make them represent String data types."

2. The second command says, "Assign the value of `"John "` (note the space at the end) to `FirstName`."

3. The third command says, "Assign the value of `"Doe"` to `LastName`."

4. The fourth command says, "Make `FullName` equal to the value of `FirstName` and the value of `LastName` smashed together." In this case, the value of `FullName` equals `"John"` & `"Doe"`, or `"John Doe"`.

Besides concatenating strings using the ampersand character (&), you can also use the plus sign (+). However, you should use the ampersand character instead because the plus sign is also used with numerical addition. Using the ampersand simply makes your code easier to read.

As a shortcut, you can also add two numbers together using the &= operator, such as:

```
FirstName &= LastName
```

This is equal to the following:

```
FirstName = FirstName & LastName
```

Converting data types

When performing arithmetic on different data types, all data types must be identical (such as all Integer data types) or compatible (such as Single and Double data types). If you need to add a Double data type variable to an Integer data type variable, you must convert your variables to like data types first, such as converting all variables to Integer or Double data types.

To convert data types, you need to use a special type conversion function, which looks like this:

```
ConversionFunction (Expression)
```

In the preceding example, you would substitute the exact type conversion function you want to use for `ConversionFunction` and the number you want to convert for `Expression`. So if you wanted to convert a Single data type variable (represented by the letter X) into an Integer data type, you would use the `CInt` type conversion function such as:

```
Dim Y As Integer
Y = CInt (X)
```

Table 17-2 lists the different data type conversion functions.

Table 17-2		Type Conversion Functions
Function	*Return Type*	*Range for Expression Argument*
CBool	Boolean	Any valid string or numeric expression.
CByte	Byte	0 to 255.
CChar	Char	0 to 65535.
CDate	Date	Any valid representation of a date and time.
CDbl	Double	-1.79769313486231E308 to -4.94065645841247E-324 for negative values; 4.94065645841247E-324 to 1.79769313486232E308 for positive values.
CDec	Decimal	+/-79,228,162,514,264,337,593,543,950,335 for zero-scaled numbers, that is, numbers with no decimal places. For numbers with 28 decimal places, the range is +/-7.9228162514264337593543950335. The smallest possible non-zero number is 0.0000000000000000000000000001.
CInt	Integer	-2,147,483,648 to 2,147,483,647; fractions are rounded.
CLng	Long	-9,223,372,036,854,775,808 to 9,223,372,036,854,775,807; fractions are rounded.
CObj	Object	Any valid expression.

Function	Return Type	Range for Expression Argument
CShort	Short	-32,768 to 32,767; fractions are rounded.
CSng	Single	-3.402823E38 to -1.401298E-45 for negative values; 1.401298E-45 to 3.402823E38 for positive values.
CStr	String	Any valid expression.

Logical Operators

Logical operators manipulate True and False values. Visual Basic .NET represents a value of True as –1 and a value of False as 0. Table 17-3 shows the most common logical operators.

Table 17-3	Logical Operators
Operator	**How to Use**
And	Variable1 And Variable2
Or	Variable1 Or Variable2
Xor	Variable1 Xor Variable2
Not	Not Variable

Using the Not operator

The Not operator simply changes a True value to False and a False value to True, as in the following example:

Variable Name	Value
Another_Computer_Book	True
Not Another_Computer_Book	False

For clarity, cool programmers like to use parentheses. If you use parentheses in the preceding example, it would look like this:

```
Not(Another_Computer_Book)
```

Using the And operator

The And operator compares the True or False values of two variables and calculates a new True or False value. This allows your program to make decisions, as the following example illustrates:

```
KicktheCat = CatPresent And CatMisbehaving
```

So when is the variable KicktheCat True or False? This depends on the True or False value of CatPresent and CatMisbehaving.

KicktheCat	CatPresent	CatMisbehaving
True	True	True
False	False	False
False	True	False
False	False	True

The And operator returns a True value only if both CatPresent and CatMisbehaving are True.

Using the Or operator

Like the And operator, the Or operator compares the True or False values of two variables and calculates a new True or False value. This allows your program to make decisions, as the following example illustrates:

```
LoafInside = GameOnTV Or WeatherBad
```

So when is the variable LoafInside True or False? This depends on the True or False values of GameOnTV and WeatherBad.

LoafInside	GameOnTV	WeatherBad
True	True	True
True	False	True
True	True	False
False	False	False

The Or operator returns a False value only if both GameOnTV and WeatherBad are False.

Using the Xor operator

As with the And and Or operators, the Xor operator compares the True or False values of two variables and calculates a new True or False value. This allows your program to make decisions, as the following example illustrates:

```
TellOffBoss = BossPresent Xor AtWork
```

So when is the variable TellOffBoss True or False? This depends on the True or False value of BossPresent and AtWork.

TellOffBoss	BossPresent	AtWork
True	True	False
True	False	True
False	True	True
False	False	False

The Xor operator returns a False value if both BossPresent and AtWork are True or if both are False.

Comparison Operators

Comparison operators compare two numbers or strings to see whether the numbers or strings are equal to, not equal to, greater than, or less than one another. Table 17-4 shows the most common arithmetic operators.

Table 17-4	Comparison Operators
Operator	*Meaning*
<	Less than
<=	Less than or equal to
>	Greater than
>=	Greater than or equal to
=	Equal to
<>	Not equal to

Comparing numbers and strings

As the following example illustrates, comparison operators compare the values of numbers and strings in order to return a value of True or False:

```
Dim Age, MinimumAge As Integer
Dim Pass As Boolean
Age = 18
MinimumAge = 21
Pass = (Age >= MinimumAge)
```

This is how Visual Basic .NET interprets these three BASIC commands:

1. The first command says, "Create variables named Age and MinimumAge and make them Integer data types."

2. The second command says, "Create a variable named Pass as a Boolean data type."

3. The third command says, "Assign the value of 18 to Age."

4. The fourth command says, "Assign the value of 21 to MinimumAge."

5. The fifth command says, "Compare the value of Age and see whether the value is greater than or equal to the value of MinimumAge. If the value of Age is greater than or equal to the value of MinimumAge, set the value of Pass to True. If the value of Age is not greater than or equal to the value of MinimumAge, set the value of Pass to False." In this case, 18 (the value of Age) is not greater or equal than MinimumAge so the value of Pass is False."

Comparing numbers is fairly easy, but comparing strings is a bit trickier. When comparing strings, Visual Basic .NET calculates the ANSI character code value of each letter.

The ANSI character set

At the simplest level, computers understand only two numbers: zero and one. Because computers only understand numbers, not letters, humans created a simple system where certain numbers represent certain letters, punctuation marks, and characters. So the number 97 represents the letter a, the number 65 represents the letter A, and the number 33 represents an exclamation mark (!).

To make sure that all computers use the same numbers to represent the same letters and punctuation marks, the American National Standards Institute (ANSI) defined an ANSI character set that specifies which number represents which letter or punctuation mark.

Comparing strings with the = and <> operators

Two strings are equal only if they are absolutely identical. As you can see in the following example, the equal to operator (=) always calculates a False value unless the operator compares two identical strings, such as "a" = "a":

Operation	Value of Operation
"a" = "a"	True
"a" = "A"	False
"a" = "aa"	False

In the next example, however, you see that the not equal to operator (<>) always calculates a True value unless this operator compares two identical strings, such as "Abott" <> "Abott":

Operation	Value of Operation
"A" <>"a"	True
"Abott" <> "Abott"	False

Visual Basic .NET always treats uppercase and lowercase letters as completely different entities when comparing strings.

Comparing strings with the >, >=, <, and <= operators

When comparing strings, Visual Basic .NET calculates the ANSI character code for each letter in each string, beginning with the first letter. The string whose character has the higher ANSI character code is considered greater.

For example, the letter *A* has an ANSI character code of 65 and the letter *a* has an ANSI character code of 97. So consider the following line:

```
Flag = ("Air" < "aardvark")
```

Test your newfound knowledge

1. What is the difference between the / operator and the \ operator?

   a. One is called a forward slash and one is called a backslash. Other than that, they both look like typos.

   b. The / operator divides two numbers and the \ operator puts them back together again.

   c. The / operator calculates a floating-point (decimal) number, such as 3.54, and the \ operator calculates an integer, such as 5 or 34.

   d. The / operator doesn't work at all, so you have to use the \ operator instead.

2. Is the following statement True or False?

   `"aeroplane" < "airplane"`

   a. False, because I don't know what to think; besides, the answer hasn't been the letter (a) for a long time.

   b. True, because the second letter in aeroplane is less than the second letter in airplane.

   c. True and False, because I'm hedging my bets.

   d. False, because an aeroplane is an old-fashioned way of saying airplane, so both strings are exactly the same.

Because the first letter in `"Air"` has a lower character code number than the first letter in `"aardvark"`, Visual Basic .NET considers the value of `"Air"` to be less than `"aardvark"`, so the value of `Flag` is going to be True.

Now consider the following example:

```
Flag = ("air" < "aardvark")
```

Here the value of `Flag` is False. How does Visual Basic .NET decide whether `"air"` is less than `"aardvark"`? First, it calculates the ANSI character code for the first letter of each string. Because both begin with *a*, Visual Basic .NET looks at the second letter. Because *i* has a higher ANSI character code than *a*, `"air"` is considered greater than `"aardvark"` and `Flag` is therefore False.

Consider one final example:

```
Flag = ("air" < "airplane")
```

In this example, the value of `Flag` is True. The first three letters of each string are identical, but the fourth letter is not. Because `"air"` doesn't have a fourth letter and `"airplane"` does, `"airplane"` is considered greater and `Flag` is therefore True.

Working with Precedence

With all these operators crowding your BASIC commands, what happens if you lump them all together on one line, like this:

```
Dim Mess As Single
Mess = 4 / 7 + 9 * 2
```

If you guessed that the value of Mess is 18.57143, congratulations! But how does Visual Basic .NET handle this? First, it calculates those operators that have higher priority, or *precedence*.

Visual Basic .NET chooses which operator to calculate first based on precedence. The higher an operator appears in Table 17-5, the higher that operator's precedence, so the exponential operator (^) has higher precedence (is calculated first) than the less than operator (<).

Table 17-5	Precedence of Operators
Operator	*Type of Operator*
Exponential (^)	Arithmetic
Negation (−)	Arithmetic
Multiplication and Division (* and /)	Arithmetic
Integer division (\ )	Arithmetic
Modulo (mod)	Arithmetic
Addition and Subtraction (+ and −)	Arithmetic
String concatenation (&)	Arithmetic
Equality (=)	Comparison
Inequality (<>)	Comparison
Less than (<) and Greater than (>)	Comparison
Greater then or equal to (>=)	Comparison
Less than or equal to (<=)	Comparison
Not	Logical
And	Logical
Or	Logical
Xor	Logical

How does Visual Basic .NET calculate the value of Mess in the following equation?

```
Dim Mess As Single
Mess = 4 / 7 + 9 * 2
```

To help you understand how Visual Basic .NET calculates a result, these are the steps it follows:

1. Multiplication and division have a higher precedence than addition, so Visual Basic .NET looks at the multiplication and division operators first.

2. Because multiplication and division have the same precedence, Visual Basic .NET starts with the one furthest to the left. So Visual Basic .NET calculates the value of 4 / 7 and comes up with 0.57143. Now the equation has been simplified to

```
Mess = 0.57143 + 9 * 2
```

3. Visual Basic .NET sees that the multiplication operator has a higher precedence than the addition operator, so it calculates the value of 9 * 2 and comes up with 18. The equation is now

```
Mess = 0.57143 + 18
```

The final value of Mess is 18.57143.

What if you really wanted Visual Basic .NET to add the two numbers first before doing any division or multiplication? For clarity, and to make sure that calculations come out the way you intend, enclose particular operations in your equations in parentheses, as shown in the following example:

```
Mess = 4 / (7 + 9) * 2
```

This is how Visual Basic .NET calculates the result:

1. The parentheses tell Visual Basic .NET to add 7 + 9 first, which creates the following equation:

```
Mess = 4 / 16 * 2
```

2. Because the division and multiplication operators have the same precedence, Visual Basic .NET begins with the leftmost operator. Visual Basic .NET calculates 4 / 16 and comes up with 0.25. The equation is now

```
Mess = 0.25 * 2
```

3. Finally, Visual Basic .NET multiplies these numbers and assigns the value of 0.5 to the variable Mess.

Whenever you use two or more operators, use parentheses to provide clarity and to ensure that Visual Basic .NET calculates everything in the exact order you want.

Chapter 18

Strings and Things

• •

In This Chapter

▶ Finding the length of a string

▶ Converting the case of a string

▶ Trimming your strings

▶ Searching a string

▶ Converting strings into ASCII values

• •

*I*n addition to manipulating numbers, your program can manipulate strings as well. *Strings* are any combination of letters, numbers, or symbols that you want the program to treat literally.

To tell your program to treat strings literally, always surround your strings with quotation marks, "like this". So if you want to assign the string 123-4567 to a variable, you use quotation marks, as in the following example:

```
Dim Phone As String
Phone = "123-4567"
```

After you designate particular data as a string, Visual Basic .NET provides all sorts of weird ways to examine, manipulate, and mutilate the string.

Counting the Length of a String

The length of a string is the total number of characters (including spaces) that the string contains. To count the length of a string, you can use the Len BASIC command such as:

```
VariableName = Len("String")
```

For example:

```
Dim Name As String
Dim NameLength As Integer
Name = "Bo the Cat"
NameLength = Len(Name)
```

In this case, the length of the string "Bo the Cat" is 10 (eight letters and two spaces), so this value is assigned to the variable called NameLength.

Converting the Case of Strings

If you don't like the way a string looks, you can convert its case to proper case or from lowercase to UPPERCASE (and vice versa). Visual Basic .NET has three commands for converting the case of strings: LCase, UCase, and StrConv.

Converting from UPPERCASE to lowercase

To convert a string to all lowercase letters, use the following BASIC command:

```
LCase("String")
```

For example:

```
Dim Name, LowerCase As String
Name = "DOESN'T THIS LOOK OBNOXIOUS?"
LowerCase = LCase(Name)
```

In this case, the value of LowerCase is the following string:

```
doesn't this look obnoxious?
```

Notice that the LCase command affects only letters. (How *do* you present a lowercase question mark, anyway?)

Converting from lowercase to UPPERCASE

To convert a string to all uppercase letters, use the following BASIC command:

```
UCase("String")
```

For example:

```
Dim Name, UpperCase As String
Name = "whisper when you speak"
UpperCase = UCase(Name)
```

In this example, the value of UpperCase is the following string:

```
WHISPER WHEN YOU SPEAK
```

Converting a string to Proper Case

Rather than make your string into all lowercase or all uppercase, you have a third option called *proper case,* which only capitalizes the first letter of every word, Kind Of Like This Part Of The Sentence.

To convert a string to proper case, use the StrConv BASIC command:

```
StrConv("String", VbStrConv.ProperCase)
```

For example:

```
Dim Name, ProperCase As String
Name = "whisper when you speak"
ProperCase = StrConv(Name, VbStrConv.ProperCase)
```

In this example, the value of ProperCase is the following string:

```
Whisper When You Speak
```

Trimming a String

Sometimes your strings may be too long, so you want to remove a few characters from the beginning or end of a string.

Strings aren't always nice and neat. Sometimes spaces lie in front of or behind the string, as the following examples illustrate:

```
"    This is an example of leading spaces"
"This is an example of trailing spaces    "
```

Trimming leading spaces from strings

To strip away leading spaces (those that appear in front of the string), use the LTrim BASIC command:

```
LTrim("TargetString")
```

For example:

```
Dim FullName As String
FullName = "   John Doe"
FullName = LTrim(FullName)
```

The value of FullName is "John Doe" with the leading spaces removed.

Trimming trailing spaces from strings

To strip away trailing spaces (those that appear at the end of a string), use the RTrim BASIC command:

```
RTrim("TargetString")
```

For example:

```
Dim FullName As String
FullName = "John "
FullName = RTrim(FullName)
FullName = FullName & " " & "Doe"
```

In the preceding example, the RTrim command removes the trailing spaces so the value of FullName is just plain "John". Then the last command adds the value of FullName ("John") to a blank space (" ") and the string "Doe" to create the string "John Doe".

Trimming both leading and trailing spaces from strings

In case you have both leading and trailing spaces, you can combine the two commands like this:

```
LTrim(RTrim("TargetString"))
```

This command says, "First, remove all trailing spaces and then remove all leading spaces."

For an even simpler method, use the following BASIC command instead:

```
Trim("TargetString")
```

For example:

```
Dim FullName As String
FullName = " John Dull "
FullName = Trim(FullName)
FullName = FullName & " " & "Doe"
```

The `Trim` command removes both the leading and trailing spaces in one quick stroke, and then the last command adds the string "John Dull" to a blank string (" ") and the string "Doe" to create "John Dull Doe".

Extracting Stuff from a String

You can selectively remove or extract characters from a string; from the front, the back, or the middle of an existing string using three special commands: `Left`, `Right`, and `Mid`.

Extracting characters from the front of a string

Sometimes a string contains more information than you want. For example, you may have stored a person's full name in a variable called `FullName`, as in the following:

```
FullName = "John Doe"
```

To extract characters starting from the left or front of the string, use the following BASIC command:

```
Microsoft.VisualBasic.Left(FullName, N)
```

In case you're wondering about the clumsy syntax needed to use the Left command, `Microsoft.VisualBasic` represents a separate class file that contains BASIC code to make the Left command work. Part VII of this book explains class files and object-oriented programming in more detail.

The preceding command says, "See that string over there called `FullName`? Yank out *N* number of characters, starting from the left." For example:

```
Dim FullName, First As String
FullName = "John Doe"
First = Microsoft.VisualBasic.Left(FullName, 4)
```

In the preceding example, the value of `First` is `John`.

Extracting characters from the end of a string

To extract characters starting from the right or end of the string, use the following BASIC command:

```
Microsoft.VisualBasic.Right(FullName, N)
```

This command says, "See that string over there called `FullName`? Yank out *N* number of characters, starting from the right." For example:

```
Dim FullName, Last As String
FullName = "John Doe"
Last = Microsoft.VisualBasic.Right(FullName, 3)
```

In this example, the value of `Last` is `Doe`.

Extracting characters from the middle of a string

Another command for extracting characters from a string is the `Mid` command, such as:

```
Microsoft.VisualBasic.Mid(FullName, X, Y)
```

This command says, "See that string over there called `FullName`? Count *X* number of characters from the left, and rip out the next *Y* number of characters. For example:

```
Dim FullName As String, Middle As String
FullName = "John Q. Doe"
Middle = Microsoft.VisualBasic.Mid(FullName, 6, 2)
```

In this example, the value of `Middle` is `Q.` (including the period).

Searching (and Replacing) Your Strings

One useful command is to search for a string within an existing string, such as trying to find a name or number buried in a longer string. To search a string, you can use one of two Visual Basic .NET commands: InStr or InStrRev.

Finding part of a string with another string

If one string is buried in the middle of another string, you can find the location of the buried string by using the InStr BASIC command, such as:

```
InStr("TargetString", "WantedString")
```

This command returns a number defining the exact location from the left where the "WantedString" begins inside the "TargetString". For example:

```
Dim FullName As String
Dim Location As Integer
FullName = "John Plain Doe"
Location = InStr(FullName, "Plain")
```

In this case, the value of Location is 6.

If the string you want isn't located inside the string you're searching for, the InStr command returns 0.

When you search for a string within another string, you have to search for the exact uppercase or lowercase string. For example, the following command returns a value of 0:

```
InStr("John Plain Doe", "PLAIN")
```

In this example, "Plain" is not the same string as "PLAIN", so InStr returns 0. Essentially, a zero is the Visual Basic .NET way of saying, "Sorry, I can't find your exact string anywhere."

Pattern-matching a string

Pattern-matching means that Visual Basic .NET can check to see if one string is equal to another using the magical Like operator, such as:

```
Dim Flag As Boolean
Dim MyString As String
MyString = "cat"
Flag = MyString Like "cat"
```

Here's how Visual Basic .NET interprets the preceding code:

1. The first line tells Visual Basic .NET to create the Flag variable so it can hold a Boolean data type, which is either True or False.

2. The second line tells Visual Basic .NET to create the MyString variable so it can hold a String data type.

3. The third line tells Visual Basic .NET to assign the MyString variable to the "cat" string.

4. The fourth line tells Visual Basic .NET, "Find out if the MyString variable is like the "cat" string. In this case, MyString is identical to "cat" so the value of the Flag variable is set to True.

Using the ? wildcard

In the previous example, the pattern is the string "cat". A slightly more complicated pattern is one that uses the question mark (?) to represent any character, such as this pattern: "c?t", which appears as:

```
Flag = MyString Like "c?t"
```

In this example, the value of the Flag variable is True if the MyString variable contains any three-letter string that begins with a "c" and ends with a "t," no matter what the second character may be. So the value of Flag would be True if the MyString variable represented the following strings: cat, cgt, cct, c5t, or c*t.

Visual Basic .NET is case-sensitive, which means the letter "C" is not the same as the letter "c." So the following strings would set a value of False to the Flag variable: Cat and caT.

The value of Flag would be False any time the MyString variable contains any string shorter or longer than exactly three characters, if the first character is not a "c" or if the last character is not a "t."

You can also use the ? wildcard in groups of two or more, such as:

```
Flag = MyString Like "c??"
```

In this case, the value of Flag would be True only if the MyString variable contained exactly three characters where the first character is "c" and the second and third characters could be anything.

Using the * wildcard

Using multiple ? wildcards to represent any character can get cumbersome, so Visual Basic .NET also offers the * wildcard, which represents zero or more characters, such as:

```
Flag = MyString Like "c*t"
```

In this case, the value of Flag would be True if the value of MyString were any of the following: cat, coast, ct, or c7398478dj48t because they all start with a "c," end with a "t," and have zero or more characters in between.

If you want to get fancy, you can combine the ? and * wildcards together, such as:

```
Flag = MyString Like "c?t*"
```

In this case, the value of Flag would be True for any value of MyString that starts with a "c," contains exactly one character after the "c," has a "t" for its third character, and zero or more characters after the "t" such as cat, cotton, c8tkjoiele, or cutlery.

Using the # wildcard

The ? and * wildcards represent any character, which can be a letter, number, or symbol. In case you just want to match a single number, you can use the # wildcard, which only represents any single number between 0 and 9, such as:

```
Flag = MyString Like "c#t*"
```

In this case, the value of Flag would be True for any value of MyString that starts with a "c," ends with a "t," and contains exactly one number as the second character, such as c7t, c9t, or c3t.

Using lists

Visual Basic .NET uses lists to see whether a character falls within a range of characters. For example, if you want to check whether a character falls within the range of A to Z, you can use the following:

```
Flag = MyString Like "[A - Z]"
```

In this case, the value of Flag would be True for any single-character string of MyString that is an uppercase letter such as A, N, V, or Y.

For greater flexibility, you can combine lists with the ? and * wildcards, such as:

```
Flag = MyString Like "c?[g - z]t*"
```

In this case, the value of Flag would be True for any value of MyString that starts with a "c"; has exactly one character following the "c"; contains a third character that falls within the range of "g" to "z" such as g, h, t, x, or z; has a fourth character of "t"; and has any number of characters following afterwards.

Lists represent a single character.

As an alternative, you can also use lists to check whether a character doesn't fall within a certain range such as [!a-z]. This tells Visual Basic .NET, "Check a single character to see if it does not fall within the range of a to z" such as:

```
Flag = MyString Like "c[!a - z]t"
```

In this case, the value of Flag would be True for any value of MyString that starts with a "c," ends with a "t," and contains a second character that is not a lowercase letter ranging from a to z such as c8t or cAt.

You can use any combination of wildcards and lists together such as:

```
Flag = MyString Like "#[a - z]?"
```

In this case, Flag is True only if MyString contains a three-letter string that begins with a number (the # wildcard), the second character is a lowercase letter ranging from a to z, and the third character can be anything.

Replacing part of a string with another string

In case you get the creative urge to write your own word processor in Visual Basic .NET (complete with search and replace features), you can do so with the following BASIC command:

```
Mid("TargetString", Position) = "NewString"
```

This command says, "See that string called TargetString? Find the value defined by Position, count that number of characters from the left, and insert the string called NewString."

Of course, you have to be careful when inserting a new string into an existing one. For example, consider the following code:

```
FullName = "John Plain Doe"
Mid(FullName, 6) = "Vanilla"
```

Here's how Visual Basic .NET interprets this code:

1. The first line tells Visual Basic .NET to assign the string "John Plain Doe" to the variable called FullName.

2. The second line tells Visual Basic .NET to look at the string "John Plain Doe", find the sixth character from the left, and insert the string "Vanilla", replacing the original string beginning with the sixth character.

So the following is what happens:

John Plain Doe	(Original string)
^	(Sixth character from the left)
John Vanillaoe	(New string)

After you tell Visual Basic .NET to replace part of a string with another one, it gets overzealous and wipes out anything that gets in the way of the new string.

Test your newfound knowledge

1. How do you tell your program to treat strings literally?

   a. Just say, "I'm not kidding, honest!"

   b. Add the word TreatLiterally to the line of code that the string resides in.

   c. Surround your strings with quotation marks.

   d. Speak clearly and slowly, so that you create no misunderstandings.

2. What does the following line of code do?

   ```
   Found = InStr("TargetString",_
       "WantedString")
   ```

   a. The line shows a list of the ten most-wanted criminals, which you can also find at the post office.

   b. This line of code inserts a bull's-eye icon, showing where to aim your dart gun when you get frustrated.

   c. The line returns a number, stored in the variable called Found, that defines the exact location from the left where the "WantedString" can be found inside the "TargetString".

   d. All of the above.

Converting Strings and Values

There may come a time when you need to convert a string into a number so that you can use the string for calculations. Or you may need to convert a number into a string so that you can manipulate the string. You also may need to convert a string into the equivalent ASCII or ANSI value.

Converting a string into a number

What if you have a text box in which users can type their hourly wages? Unfortunately, the Text property of any text box stores data as a string, not as a number. To convert this string into a number, you have to use a data-conversion function such as:

```
CDbl("TargetString")
```

or

```
CInt("TargetString")
```

CDbl and CInt aren't the only Numeric data type conversion functions you can use. You can use other data type conversion functions as well, such as CSng (to convert text into Single data types). It all depends on the data type you want to convert your number into.

The first command says, "Take the string called TargetString and convert it to a Double data type."

The second command says, "Take the string called TargetString and convert it to an Integer data type."

For example:

```
Dim GetNumber As Double
GetNumber = CDbl(txtHourlyWage.Text)
```

The following is how Visual Basic .NET interprets this code:

1. The first line says, "Declare a variable called GetNumber as a Double data type."
2. The second line says, "Get the string stored in the Text property of a text box called txtHourlyWage and convert the string to a number that's a Double data type. Finally, store the value in the txtHourlyWage.Text property to the GetNumber variable."

So if the user types **6.25** in the txtHourlyWage text box, the value of GetNumber is 6.25.

If the user types **6.25 Hourly wage** or **My hourly wage is 6.25** in the txtHourlyWage text box, Visual Basic .NET chokes and screams about a type mismatch error because Numeric data type conversion functions don't know how to handle characters.

Converting a number into a string

What if you have a number and need to convert it into a string so that you can do fancy string manipulations to the number? Then you have to use the following BASIC command:

```
CStr(Number)
```

This command says, "Take the number represented by Number and turn this number into a string."

For example, Visual Basic .NET considers these to be two completely different creatures:

```
10 ' This is a number
"10" ' This is a string
```

The following converts a number into a string:

```
CStr(10) ' The string " 10"
CStr(10.5) ' The string " 10.5"
CStr( - 10) ' The string "-10"
```

When Visual Basic .NET converts a number into a string, the string has an extra leading space if the string is a positive number or a minus sign (–) if the string is a negative number.

The CStr type conversion function is especially useful to display numbers in the Text property of a label or text box.

Converting a string into an equivalent ASCII value

As a programmer, you have to practically memorize the ASCII table at some point, so you may as well find a copy of one and hang it near your computer somewhere so that you can find this table easily.

An ASCII table shows the codes that computers use to represent most of the characters you need. For example, the letter *A* has an ASCII value of 65, and the letter *a* has an ASCII value of 97.

Whenever you need the ASCII value of a one-character string, you can use this BASIC command:

```
Asc("Character")
```

The following shows how to convert a character into its ASCII value:

```
X = Asc ("A") ' X = 65
X = Asc ("a") ' X = 97
```

Converting an ANSI value into a string

Microsoft Windows doesn't use the ASCII table. Instead, it uses the ANSI table, which is practically the same as the ASCII table anyway.

To use an ANSI value, use the following BASIC command:

```
Dim X As String
X = Chr("Character")
```

The only time you need to use the ANSI value of anything is for special control codes, such as for line feeds, carriage returns, and new lines.

The following commands show common ANSI values:

```
LineFeed = Chr(10)
FormFeed = Chr(12)
Carriage = Chr(13)
```

By using all these fancy string-manipulation commands, you can make sure that your strings look exactly the way you want them to before displaying them in a text box or label. Either that, or you can just have fun playing with words and numbers and pretend you're doing serious research on your job.

Chapter 19

Defining Constants and Using Comments

• •

In This Chapter

▶ Naming and calculating constants

▶ Declaring the scope of constants

▶ Creating and using the three types of comments

• •

A *constant* is a fixed value that never changes, no matter what happens to your program. Numbers, strings, and dates can be constant values.

But why bother using constants? Several good reasons exist, none of which make any sense until you start writing your own programs.

For example, suppose that you want to write a program that pays employees according to the current minimum wage. If the minimum wage is $5.95, you have to type the number 5.95 everywhere in your program.

Unfortunately, the number 5.95 means nothing in itself. Even worse, if the minimum wage changes from $5.95 to $6.25, you have to change 5.95 to 6.25 everywhere in your program. If you forget to change just one use of 5.95 to 6.25, your program won't work properly and you could wind up spending hours wondering why.

To overcome these problems, you can use constants. A constant is simply a word that represents a specific value. A constant can not only use plain English to describe what the value means, but it also lets you change values quickly and easily throughout an entire program.

Naming Constants

Constant names must meet the following criteria. They must

- ✔ Begin with a letter
- ✔ Be 40 characters or fewer
- ✔ Contain only letters, numbers, and the underscore character (_); punctuation marks and spaces aren't allowed
- ✔ Be any word except a Visual Basic .NET-reserved keyword

To make constant names stand out, use all uppercase letters. For example, the following are acceptable constant names:

```
AGE                    MINIMUM_WAGE
MY_BIRTHDAY            LIFEBOAT_CAPACITY
```

To provide additional information about the type of data a constant represents, use a three-letter prefix as part of the constant name such as:

```
intAGE                 (int represents an Integer data value.)
decMINIMUM_WAGE        (dec represents a Decimal data value.)
sngGPA                 (sng represents a Single data value.)
```

Table 19-1 provides a list of common three-letter prefixes for naming constants (or variables, for that matter). Feel free to invent your own just as long as you use them consistently.

Table 19-1	Three-Letter Prefixes for Naming Constants and Variables	
Data Type	*Prefix*	*Example*
Boolean	bln	blnIsItDeadYet
Byte	byt	bytThisNumber
Date (Time)	dtm	dtmAnniversary
Decimal	dec	decCEOBonus
Double	dbl	dblHeight
Integer	int	intTotalNumber
Long	lng	lngWidth

Data Type	Prefix	Example
Short	sht	shtPeople
Single	sng	sngAverage
String	str	strMyName

Some people even go one step further and just use one-letter prefixes for their variables such as using the letter "i" to identify Integer data types:

```
iNumberofMorons As Integer
```

Just be aware that one-letter prefixes may be simpler to write but could cause confusion later because some data types share the same first letter, such as Boolean and Byte or Single and String.

Declaring Constants

Constants can represent any of the following:

- Numbers
- Strings
- Dates

Before you can use a constant, you have to *declare* the constant. To declare a constant, you just give the constant a name, assign it a specific value, and declare it as a specific data type such as:

```
Const ConstantName As DataType = ConstantValue
```

The following code declares number, string, and date constants:

```
Const intAGE As Integer = 21
Const strCOMPANY As String  = "Acme Manufacturing"
Const dtmCHRISTMAS As Date = #12/25/95#
```

Instead of typing one constant declaration on each line, you can smash them all together on a single line and separate them with commas, as shown in the following code:

```
Const intAGE As Integer = 21, strCOMPANY As String = "Acme"
```

Note *string constants* are anything enclosed in quotation marks (" "), and *date constants* are dates surrounded by the pound sign (#).

Here are some of the ways in which dates can display:

```
#12-25-95#
#December 25, 1995#
#Dec-25-95#
#25 December 1995#
```

Calculating constants

Constants normally represent a fixed value. However, they can also be mathematic values based on other constants. For example:

```
Const intRETIREMENT_AGE As Integer = 65
Const sngHALFWAY_THERE As Single = intRETIREMENT_AGE / 2
```

In this case, the value of the constant `intRETIREMENT_AGE` is 65 and the value of the constant `sngHALFWAY_THERE` is 65/2, or 32.5.

Using constants

After you declare a constant, you can use it just like any other value. Consider the following:

```
Dim Salary As Single
Const sngMINIMUM_WAGE As Single = 5.75
Salary = sngMINIMUM_WAGE * 20
```

Here's how Visual Basic .NET interprets this code:

1. The first command says, "Create a variable named `Salary` and make it a Single data type."

2. The second command says, "Create a constant named `sngMINIMUM_WAGE`, declare the constant as a Single data type, and set the value of `sngMINIMUM_WAGE` to 5.75."

3. The third command says, "Multiply the value of `sngMINIMUM_WAGE` by 20 and store this value in the variable called `Salary`." In this case, the value of `sngMINIMUM_WAGE` is 5.75, so you multiply 5.75 by 20, which equals 115. Then Visual Basic .NET stores this value in `Salary`.

After you assign a value to a constant, you can never change the value of that constant ever again in your program. (That's why they're called "constants.")

Defining the Scope of Constants

Visual Basic .NET lets you declare the scope of constants in the following three ways:

- Private (also called local)
- Module
- Public

Private (local) constants

You can use a *local* constant only within the procedure in which you declare the constant. The purpose of local constants is to isolate specific constants in a single procedure where they are used.

Declare a local constant within an event-handling procedure, as in the following:

```
Private Sub Button1_Click(ByVal sender As System.Object,_
        ByVal e As System.EventArgs) Handles Button1.Click
   Const intSPEED_LIMIT As Integer = 55
End Sub
```

Visual Basic .NET declares constants as private by default, however, you may want to explicitly state that in your code, such as:

```
Private Sub Button1_Click(ByVal sender As System.Object,_
        ByVal e As System.EventArgs) Handles Button1.Click
   Private Const intSPEED_LIMIT As Integer = 55
End Sub
```

You can use a local constant only in the one event-handling procedure in which you declare the constant. However, what if you want to create a constant that two or more event procedures can share? In that case, you have to create a module constant.

Module constants

A *module* constant can be used by all procedures stored in the same file. To declare a module constant in a form file, just add your constant declaration directly underneath the `Public Class Form1` statement like this:

```
Public Class Form1
   Const intDRINKING_AGE As Integer= 21
```

Form1 is just the generic name of the form. If you've changed the name to something else, the name you chose appears in the `Public Class` line instead.

If you want to create a module constant in a module file, just type your constant declaration directly underneath the `Module Module1` (where `Module1` is the actual name of your module file) line, such as:

```
Module Module1
   Const intDRINKING_AGE As Integer= 21
```

Module constants are useful for sharing a constant value among all procedures stored in a single file. If you want a constant that *any* procedure in your program can use, you need to create a public constant.

To help you identify module constants buried in your code, some programmers like to put the letter *m* in front of the constant name, such as:

```
Const mintDRINKING_AGE = 21
```

Public constants

A *public* constant (also called a global constant) can be the most convenient to use because every procedure in your Visual Basic .NET program can access such a constant. However, cool programmers use public constants only when absolutely necessary; cluttering up your program with public constants that only a few procedures ever use is bad programming practice.

Using public constants is poor programming etiquette because changing a public constant can affect your entire program. Experienced programmers may blush in embarrassment for you if they catch you using public constants needlessly, and you may never get invited to any of the really great programmer parties as a result.

You need to declare public constants in a .BAS (module) file. To declare a public constant, add the word `Public` in front of your constant declaration, such as:

```
Public Const AGE_LIMIT As Integer = 18
```

You can create a public constant in any file, such as a form or module file.

To help you identify public (or global) constants buried in your code, you may want to add another letter (such as the letter *g*) in front of your constant name, such as:

```
Public Const gsngHEIGHT_LIMIT As Integer = 21.67
```

Using Comments

When you're coding your program (note the proper use of the word *coding*), the way your program works may be clear to you. Unfortunately, if you put your program aside and try to modify it five years later, you may have forgotten why you wrote certain commands and even how some of those commands work.

For just this reason, add plenty of comments to your programs. *Comments* are short descriptions that programmers add to their program to explain what certain commands mean or to explain what is supposed to happen in a particular part of the program.

As far as the computer is concerned, comments do absolutely nothing to help or hinder the way your program works. However, from a programmer's point of view, comments help explain how and why a program functions.

Creating comments

Visual Basic .NET lets you create comments by using the apostrophe (') symbol, followed by anything you care to type. The following, for example, is a valid comment:

```
' This line does absolutely nothing
```

As far as Visual Basic .NET is concerned, the computer ignores anything that appears to the right of the apostrophe symbol.

If using the apostrophe symbol bothers you, you can also create comments using the REM command (short for REMark), such as:

```
REM This line does absolutely nothing
```

Like the apostrophe symbol, the computer ignores anything that appears to the right of the REM command.

Comments can appear on a separate line or on a line that contains actual working BASIC code.

Comments can appear on separate lines or they can appear as part of another line, as in the following example:

```
X = Y * 2 ' Y represents the number of employees
```

You can also cram several comments together on multiple lines:

```
Y = 200    ' Y represents the number of employees
X = Y * 2
' X represents the number of employees who would like
' to slash the tires on the boss's car.
```

Just remember that the computer ignores anything that appears to the right of the apostrophe symbol and considers it a comment.

Comments for readability

The main reason for using comments is to make your programs easy to understand. For this reason, most cool programmers put comments at the beginning of every procedure.

These comments explain what data the procedure gets (if any) and what calculations the procedure performs. By just looking at the comments, anyone can quickly see what the procedure does without needing to decipher several lines of cryptic BASIC code. For example, can you figure out what the following does?

```
A = SQR(B ^ 2 + C ^ 2)
```

To make this line easier to understand, add a bunch of comments at the top of this procedure:

```
' The following equation uses the Pythagorean theorem
' for calculating the length of a side of a right
' triangle if the lengths of two sides are known. In
' this case, the length of one side of the triangle is
' represented by B and the length of the second side of
' the triangle is represented by C.
A = SQR(B ^ 2 + C ^ 2)
```

If several people share the responsibilities for writing procedures, you can use comments to note the name of the programmer and the date each procedure was last modified. (That way, you know who to blame when the procedure doesn't work.) For example:

```
' Programmer: JOHN DOE
' Last modified: 1/1/80 (our computer clock doesn't work)
A = SQR(B ^ 2 + C ^ 2)
```

Of course, if you get too wordy, your comments can be more intrusive than helpful — like billboards along the highway. Just remember: Provide enough information to be helpful, but not so much that people nod off to sleep while reading your comments. You're not writing a classic novel here, just a brief description that other people can understand.

Test your newfound knowledge

1. Why do you want to add comments to your program?

  a. To summarize and explain how your BASIC code works.

  b. To exercise your literary skills and prove that programmers can write, too.

  c. To prove that you have something to say besides BASIC commands.

  d. So that you can leave cryptic messages for other programmers to decipher.

2. Comment on the simplicity and brevity of this lesson.

  a. All right! Now I can quit and go home early.

  b. Why can't all the lessons in this book be this simple and short?

  c. I still can't write a program, but I know how to use comments. Maybe I need to get a job as a commentator.

  d. Comments are cool. If we can write comments in our programs, does that mean we can write programs with our word processors?

Comments for legibility

If your program contains lots of BASIC code, you can use comments and blank lines to make your code easy to read. For example, to make each chunk more easily seen, separate chunks of code:

```
Const dblINTEREST_RATE = .055 ' 5.5% interest rate
Dim Msg As String ' Declares Msg as a string
                  ' variable
Dim BankBalance, BankFees As Decimal

BankBalance = 500
BankBalance = BankBalance * dblINTEREST_RATE

' Subtract bank fees
BankFees = BankBalance * 2
BankBalance = BankBalance - BankFees

' Display a message box saying that the user owes the
' bank a certain amount of money.
Msg = "Please pay this amount: " & -BankBalance
MsgBox Msg, vbCritical, "Amount You Owe"
```

As the preceding example shows, you can insert hard returns to add blank lines between chunks of code, thereby enabling yourself to see more easily what each chunk actually does.

Stripping out all comments and blank lines gives you the following equivalent, but uglier, version:

```
Const dblINTEREST_RATE = .055
Dim Msg As String
Dim BankBalance, BankFees As Decimal
BankBalance = 500
BankBalance = BankBalance * dblINTEREST_RATE
BankFees = BankBalance * 2
BankBalance = BankBalance - BankFees
Msg = "Please pay this amount: " & -BankBalance
MsgBox Msg, vbCritical, "Amount You Owe"
```

Notice how this new version seems cramped and cluttered, much like your bathroom counter or your garage.

Comments for disability

With comments, you can not only add explanations about your program and visually break up your code but also temporarily disable one or more BASIC commands.

For example, as you're writing a program, you may find that a command isn't working as you want it to. To test how your program works without this command, you have two choices:

✔ Erase the command.

✔ Comment the command out.

If you erase a command and then decide you need it, you have to type the command all over again. If you *comment the command out,* however, you only have to erase the apostrophe symbol in order to put the command back in.

The following example contains a fairly long line of numbers:

```
Private Sub Button1_Click(ByVal sender As System.Object,_
          ByVal e As System.EventArgs) Handles Button1.Click
  X = 3.14 * 650 - (909 / 34.56) + 89.323
End Sub
```

If you erase the second line, typing the line again can be a real pain in the neck. However, you can just comment the line out, as follows:

```
Private Sub Button1_Click(ByVal sender As System.Object,_
          ByVal e As System.EventArgs) Handles Button1.Click
  ' X = 3.14 * 650 - (909 / 34.56) + 89.323
End Sub
```

Remember, the computer ignores anything that appears to the right of the apostrophe symbol. So, to the computer, this procedure now looks like the following:

```
Private Sub Button1_Click(ByVal sender As System.Object,_
          ByVal e As System.EventArgs) Handles Button1.Click
End Sub
```

Placing the apostrophe in front of this statement turns the statement into a comment and disables this new comment as a BASIC command. By removing the apostrophe symbol, you can quickly turn the comment back into a real-life BASIC command.

By using comments wisely, you can ensure that you or another programmer can easily understand any programs you write. Then again, if you really want to sabotage a programming project, add comments that don't make any sense or leave them out altogether and see what happens.

If you want to comment multiple lines of code quickly without having to type an apostrophe symbol in front of each line yourself, follow these steps:

1. **Highlight the lines of code you want to turn into a comment.**

2. **Choose <u>V</u>iew⇔<u>T</u>oolbars⇔Text Editor.**

   The Text Editor toolbar appears, as shown in Figure 19-1.

Figure 19-1:
The Text Editor toolbar allows you to comment out blocks of text quickly and easily.

Uncomment out the selected lines

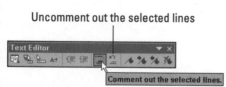

Comment out the selected lines.

3. **Click on the Comment out the selected text icon.**

   Visual Basic .NET adds an apostrophe to the front of each line that you highlighted in Step 1.

To uncomment blocks of code, just repeat the above three steps except click on the Uncomment the selected text icon on the Edit toolbar in Step 3.

Chapter 20

Storing Stuff in Data Structures

●　●

In This Chapter

▶ Using an array

▶ Creating a structure

▶ Using a collection data structure

●　●

A variable can just hold one item, but what if you want to store a bunch of related information such as a list of all the people you don't like at work? While you could create separate variables for each person, that would be time-consuming and tedious, and programmers hate anything that wastes time (which often includes cooking and grooming as well).

Ideally, you should be able to create a single variable that can hold any number of related items. If you haven't guessed by now, Visual Basic .NET offers magical variables that can hold multiple items, but instead of calling this a magical variable, it calls these wonderful creations *data structures*. In Visual Basic .NET, you can create three wonderful data structures called arrays, structures, and collections.

Think of a data structure as a way for your computer to temporarily store and organize data in its memory while your program is running. The moment you shut off your computer or exit the program, all the data stored in those data structures disappear unless you've specifically written BASIC code to save this data on a disk somewhere.

Making an Array

One of the simplest data structures that programmers have created is called an *array*. An array acts like a row of buckets that can hold multiple items. Each bucket is called an array element and each array element is identified by a unique number, called an *array index* (see Figure 20-1).

Figure 20-1:
An array consists of multiple array elements that can hold a single chunk of data such as a number.

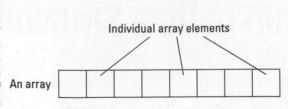

Individual array elements

An array

To create an array, you need to define:

- The array name
- The size of the array
- The type of data the array can hold

The magical BASIC command to create an array looks like this:

```
Dim ArrayName(Size) As DataType
```

If you replace the `Dim` keyword with `Public`, you can create an array that any part of your program can access.

So if you wanted to create an array named `MyStuff` and have it hold four items that only hold Integer data types, the command would look like this:

```
Dim MyStuff(3) As Integer
```

In the preceding example, Visual Basic .NET creates an array that can hold four items, although the array size is 3. The reason is because the array size ranges from 0 to 3. So the first item in the array is represented by 0, the second item by 1, the third item by 2, and the fourth item by 3.

In previous versions of Visual Basic .NET, you could specify the upper and lower bounds of an array such as:

```
Dim MyStuff(1 To 3) As Integer
```

In Visual Basic .NET, the lower bound of an array is always (yes, always) zero (0) so this command is invalid and Visual Basic .NET will scream if you try to use it.

Stuffing data into an array

When you create an array, the array doesn't hold anything until you start stuffing data into that array. To stuff data into an array, you need to assign the location in the array where you want your data to go.

For example, suppose you created an array to hold five strings such as:

```
Dim Losers(5) As String
```

If you wanted to fill the first location of the array with the string "Bobby Lee", you would use this command:

```
Losers(0) = "Bobby Lee"
```

The first element in an array is always number zero (0).

After creating an array, many programmers like to initialize an array, which means stuffing it with zeroes or empty strings. To initialize an array, you can use a For-Next loop (explained in Chapter 25), such as:

```
Dim Losers(5) As String
Dim I As Integer
For I = 0 To 4
  Losers(I) = ""
Next I
```

Note that the size of the Losers array is five (5), which means that the first element in the array is number zero (0), the second is number (1), the third is number two (2), the fourth is number three (3), and the fifth is number four (4), as shown in Figure 20-2.

Figure 20-2:
How Visual Basic .NET identifies elements in an array.

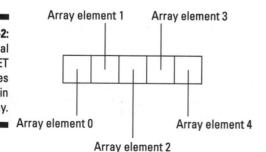

Array element 1   Array element 3

Array element 0   Array element 4

Array element 2

You can also assign the contents of an array element to a variable such as:

```
Dim Losers(5) As String
Dim Moron As String
Losers(3) = "Bobby Lee"
Moron = Losers(3)
```

1. The first line creates an array named Losers, which can hold five strings.

2. The second line creates a variable named Moron, which can hold a string.

3. The third line assigns the string "Bobby Lee" to the fourth array element, Losers(3). (Remember that the first array element is number zero, the second is one, the third is two, and the fourth is three.)

4. The fourth line assigns the contents of the Losers(3) array element to the Moron variable. Since the previous line stored the string "Bobby Lee" into the Losers(3) array element, the fourth line also assigns the string "Bobby Lee" to the Moron variable.

Normally arrays can only hold one data type, such as all integers or all strings. If you want an array that can hold different data types, you need to declare your array as an Object data type such as:

```
Dim MyStuff(3) As Object
```

Then you can stuff different data types in each array element such as:

```
MyStuff(0) = "Hello"
MyStuff(1) = 54
MyStuff(2) = 3.1415
```

Creating multidimensional arrays

When you create an array and define its size, you're creating a one-dimensional array, because the array resembles a row of buckets. For more flexibility, Visual Basic .NET also lets you create multidimensional arrays. Although you can create arrays with up to 60 dimensions, the most common multidimensional array is a two-dimensional array, which resembles a grid, as shown in Figure 20-3.

Dim My Array (Rows, Columns) As Data Type

Figure 20-3:
What a two-
dimensional
array
looks like.

(0,0)	(0,1)	(0,2)	(0,3)	(0,4)
(1,0)	(1,1)	(1,2)	(1,3)	(1,4)
(2,0)	(2,1)	(2,2)	(2,3)	(2,4)

Creating a multidimensional array is much like creating a one-dimensional array except you add another number to create an additional dimension. So to create a two-dimensional array, you would use two numbers to define the size of your array, such as:

```
Dim TwoDArray(Rows, Columns) As DataType
```

To create a three-dimensional array, you would use three numbers to define the size of your array and so on, such as:

```
Dim ThreeDArray(X, Y, Z) As DataType
```

With multidimensional arrays, each array element reserves space in memory to hold data, even if the data is a zero or an empty string. As a result, multi-dimensional arrays gobble up lots of memory in a hurry. So if you plan on using multidimensional arrays, use them sparingly.

Resizing an array

After you define the size of an array, you can always expand (or shrink) it later. For example, suppose you created an array of five elements that contain string data types such as:

```
Dim ArrayName(4) As String
```

Whenever you want to expand the size of your array, you can use the magical ReDim command such as:

```
ReDim ArrayName(7) As String
```

This command simply adds three (7 – 4) additional elements to the array previously defined by the ArrayName variable. As an alternative, you can also shrink your array using the ReDim command such as:

```
ReDim ArrayName(2) As String
```

You can also resize a multidimensional array using the ReDim command. However, you can never eliminate or add additional dimensions to a multi-dimensional array.

Each time you use the ReDim command to expand or shrink an array, Visual Basic .NET tosses out any data stored in that array before resizing the array. In case you want to keep the data in your array while expanding (but not shrinking) an array, you have to use the ReDim command along with the Preserve command such as:

```
ReDim Preserve ArrayName(25) As String
```

By shrinking the size of your arrays whenever possible, you can reduce the amount of memory your program needs to run.

When resizing multidimensional arrays with the ReDim Preserve commands, you can only resize the last dimension of the multidimensional array. So if you created a two-dimensional array such as:

```
Dim ArrayName(2, 5) As String
```

You can only resize the last dimension such as:

```
ReDim Preserve ArrayName(2, 17) As String
```

If you try to resize and preserve any dimension but the last dimension of a multidimensional array, Visual Basic .NET will scream and refuse to let you make such a horrid mistake.

Creating a Structure

If you want to store related information in one location, tough. An ordinary variable can only hold one item at a time, such as a string or a number. While an array can hold multiple chunks of data, what you really need is to store multiple chunks of data in one variable. Fortunately, Visual Basic .NET offers you this feature through a data structure called (this is going to sound redundant) a structure.

Creating a variable to represent your structure

A structure essentially lumps two or more variables together, regardless of the data type they represent. The BASIC code needed to create a structure looks like this:

```
Structure NameOfStructure
   VariableDeclaration1
   VariableDeclaration2
End Structure
```

So if you wanted to keep a person's name, address, and IQ together, you could create a structure like this:

```
Structure PeopleIHate
   Public Name As String
   Public Address As String
   Public IQ As Integer
End Structure
```

Structures are called user-defined data types because after you've created a structure, you need to define a variable to represent your structure, such as:

```
Variable As StructureName
```

So if you wanted to create a variable to represent your PeopleIHate structure, you could do the following:

```
Losers As PeopleIHate
```

This tells Visual Basic .NET, "Create a variable named Losers that represents a structure named PeopleIHate. This structure holds a Name variable, an Address variable, and an IQ variable."

The two-step process for using structures is this:

1. Define a structure.

2. Declare a variable to represent your structure.

Storing stuff in a structure

After you've created a structure and declared a variable to represent your structure, the final step is to stuff data into that structure. To store data into a structure's variable, you have to identify the variable (which represents your structure) followed by a period and the specific structure variable to store your data, such as:

```
VariableName.StructureVariable = NewValue
```

So let's say you defined a new structure as follows:

```
Structure Pets
   Public Name As String
   Public Age As Integer
   Public Fixed As Boolean
End Structure
```

Remembering the two-step process for using structures, after defining a structure, your next step would be to declare a variable to represent that structure, such as:

```
Structure Pets
   Public Name As String
   Public Age As Integer
   Public Fixed As Boolean
End Structure

Dim MyPet As Pets
```

After declaring a variable to represent your structure, storing data in your structure means identifying the variable (which represents your structure) and the specific structure variable to hold your data, such as the following:

```
Structure Pets
   Public Name As String
   Public Age As Integer
   Public Fixed As Boolean
End Structure

Dim MyPet As Pets

MyPet.Name = "Fluffy"
MyPet.Age = 6
MyPet.Fixed = True
```

The preceding Visual Basic .NET code tells your computer to do the following:

1. The first through fifth lines define a structure named Pets. The Pets structure can hold three variables named Name (String data type), Age (Integer data type), and Fixed (Boolean data type).

2. The sixth line declares a variable called MyPet, which represents the Pets structure.

3. The seventh line assigns the string "Fluffy" to the Name portion of the MyPet variable.

4. The eighth line assigns the number 6 to the Age portion of the MyPet variable.

5. The ninth line assigns the value True to the Fixed portion of the MyPet variable.

Think of structures as a single variable that can hold multiple, but related, data.

Combining structures with arrays

A structure by itself isn't of much use. So most programmers use structures in combination with arrays. That way, they can create an array that can hold multiple, but related, chunks of data in a list.

To create an array of structures, all you have to do is define your structure and then define your array as that structure type, such as:

```
Structure Pets
   Public Name As String
   Public Age As Integer
   Public Fixed As Boolean
End Structure

Dim PetArray(4) As Pets
```

Figure 20-4 shows what the PetArray looks like.

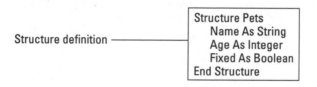

Figure 20-4: An array of structure can organize groups of related data in a list.

Tossing Stuff in a Collection

A *collection* is a special data structure that acts like a super array that can grow to any size and hold any type of data such as strings, numbers, or even other data structures such as arrays or structures.

One problem with arrays is that if you store something in a large array, trying to find that item later can be difficult because you may have to search through the entire array. To solve this problem, collections allow you to assign a special "key" to each item that you store in the collection. Now you can use this "key," which must be a unique string, to find any item in a collection quickly.

To create a collection, you just need to declare a variable to represent the collection, such as:

```
Dim LoserList As New Collection()
```

The preceding command tells Visual Basic .NET, "Create a variable named LoserList and make it represent a collection data structure (also called an object)."

Adding stuff to a collection

After you've created a collection, the next step is to toss junk into that collection. To add any item in a collection, you need to specify the data itself along with its unique "key" to help you retrieve that item later. Both the data you're adding and the unique "key" must be String data types.

Adding stuff to a collection means using BASIC code that looks like this:

```
CollectionName.Add (DataToAdd, Key)
```

You just need to replace CollectionName with the actual name of your collection, Key with a unique string or number, and DataToAdd with your actual data (a number, string, or other data structure).

So if you wanted to add the name "Bill McPherson" and the key "666" to your collection named LoserList, you could use the following BASIC code:

```
Dim LoserList As New Collection()
LoserList.Add ("Bill McPherson", "666")
```

As an alternative to putting quotes around your key, you can also use the ToString function, which converts a number into a string, such as:

```
Dim LoserList As New Collection()
LoserList.Add ("Bill McPherson", 666.ToString)
```

Counting the number of items in a collection

After you've tossed stuff into a collection, you might be curious to know how much junk your collection has accumulated. To retrieve the total number of items in a collection, use this BASIC code:

```
CollectionName.Count
```

The preceding code returns an integer that tells you the exact number of items stored in your collection. You can assign a variable to represent that value, such as:

```
Dim X As Integer
X = CollectionName.Count
```

As an alternative, you can also use this value directly in other parts of your BASIC code, such as part of a For-Next loop (explained in Chapter 25), as follows:

```
Dim x As Integer
For x = 0 to CollectionName.Count
   ' Do something here
Next x
```

Retrieving stuff from a collection

To help you retrieve stuff stored in a collection, you can use this BASIC command:

```
CollectionName.Item(X)
```

Where X represents the unique key you used to identify each item you stored in the collection. So if you want to search a collection named LoserList to find an item that has a key of "666", you would use this command:

```
LoserList.Item("666")
```

This would return the item stored in your collection and identified by the key "666".

For example, to retrieve the string identified by the key "666", you would use the following commands:

```
Dim WhichLoser As String
Dim LoserList As New Collection()
LoserList.Add ("Bill McPherson", "666")
WhichLoser = LoserList.Item("666")
```

In this case, the value of the WhichLoser variable is "Bill McPherson".

Removing stuff from a collection

Visual Basic .NET offers two magical commands for removing stuff from a collection. If you just want to remove a specific item, you can use this command:

```
CollectionName.Remove(X)
```

Where X represents the key used to identify that item. So if you wanted to remove an item identified by a key of "666", you would use this command:

```
CollectionName.Remove("666")
```

Chapter 21

Killing Bugs

● ●

● ●

*E*ven if you've written millions of different programs before, you are still going to make a mistake at one time or another. You may misspell a word or forget to type a command. So no matter how carefully you write your program, the program may not work exactly as you design it to. The problems hindering your program from working are called *bugs*.

Every program in the world has bugs, including WordPerfect, Linux, Quicken, Tomb Raider, and Microsoft Windows XP. The only difference between the bugs in your program and the bugs in a commercial program is that nobody is paying you to eliminate bugs in your program. However, with a fair amount of planning, application design, and just plain common sense, you can avoid quite a few bugs.

Don't worry. Many bugs are relatively harmless. These minor bugs normally aren't going to prevent you from using a program correctly, but they may slow down your computer or display odd colors or objects on the screen at random times.

Major bugs are more devastating. For example, a major bug allegedly blew up one of NASA's multimillion-dollar weather satellites because someone mistyped a single command in the program.

Nobody is perfect, so no program can be guaranteed to be completely bug-free. Even an experienced professional with a doctorate in computer science regularly writes bug-ridden programs.

Bugs are a fact of life, like cockroaches in a kitchen. You may never get rid of them all, but you can kill as many as possible along the way.

Why computer problems are called bugs

The first computer in the world used mechanical relays instead of modern electronics. One day the computer stopped working for no apparent reason. The scientists checked their programming (the program was supposed to have worked), the electric cord (it was plugged in), and the wires inside the computer (they were still connected).

Eventually, someone noticed that a moth had gotten smashed in one of the relays, preventing the relay from closing all the way. Because the moth's dead body prevented the computer from working, problems with computers were henceforth known as bugs (which is a lot easier to say than Chihuahuas, so we should be glad that a dog didn't get smashed in the first computer).

Types of Bugs

The art of killing bugs is known as *debugging*. Before you can kill a bug, you first have to find the bug. With small programs, such as ones that display `Hello, world!` on the screen, there are only so many places a bug can hide. With large programs, a bug can be hiding anywhere, and this can be as frustrating as trying to find a single Tsetse fly in a high-rise apartment building.

To make hunting for bugs easier, computer scientists classify bugs in three categories:

- Syntax errors
- Run-time errors
- Logic errors

Syntax errors

A *syntax* error is a bug that occurs when you misspell a command. If you type INTTEGER instead of INTEGER, for example, Visual Basic .NET is going to have no idea what INTTEGER means and isn't going to even bother trying to run the rest of your program.

When Visual Basic .NET runs across a syntax error, it politely highlights the misspelled word on the screen to show you exactly what the problem is. Just type the correct spelling and run your program again.

Even one syntax error will keep your program from running. When you finally get your program to run for the first time, you know that your program is completely free of syntax errors. Then you have to worry only about run-time and logic errors.

Run-time errors

A *run-time* error is more subtle than a syntax error because they only occur when your program gets data that the program doesn't quite know how to handle. Your program may be riddled with run-time errors, but you may never know this until you actually run your program.

To simulate a run-time error in your own life, pull into the drive-through window at your nearest Burger King. When the cashier asks, "May I help you?" order a Big Mac. Because the cashier expects you to order something from Burger King's menu, this person has no idea how to respond to your question and is likely to suffer a run-time error.

For an example of a run-time error in a program, consider this formula for calculating a result:

```
TaxRate = TaxesOwed / YearlyIncome
```

This equation normally works — unless the YearlyIncome equals 0. Because dividing any number by 0 is impossible, the program stops running if the value in YearlyIncome is 0.

To discover a run-time error, you must test your program for every possible occurrence: from someone pressing the wrong key to some idiot typing a negative number for his or her age.

Because the number of things that can ever go wrong is nearly infinite (Murphy's Law), you can understand why every large program in the world has bugs. (Now isn't this a comforting thought to remember the next time you fly in a computer-controlled airplane?)

Logic errors

The trickiest type of bug is a *logic* error. A logic error occurs when the program doesn't work correctly because you gave it the wrong commands or the commands you issued are out of sequence with other commands. Huh? How can you give a program the wrong commands when you're the one writing the program? Believe it or not, entering the wrong commands is easy.

Anyone raising teenagers knows that when you tell them to mow the lawn or clean up their rooms, they may do the task — but not quite the way you wanted the task accomplished. Instead of mowing the lawn in neat rows, a teenager may move around in circles and give up. Or instead of cleaning a room by picking up dirty clothes and tossing out papers, a teenager may shove the whole mess under the bed or out into the hallway.

In both cases, the teenager followed your instructions, but your instructions weren't specific enough. If a teenager can find a loophole in your instructions, he or she will, and a computer is no different.

Because you thought you gave the computer the right commands to follow, you have no idea why your program isn't working. Now you have to find the one spot where your instructions aren't clear enough. If you have a large program, this may mean searching the entire program, line by line. (Isn't programming fun?)

Bug Hunting

Basically, you need to go through four steps to hunt down and kill bugs in your program:

1. **Realize that your program has a bug.**
2. **Find the bug.**
3. **Find what's causing the bug.**
4. **Squash the bug.**

What can make bug hunting even more maddening is that the moment you fix one bug, you may have created two or three more by mistake. Now you have to repeat the whole process all over again for all the new bugs you just introduced into your program. Have fun!

Realizing that your program has a bug

The best way to discover bugs in your program is to let unsuspecting individuals use your program. (In the world of commercial software, these unsuspecting individuals are often called *paying customers*.)

The more people you find to test your program, the more likely that these guinea pigs are going to uncover bugs you never knew existed. Bugs can be as glaring as ones that cause the computer to crash, or they can be as sneaky as ones that round off numbers to the wrong decimal place.

After you conclude that your program has a bug, you have to track down the bug. (For the optimists in the group, you can call your program's bugs *undocumented features*.)

Finding the bug

Finding where a bug is hiding is the toughest part. The simplest (and most tedious) way to find a bug's hiding place is to run your program and examine it line by line. The moment the bug appears, you know exactly which line caused the bug.

For small programs, this approach is acceptable. For large programs, this is crazy.

As a faster alternative, just examine the parts of your program in which you think the bug may be hiding. If your program doesn't print correctly, for example, the bug may be in that portion of your BASIC code that tells the computer how to print.

Finding what's causing the bug

After you isolate where you think the bug is hiding, you have to figure out what is causing the bug in the first place.

Suppose that your program is to print your name on the screen but is printing your social security number instead. The program may seem to be *printing* everything correctly but is simply getting the wrong type of information to print.

By using your incredible powers of deductive reasoning, you realize that the bug is (probably) either where your program is first trying to get your name or where your program is trying to retrieve your name that it stored somewhere on disk or in memory.

Squashing the bug

After you find the cause of your bug, you've reached the time to correct your program. But be careful! Sometimes correcting one bug introduces two or three more by mistake. Huh? How can that be?

Compare bug squashing to repairing a problem with the plumbing in your house. The easiest solution may be to tear out a wall and put in new pipes. This may solve the plumbing problem, but tearing out a wall can also tear out electrical wires inside the wall. So now you've fixed your plumbing problems but you've also created a new electrical problem. If you put up a new wall with electrical wiring, you may inadvertently block a vent for the central air conditioning. Move the wall back three feet, and now the roof may be too weak in the middle to hold up the wall. See — your small plumbing "bug" has just multiplied.

So when fixing a bug, be careful. Sometimes rewriting a huge chunk of code is easier than trying to fix a bug within the code.

The best way to avoid bugs is to not have any in the first place. Of course, that's like saying, to avoid money problems, just make sure you always have enough money.

Because bugs appear in even the best of programs, the most you can hope for is to reduce the number of bugs that can pop up in your programs. Here are some tips that may help:

✔ To avoid bugs, write (and test) lots of tiny programs and paste them together to make one huge program. The smaller your programs, the easier isolating any bugs is going to be. This is the principle behind object-oriented programming (as explained in Part VII).

✔ Test your program each time you modify it. If your program worked fine until you changed three lines, the problem probably can be isolated to those three lines.

✔ Have someone you can pin the blame on. If your program refuses to work, blame your spouse, your dog, or your favorite deity. This isn't going to help fix your program, but blaming someone or something else can make you feel better for a moment or two.

Setting an Error Trap

A program needs explicit instructions to tell it how to do anything at any given moment. The moment your program runs across a problem that it doesn't know how to handle, it usually fails, which can be as simple as doing nothing (so your program appears to be "frozen") or as drastic as crashing your computer.

So to help you eliminate any problems in your program, Visual Basic .NET offers you the option of setting error traps. An error trap tells the computer, "Here's a set of generic instructions to follow in case you run into a problem that you can't handle." These generic instructions can be as simple as displaying a message on the screen. But at least the computer will be happy following some instructions rather than crashing or freezing your computer.

The simplest Visual Basic .NET error trap looks like this:

```
Try
    ' Code you want to test
Catch
    ' Instructions to notify you that an error has occurred
End Try
```

For example, you may have the following BASIC code:

```
Try
    Dim intX As Integer
    intX = 9 / CInt(TextBox1.Text)
Catch
    MsgBox ("An error has occurred.")
End Try
```

When Visual Basic .NET runs the preceding BASIC code, this is what happens:

1. Visual Basic .NET runs the lines sandwiched between the `Try` command (the first line) and the `Catch` command (the fourth line). In this case, the second line creates an integer variable named `intX` and the third line divides 9 by the number that the user types into a text box named `TextBox1`.

2. The lines sandwiched between the `Catch` command (the fourth line) and the `End Try` command (the sixth line) tell Visual Basic .NET, "Display an message dialog box that displays the string, `An error has occurred.`" This message dialog box only appears if an error has occurred in any of the code sandwiched in between the `Try` and `Catch` commands. In this case, an error occurs if the user types a 0 into the `TextBox1` text box.

   If an error occurs in any code outside of the `Try-Catch` commands, the error trap won't catch it.

3. The sixth line tells Visual Basic .NET, the `End Try` command marks the end of the error trap.

Error traps essentially keep your program from crashing so that way you don't have to go through the hassle of rebooting your computer each time your program runs into an error.

How Visual Basic .NET Tracks and Kills Bugs

Visual Basic .NET provides two primary ways to help you track and kill bugs: stepping and watching.

- *Stepping* means that you go through your program line by line and examine each instruction. After each line runs, look to see what the program did. If your program works the way you wanted it to, the line is okay. If not, you just located a bug.

- *Watching* lets you see what data your program is using at any given time. If you watch for specific data, such as a name or phone number, you can see whether your program is storing, printing, or modifying the specific data correctly.

Stepping and watching usually work together. By stepping through a program line by line and watching to see what data your program is using, you can find any bugs in your program.

Stepping through a program line by line

If you have absolutely no idea where your bug may be, you need to examine your entire program line by line, starting from the beginning. To step through a program, Visual Basic .NET provides three commands:

- ✔ **Debug⇨Step Into (or press F11):** The Step Into command runs through your entire program one line at a time, including every line stored in every procedure in your program.

- ✔ **Debug⇨Step Over (or press F10):** The Step Over command runs through your entire program but whenever Visual Basic .NET runs into a procedure, it runs all the instructions in that procedure without forcing you to view them line by line. If you are positive that there isn't a bug in a particular procedure, you can save time by stepping over it.

- ✔ **Debug⇨Step Out (or press Shift+F11):** The Step Out command is used to prematurely exit out of a procedure so you don't have to step through all the instructions stored in a procedure.

You can combine the three commands at any time. First, use the Step Into command to examine your program line by line. Then, use the Step Out command to exit out of a procedure so you don't have to examine a procedure's instructions line by line. Finally, use the Step Over command to skip over any procedures that you're positive already work.

To use the Step Into or Step Over commands, follow these steps:

1. **Choose Debug⇨Step Into (or press F11), or choose Debug⇨Step Over (or press F10).**

   Visual Basic .NET displays the BASIC code of your program and highlights the currently running line with a yellow arrow in the left margin, as shown in Figure 21-1.

2. **Repeat Step 1 for each line you want to examine. If you want to exit out of a procedure without having to view every line in the procedure, choose Debug⇨Step Out.**

3. **Choose Debug⇨Stop Debugging (or press Shift+F5) when you want to stop debugging.**

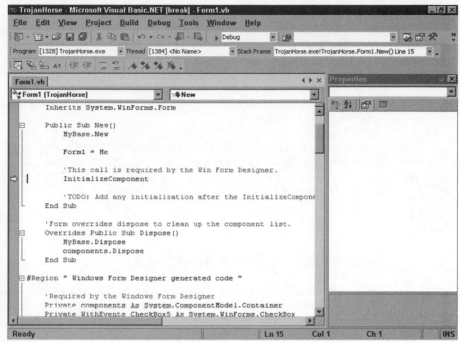

Figure 21-1:
Visual
Basic .NET
stepping
through a
program line
by line.

If your program's user interface is visible, you can also stop debugging by choosing the Exit command in your program to stop the entire program from running.

Setting breakpoints

Both the Step Into and Step Over commands start from the beginning of your program and continue until they reach the end. This is acceptable for small programs, but the process can get tedious for large programs.

To skip over large sections of your program that you know (or hope) already work, you can set a breakpoint. A *breakpoint* tells Visual Basic .NET, "Run the program up until you reach the breakpoint. Then wait until I give you the Step Into or Step Over command so I can start examining the program line by line, starting from the breakpoint."

To set a breakpoint, follow these steps:

1. **Open the Code window by pressing F7, choosing View⇨Code, or clicking on the View Code icon in the Solution Explorer window.**

2. **Click on the line where you want to set your breakpoint.**

3. **Press F9 (or right-click and choose Insert Breakpoint).**

    Visual Basic .NET displays a red dot in the left margin to show you which lines have a breakpoint.

After you set a breakpoint, press F5 (or choose Debug➪Start) so your program will skip over all the instructions from the start of your program until it reaches your breakpoint. At this point, you can use the Step Into (F11) or Step Over (F10) commands.

To remove a breakpoint, just follow the preceding three steps again, clicking on the line that contains the breakpoint you want to remove.

To quickly remove all breakpoints in your program, press Ctrl+Shift+F9 or choose Debug➪Clear All Breakpoints.

Watching your variables

Stepping through your program line by line can be even more useful if you watch how your program handles data at the same time. To help you see what values your variables contain at any given time, Visual Basic .NET provides a Watch window.

The Watch window tells Visual Basic .NET, "These are the variables I want to examine. Show me the contents of these variables as I step through my program line by line."

Test your newfound knowledge

1. What is a bug?

    a. A mistake that prevents a program from working correctly.

    b. An ugly little creature with six or more legs and a hard shell that crunches when you step on it.

    c. A moth that kills itself by crashing into your computer.

    d. Something little boys eat to frighten little girls.

2. How does Visual Basic .NET help trap bugs?

    a. By coming loaded with several bugs of its own.

    b. With glue and bug bait.

    c. By making programming so difficult that you can't write a bug even if you want to.

    d. By stepping through your program and watching to see whether the program handles data correctly.

To use the Watch window to watch your variables, follow these steps:

1. **Choose Debug⇨Step Into (or press F11), or choose Debug⇨Step Over (or press F10).**

   Visual Basic .NET displays the BASIC code of your program.

2. **Right-click on the variable that you want to watch.**

   A pop-up menu appears.

3. **Choose Add Watch.**

4. **Choose Debug⇨Windows⇨Watch (or press Ctrl+Alt+W) to display the Watch window, as shown in Figure 21-2.**

   The Watch window displays the value of your watched variable each time you choose the Step Into or Step Over command.

Breakpoint

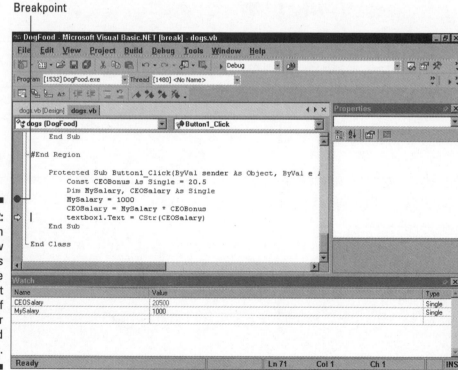

Figure 21-2:
The Watch window shows you the current value of your watched variables.

5. **Choose Debug⇨Step Into (or press F11), or choose Debug⇨Step Over (or press F10).**

   The moment a line of code changes the value of a variable that you chose to watch in Step 2, the Watch window shows you the new value of that variable.

6. **Choose Debug⇨Stop Debugging (or press Shift+F5) when you want to stop debugging.**

   When you stop debugging, you can go back to editing your program.

Part V
Making Decisions and Getting Loopy

The 5th Wave   By Rich Tennant

WANDA HAD THE DISTINCT FEELING HER HUSBAND'S NEW SOFTWARE PROGRAM WAS ABOUT TO BECOME INTERACTIVE.

In this part . . .

Programs contain nothing more than instructions that tell the computer what to do next. The simplest programs just contain one massive list of instructions that the computer follows, one instruction after another, like a shopping list.

But blindly following instructions doesn't make for a very useful program. Most programs need to receive data and then decide how to use the data.

So this part of the book shows you how your program can make decisions all by itself. In addition, this part of the book also shows you how to write instructions that run over and over again. That way if you need the computer to repeat itself, you can create something magical called a loop, which tells the computer, "See those instructions over there? I want you to keep following them a certain number of times until I tell you to stop."

By making decisions and repeating instructions in a loop, your Visual Basic .NET programs can seem alive, responsive, and intelligent. (Well, alive, anyway.) When a program can tell your computer how to make its own decisions, your computer can begin doing something useful.

Chapter 22

Making Decisions with If-Then Statements

In This Chapter

▶ Having fun with Boolean values

▶ Using If-Then and If-Then-End If statements

▶ Using If-Then-Else and If-Then-ElseIf statements

---

*A*t the simplest level, a program follows one instruction after another and then stops. But a program that does the same thing over and over again is pretty limited (and usually useless), so you need to give your program the ability to respond to outside input. That input can be in the form of a mouse click or key pressed, the movement of a joystick, or names and addresses retrieved from a database file.

After a program receives data, it needs to decide how to react to that data. Most decisions that a program makes appear in the form of an If-Then statement, such as, "If the license plate of a stolen car appears in the database file, then display a message to warn the police officer." By examining data and then deciding what to do based on that data, your program can respond to the user and actually appear to be smarter than it really is.

Understanding Boolean Values

Before your program can make a decision, it needs data. After it receives certain data, your program can decide what to do next. Which action your program follows is determined by a *condition,* which represents either a True or False value. Anything that represents either a True or False value is called a *Boolean* value.

In the world of Visual Basic .NET, a Boolean value can be represented by:

- A single variable
- An expression

Assigning a Boolean value to a variable

If a Boolean value is a single variable, that variable must be a Boolean data type, which means it can only have a value that is either True or False. You can declare a variable as a Boolean data type by using the following:

```
Dim Flag, CheckMe As Boolean
```

If you declare a variable as a Boolean data type, you can assign one of two values to that variable: True or False, such as:

```
Flag = True
CheckMe = False
```

You can check the value of a variable in two ways. The first way is to specifically check whether a variable is equal to True, as in the following example:

```
If TooHot = True Then
```

The second way (which is shorter to write) lets you eliminate `= True` and just write the following:

```
If TooHot Then
```

You don't have to specify whether this variable is equal to True because Visual Basic .NET checks whether the value is True or False anyway.

If you want to specifically test whether a variable is False, you can do the following:

```
If TooCold = False Then
```

As a shortcut, eliminate `= False` and just write

```
If Not TooCold Then
```

Assigning a Boolean value to an expression

Besides single variables, entire groups of variables (called an expression) can also represent a True or False values. A typical expression compares a variable with a specific value, such as:

```
Age > 21
```

In this case, the expression `Age > 21` is True only if the value of the `Age` variable is greater than 21. If the value of the `Age` variable is 21 or less, the value of this expression is False.

Since entire expressions can represent True or False values, you can use an expression to check for a True or False value, such as

```
If Age >= 21 Then
```

If you want to get fancier, an expression can compare the value of one variable with another variable, such as:

```
If Age >= LegalAge Then
```

Now the value of the `Age >= LegalAge` expression is True or False depending on the different values that the `Age` and `LegalAge` variables may represent at the time.

Besides numbers, you can also compare strings. In the following example, if the string stored in the `Text` property of a text box called `txtName` contains the string `"Captain Mike"`, the expression is True. Otherwise, the expression is False.

```
If (txtName.Text = "Captain Mike") Then
```

The parentheses in the preceding line of code don't affect your precious code one bit; they just help make the condition easier to identify.

Now that you understand what Boolean values are and how they work, you can find out how to plug them into an If-Then statement in the following section, "The If-Then Statement."

You may want to review the "Logical Operators" section in Chapter 17 to study how you can manipulate two or more Boolean values.

The If-Then Statement

The simplest way Visual Basic .NET makes a decision is with something called an If-Then statement. An *If-Then* statement checks whether a Boolean value is True. If so, Visual Basic .NET follows one instruction. If the Boolean value is False, Visual Basic .NET ignores that same instruction.

All of this may look rather wordy, so here's the condensed version of the statement:

```
If BooleanValue Then Instruction
```

Here are a few real-life examples:

```
If Number > 25 Then txtNote.Text = "Full"
```

Here's how Visual Basic .NET interprets this code:

1. This command says, "Check a variable called Number and see whether its value is greater than 25. If the value is greater than 25, then stuff the string "Full" into the Text property of the txtNote object."

2. "If the value of the Number variable is equal to or less than 25, skip to the next instruction in your Visual Basic .NET program."

Here's another example:

```
If Hungry Or Bored Then Message = "Let's eat."
```

Here's how Visual Basic .NET interprets this code:

1. This command says, "Check the values of the variables Hungry and Bored. If either one has a value of True, set the value of a variable called Message equal to the string "Let's eat.".

2. "If both the variable Hungry and the variable Bored are False, skip to the next instruction in your Visual Basic .NET program."

The typical If-Then statement tests whether a certain condition is True or False and then follows a single instruction. But what happens if you want the computer to follow two or more instructions? In that case, you have to use a different form of the If-Then statement, which is called the If-Then-End If statement.

The If-Then-End If Statement

The If-Then-End If statement lets Visual Basic .NET check a Boolean value. If that Boolean value is True, the program follows a bunch of instructions. Here's the proper If-Then-End If syntax:

```
If BooleanValue Then
  Instruction1
  Instruction2
End If
```

Essentially, this code tells Visual Basic .NET, "Check to see if a Boolean value is True. If so, follow all the instructions sandwiched between the Then statement and the End If line."

Here is an honest-to-goodness example:

```
If Electricity_is_Out = True Then
  Light_candles = True
  txtWarning.Text = "You just lost all your work."
End If
```

And here's how Visual Basic .NET interprets this code:

1. The first line says, "Check the value for a variable called Electricity_ is_Out. If the variable's value is True, follow the next two instructions. If the value is False, skip over these instructions."

2. The second line says, "Assign a value of True to the variable Light_candles."

3. The third line says, "Assign the string "You just lost all your work." to the Text property of the txtWarning text box."

4. The fourth line says, "This is the end of the If-Then-End If statement."

If-Then-Else Statement

The If-Then statement and If-Then-End If statement only follow instructions if the Boolean value they check is True. So what if you want your program to follow one set of instructions if a certain Boolean value is True, but follow a different set of instruction is in case the Boolean value is False?

In this case, you have to use an If-Then-Else statement. The simplest If-Then-Else statement looks like this:

```
If BooleanValue Then
  Instructions1
Else
  Instructions2
End If
```

This statement tells Visual Basic .NET, "If the BooleanValue is True, follow the first batch of instructions. If the BooleanValue is False, follow the second batch of instructions."

Test your newfound knowledge

1. What is a Boolean value?

   a. A mysterious entity that secretly controls how your computer is really going to work.

   b. One of those oddball currencies from a country that nobody has heard of before.

   c. Something valuable that only a person named Boole might be interested in.

   d. A variable or expression that represents a True or False value.

2. What is the alternative to the following?

   ```
   If MoneyGone = False Then
   ```

   a. `If MoneyGone Then "Complain about overseas competitors."`

   b. `If MoneyGone Then "Reelect a new President."`

   c. `If Not MoneyGone Then`

   d. `If MoneyGone = True Or False Then "I don't know what I'm doing."`

If you relied solely on ordinary If-Then statements, you might have the following:

```
If Day > 15 Then txtReadMe.Text = "Bills are past due!"
If Day <= 15 Then txtReadMe.Text = "Pay your bills!"
```

While this is perfectly functional, it looks a bit messy and confusing. To simplify matters, use the If-Then-Else statement instead, such as:

```
If Day > 15 Then
 txtReadMe.Text = "Bills are past due!"
Else
 txtReadMe.Text = "Pay your bills!"
End If
```

Rather than use Day > 15, you can switch things around and use Day <= 15 instead, such as:

```
If Day <= 15 Then
 txtReadMe.Text = "Pay your bills!"
Else
 txtReadMe.Text = "Bills are past due!"
End If
```

Both types of If-Then-Else statements are perfectly acceptable. Which statement you use is just a matter of personal preference.

You can shove as many instructions as you want between the If-Then and Else lines and the Else and End If lines.

One possible drawback with an If-Then-Else statement is that if the first condition is False, Visual Basic .NET blindly follows the second group of instructions. If you don't want this to happen, you have to specify a Boolean value to check for each set of instructions. To do that, you have to use an If-Then-ElseIf statement.

The If-Then-ElseIf Statement

An If-Then-ElseIf statement looks like the following:

```
If BooleanValue1 Then
  Instructions1
ElseIf BooleanValue2 Then
  Instructions2
End If
```

This code tells Visual Basic .NET, "If `BooleanValue1` is True, follow the first set of instructions. But if `BooleanValue1` is False, check to see if `BooleanValue2` is True. If `BooleanValue2` is True, follow the second set of instructions. If `BooleanValue2` is False, don't do anything at all."

With an If-Then-Else statement, the computer always follows at least one set of instructions (the ones that follow the Else line). But with an If-Then-ElseIf statement, the computer could possibly ignore all instructions — much like a rebellious teenager.

For example:

```
If Day > 15 Then
  txtReadMe.Text = "Bills are past due!"
ElseIf Day > 10 Then
  txtReadMe.Text = "Pay your bills!"
End If
```

So what happens if the value of `Day` is 12?

1. Visual Basic .NET checks the first Boolean value and concludes that the expression 12 > 15 is False (because the value of `Day` is 12).

2. Then Visual Basic .NET checks the second Boolean value and concludes that the expression 12 > 10 is True, so Visual Basic .NET assigns the string, `"Pay your bills!"` to the Text property of an object named `txtReadMe`.

BLOW BY BLOW

Here's the tricky part. What happens if the value of Day is 6?

1. Visual Basic .NET checks the first Boolean value and concludes that the statement 6 > 15 is False, so it ignores the first set of instructions.

2. Next, Visual Basic .NET checks the second Boolean value and concludes that the statement 6 > 10 is False, so it ignores the second set of instructions.

3. Finally, Visual Basic .NET reaches the end of the If-Then-ElseIf statement. Because none of the statements were True, none of the instructions were followed.

To handle multiple possibilities, you need to add more ElseIf conditions.

Making multiple choices with If-Then-ElseIf

For checking multiple conditions, you can use multiple ElseIfs, as follows:

```
If BooleanValue1 Then
  Instructions1
ElseIf BooleanValue2 Then
  Instructions2
ElseIf BooleanValue3 Then
  Instructions3
End If
```

This code tells Visual Basic .NET, "If BooleanValue1 is True, follow Instructions1. But if BooleanValue1 is False, check whether BooleanValue2 is True. If BooleanValue2 is True, follow Instructions2. If BooleanValue1 is False and BooleanValue2 is False, check to see whether BooleanValue3 is True. If BooleanValue3 is True, follow Instructions3."

Once again, the possibility exists that all conditions are going to be False, so the computer may never follow any of the instructions.

You can use as many ElseIf lines as you need. Of course, the more you use, the more confusing your entire If-Then-ElseIf statement gets. ("Now if Condition3 is False but Condition4 is True, wait a minute, what's supposed to happen?")

Making sure that the computer follows at least one set of instructions

You can have a huge If-Then-ElseIf statement and still not have a single instruction that the computer follows. To make sure that the computer follows at least one set of instructions, add an Else statement at the end, as shown in the following:

```
If Condition1 Then
  Instructions1
ElseIf Condition2 Then
  Instructions2
Else
  InstructionsDefault
End If
```

This code tells Visual Basic .NET, "If Condition1 is True, follow the first set of instructions (Instructions1). But if Condition1 is False, check the value of Condition2. If Condition2 is True, follow the second set of instructions (Instructions2). If all conditions are False, go ahead and follow the last set of instructions (InstructionsDefault)."

Nesting If-Then Statements

If you want, you can *nest* your statements, which means cramming multiple If-Then statements inside one another, such as

```
If Age > 21 Then
  If Rating = 10 Then
    txtAction.Text = "Ask for a date."
  End If
Else
  txtAction.Text = "Sorry, you're too young."
End If
```

If the value of Age were 23 and the value of Rating were 10, Visual Basic .NET interprets this code as follows:

1. Visual Basic .NET checks the first Boolean value and concludes that the expression Age > 21 is True (because the value of Age is 23).

2. Then Visual Basic .NET checks the second Boolean value and concludes that the expression Rating = 10 is True, so Visual Basic .NET assigns the string, "Ask for a date." to the Text property of a text box called txtAction.

If the value of Age were 23 but the value of Rating were only 9, Visual Basic .NET interprets this code as follows:

1. Visual Basic .NET checks the first Boolean value and concludes that the expression Age > 21 is True (because the value of Age is 23).

2. Then Visual Basic .NET checks the second Boolean value and concludes that the expression Rating = 10 is False, so nothing happens.

Finally, if the value of Age were 13 and the value of Rating were 10, Visual Basic .NET interprets this code as follows:

1. Visual Basic .NET checks the first Boolean value and concludes that the expression Age > 21 is False (because the value of Age is 13).

2. Visual Basic .NET skips to the Else part of the If-Then-Else statement and stuffs the string "Sorry, you're too young." in the Text property of the text box called txtAction. Notice that in this case, the value of Rating is irrelevant.

Be careful when nesting If-Then statements inside one another because nested If-Then statements may act in ways that you didn't expect. For example, in the preceding code, if the value of Age were 23 but the value of Rating were only 9, you may be surprised to find that this code isn't going to put any string in the Text property of the text box called txtAction.

Chapter 23

The Select Case Statement

*T*he main problem with If-Then-ElseIf statements (which are explained in Chapter 22) is that these statements can be ugly, hard to read and understand, and cumbersome to write. Consider the following:

```
If Caller = "Frank" Then
  txtReply.Text = "Yes!"
ElseIf Caller = "Matt" Then
  txtReply.Text = "Okay, but only if you buy."
ElseIf Caller = "Jeff" Then
  txtReply.Text = "I'm washing my hair tonight."
ElseIf Caller = "Bobby" Then
  txtReply.Text = "This is a recording."
End If
```

So what's the alternative to an endless proliferation of ElseIfs that can be confusing to look at?

One alternative is to toss your copy of Visual Basic .NET out the window and find someone to write your programs for you. But the more practical alternative is to use something called the Select Case statement.

Using the Select Case Statement

The *Select Case* statement looks like the following:

```
Select Case VariableName
  Case X
    Instructions1
  Case Y
    Instructions2
  Case Z
    Instructions3
End Select
```

This statement tells Visual Basic .NET, "Look at the value of the variable called VariableName. If this value is equal to X, then follow Instructions1. If this value is equal to Y, then follow Instructions2. If this value is equal to Z, then follow Instructions3."

Replacing the multiple If-Then-ElseIf statement at the beginning of this chapter with the Select Case statement changes the code to look like the following:

```
Select Case Caller
  Case "Frank"
    txtReply.Text = "Yes!"
  Case "Matt"
    txtReply.Text = "Okay, but only if you buy."
  Case "Jeff"
    txtReply.Text = "I'm washing my hair tonight."
  Case "Bobby"
    txtReply.Text = "This is a recording."
End Select
```

Notice the cleaner look and the elimination of repetitive words such as ElseIf and Then.

Depending on how many values you need to check, you can sandwich as many Case lines in a Select Case statement as you want.

Using the Select Case Statement with Comparison Operators

Normally, the Select Case statement requires an exact value to examine. However, by using comparison operators, such as <, <=, or <>, you can make the Select Case statement examine whether a variable falls within a range of values.

To make a Select Case statement use comparison operators, you have to use the magic reserved word `is`. Therefore, the following Select Case statement

```
Select Case Day
  Case is > 15
    txtReadMe.Text = "Bills are past due!"
  Case is > 10
    txtReadMe.Text = "Pay your bills!"
End Select
```

is equivalent to the following If-Then statement:

```
If Day > 15 Then
  txtReadMe.Text = "Bills are past due!"
ElseIf Day > 10 Then
  txtReadMe.Text = "Pay your bills!"
End If
```

Making Sure the Computer Follows at Least One Set of Instructions

Like the If-Then-ElseIf statement, the possibility that none of the instructions within the Select Case statement are going to be followed exists. To make sure that the computer follows at least one set of instructions, you have to use the magical `Else` command again. Take a look at the following example:

```
Select Case Day
  Case 1
    Instructions1
  Case 2
    Instructions2
  Case 3
    Instructions3
  Case Else
    InstructionsDefault
End Select
```

The preceding code tells Visual Basic .NET, "If the value of `Day` equals 1, then follow the first set of instructions. If the value of `Day` equals 2, then follow the second set of instructions. If the value of `Day` equals 3, then follow the third set of instructions. If the value of `Day` doesn't equal 1, 2, or 3, then follow the last set of instructions."

Nesting Case Statements

Some of the simplest toys that amuse children to no end are those Chinese boxes stacked one inside the other. Each time you open a box, you find a smaller one inside. Eventually, you reach a point where no more boxes remain and you have to stop.

Normally an ordinary Select Case statement contains one or more groups of instructions, such as the following:

```
Select Case ID
  Case 123
    chkFrank.Value = True
  Case 124
    chkBob.Value = True
  Case 125
    chkMartha.Value = True
End Select
```

Rather than shoving boring old instructions inside a Select Case statement, however, you can shove If-Then and Select Case statements within a Select Case statement, as the following example illustrates:

```
Select Case IQ
  Case 120
    Select Case Age
      Case is <= 9
        txtAnalysis.Text = "You must be a smart kid."
    End Select
End Select
```

Here's how Visual Basic .NET interprets this code:

1. The first line says, "Check the value stored in a variable called IQ. Then continue to the second line."

2. The second line says, "If the value of IQ is exactly equal to 120, continue to the third line. If the value of IQ is anything else (such as 119, 121, or 3), skip to the seventh line.

3. The third line says, "Check the value stored in a variable called Age. Then continue to the fourth line."

4. The fourth line says, "If the value stored in the variable called Age is equal to or less than 9, continue to the fifth line. If the value of Age is anything greater than 9 (such as 13, 86, or 10), skip to the sixth line."

5. The fifth line says, "Assign the string, "You must be a smart kid." to the Text property of an object named txtAnalysis."

6. The sixth line says, "This is the end of one Select Case statement."

7. The seventh line says, "This is the end of another Select Case statement."

For kicks and grins, you can put an If-Then statement inside a Select Case statement or a Select Case statement inside an If-Then statement. (Some fun, huh?)

Although no theoretical limit exists as to how many If-Then or Select Case statements you can place inside one another, the fewer you use, the easier your code is going to be to figure out. As a general rule, if you have nested more than three If-Then or Case Select statements inside one another, you probably don't know what you're doing.

When nesting multiple statements, you should indent statements so that seeing where they begin and end is easier. For example, notice how confusing the following program appears without indentation:

```
Select Case Salary
Case 1200
If Name = "Bob" Then
txtReview.Text = "No raise this year, ha, ha, ha!"
ElseIf Name = "Karen" Then
txtReview.Text = "Okay, how about a 5% raise?"
End If
End Select
```

Here's what the same program looks like with indentation:

```
Select Case Salary
  Case 1200
    If Name = "Bob" Then
      txtReview.Text = "No raise this year, ha, ha, ha!"
    ElseIf Name = "Karen" Then
      txtReview.Text = "Okay, how about a 5% raise?"
    End If
End Select
```

From the computer's point of view, both programs are the same. But from a programmer's point of view, the program using indentation is much easier to read and understand.

Test your newfound knowledge

1. What is the limit to the number of control structures (If-Then or Select Case statements) you can nest?

   a. The limit is determined by the restrictions your government may place upon you.

   b. The limit is determined by the theoretical applications pursuant to the implications of Einstein's theory of relativity, as reworded by a lawyer.

   c. The limit is 65. If you go over that, you risk getting pulled over by a state trooper.

   d. No limit exists. But if you have too many nested control structures, your program is going to be harder to read and understand.

2. To make nested control structures easier to read and understand, what do you need to do?

   a. Avoid using nested control structures.

   b. Avoid programming altogether.

   c. Limit the number of nested control structures you use, and use indentation to make each If-Then or Select Case statement easy to find.

   d. Print in big, bold, block letters and use short statements like "See Dick run. Dick runs fast."

Chapter 24

Repeating Yourself with Loops

● ●

In This Chapter

▶ Running a loop zero or more times

▶ Looping one or more times

▶ Comparing different loops

● ●

S ometimes you may want your program to repeat one or more instructions over and over again. While you could write the same instructions over and over again, a simpler and more efficient way is to write your instructions just once. Then tell Visual Basic .NET to repeat that group of instructions several times.

To make Visual Basic .NET repeat one or more instructions over and over again, you need to create something called a loop. Visual Basic .NET provides three types of loops:

▸ Loops that run zero or more times

▸ Loops that run at least once or more

▸ Loops that run a fixed number of times and then stop

This chapter discusses the first two types of loops. Chapter 25 explains the third type of loops that can repeat themselves a fixed number of times.

Looping Zero or More Times

Looping allows your program to repeat one or more instructions over and over again. So how can you determine exactly how many times your loop repeats your instructions? Easy, you use a Boolean value (remember those from Chapter 22?).

The Boolean value tells Visual Basic .NET to keep looping while the Boolean value remains True or until the Boolean values become False. To loop while a Boolean value remains True, you would use a loop called a Do-While loop. To loop until a Boolean value becomes False, you would use a Do-Until loop.

Using a Do-While loop

A Do-While loop keeps running while something is True and looks like this:

```
Do While BooleanValue
 ' Instructions to repeat
Loop
```

The first time Visual Basic .NET sees a Do-While loop, it says, "Okay, is the Boolean value True or False? If it's False, ignore all the instructions inside the Do-While loop. If it's True, follow all the instructions inside the Do-While loop."

For example, study the following Do-While loop:

```
Dim Counter As Integer
Counter = 0
Do While Counter <> 5
 Counter = Counter + 1
 txtCounter.Text = CStr(Counter)
Loop
```

Visual Basic .NET interprets the code like this:

1. The first line says, "Create a variable called Counter and make it an Integer data type."

2. The second line says, "Stuff the value of 0 (zero) inside the Counter variable."

3. The third line says, "As long as Counter is not equal to 5, keep repeating all the instructions sandwiched between the Do-While line and the Loop line."

4. The fourth line says, "Add 1 (one) to the value of the Counter variable."

5. The fifth line says, "Take the value of Counter, convert it into a String, and stuff it in the Text property of a text box called txtCounter."

6. The sixth line says, "This is the end of the Do-While loop. Go back to the second line where the Do-While loop begins as long as the condition that Counter <> 5 remains True."

Each time this loop runs, it increases the value of Counter by one. As soon as the value of Counter equals 5, the condition Counter <> 5 suddenly becomes False and the Do-While loop stops.

If the condition in your Do-While loop never changes from True to False, your loop will keep repeating, creating an endless loop that will freeze your program (and possibly crash your computer). To avoid an endless loop, always make sure that at least one instruction inside your Do-While loop changes the True or False value of the Boolean value that the loop checks.

Using a Do-Until loop

A Do-Until loop keeps running until something is True and looks like this:

```
Do Until BooleanValue
  ' Instructions to repeat
Loop
```

The first time Visual Basic .NET sees a Do-Until loop, it says, "Let me check whether the value of the Boolean value is True or False. If it's False, follow all the instructions inside the Do-Until loop. If it's True, exit the Do-Until loop."

For example, the following is a typical Do-Until loop that counts:

```
Dim Counter as Integer
Counter = 0
Do Until Counter > 4
  Counter = Counter + 1
Loop
```

Here's an explanation of the code:

1. The first line says, "Create a variable called `Counter` and make it an Integer data type."

2. The second line says, "Stuff the value of 0 inside the `Counter` variable."

3. The third line says, "This is the beginning of the Do-Until loop. As long as the value of `Counter > 4` is False, keep repeating all the instructions sandwiched between the `Do` line and the `Loop` line. Otherwise, if the value of `Counter > 4` is True (when `Counter` is 5), exit the loop."

4. The fourth line says, "Take the value of `Counter` and add 1 (one) to it. Now store this new value in the `Counter` variable."

5. The fifth line says, "This is the end of the Do-Until loop."

Each time this loop runs, it increases the value of `Counter` by one. As soon as the value of `Counter` equals 5, the condition `Counter > 4` suddenly becomes True and the Do-Until loop stops.

To avoid an endless Do-Until loop, make sure that at least one instruction inside your Do-Until loop changes the True or False value of the Boolean value that the loop checks. Otherwise, your loop may run endlessly and freeze or crash the computer.

Looping at Least Once

Sometimes you may want to repeat certain instructions at least once. In that case, neither the Do-While nor Do-Until loops will work because they may never loop at all. So to solve this problem, Visual Basic .NET offers two additional loops that will always (yes, always) loop at least once before checking to see if a Boolean value is True or False.

Using a Do-Loop Until loop

A Do-Loop Until loop not only sounds like you're stuttering, but it keeps repeating until a condition becomes True.

A Do-Loop Until loop keeps running until something is True and looks like this:

```
Do
  ' Instructions to repeat
Loop Until BooleanValue
```

The first time Visual Basic .NET sees a Do-Loop Until loop, it says, "Follow all the instructions inside the loop once. Then check whether the Boolean value is True or False. If it's True, stop. If it's False, follow all the instructions inside the Do-Loop Until loop again."

For example, the following is a typical Do-Loop Until loop that counts:

```
Dim Counter As Integer
Counter = 0
Do
 Counter = Counter + 1
Loop Until Counter > 4
```

Here's what this code means:

1. The first line says, "Create a variable called Counter and make it an Integer data type."

2. The second line says, "Stuff the value of 0 inside the Counter variable."

3. The third line says, "This is the beginning of the Do-Loop Until loop."

4. The fourth line says, "Take the value of Counter and add 1 (one) to it. Now store this new value in the Counter variable."

5. The fifth line says, "This is the end of the Do-Loop Until loop. As long as the value of Counter is 4 or less, keep repeating all the instructions sandwiched between the Do line and this Loop Until line. Otherwise, exit the loop."

Test your newfound knowledge

1. If you need to loop until a certain condition becomes True, which type of loop would you use?

   a. A Do-Until loop.

   b. A loop twisted in the shape of a pretzel.

   c. A loop-the-loop.

   d. Have you noticed that if you stare at the word loop long enough, it starts to look funny?

2. Why is it possible for a Do-While loop to run zero or more times?

   a. Because it's the numero uno loop used by two out of three programmers employed at Microsoft, IBM, and Symantec.

   b. Nobody knows, but I remember seeing a segment on *Unsolved Mysteries,* asking viewers to call in if they had any information that might help resolve this question.

   c. Because it checks its condition before it runs even once.

   d. Because it uses steroids: So not only does it run once, it runs faster than any other loop that isn't doped up.

Each time this loop runs, it increases the value of Counter by one. As soon as the value of Counter equals 5, the condition Counter > 4 suddenly becomes True and the Do-Loop Until loop stops.

To avoid an endless Do-Loop Until loop, make sure that at least one instruction inside your Do-Loop Until loop changes the True or False value of the Boolean value that the loop checks. If your loop runs endlessly, it can freeze or crash the computer.

Using a Do-Loop While loop

You can find Do-Loop While loops in everyday experiences, such as when office workers tell themselves, "Keep stuffing office supplies in my briefcase while no one is looking. The moment someone looks in my direction, stop and do something else."

A Do-Loop While loop keeps running while something is True and looks like this:

```
Do
   ' Instructions to repeat
Loop While BooleanValue
```

Do-Loop While loops essentially tell Visual Basic .NET, "Go ahead and do something until a certain condition tells you to stop."

The first time Visual Basic .NET sees a Do-Loop While loop, it says, "Let me follow all the instructions inside the loop first. After this, check whether the value of the condition is True or False. If it's False, stop. If it's True, repeat all the instructions inside the Do-Loop While loop again."

For example, the following code has a Do-Loop While loop.

```
Dim Counter As Integer
Counter = 0
Do
  Counter = Counter + 1
Loop While Counter < 5
```

Visual Basic .NET interprets the code like this:

1. The first line says, "Create a variable called `Counter` and make it into an Integer data type."

2. The second line says, "Set the value of the `Counter` variable to 0."

3. The third line says, "This is the beginning of the Do-Loop While loop."

4. The fourth line says, "Take the value of `Counter` and add 1 (one) to it. Now store this new value in the `Counter` variable."

5. The fifth line says, "This is the end of the Do-Loop While loop. As long as the value of `Counter` is less than 5, keep repeating all the instructions sandwiched between the `Do` line and the `Loop While` line. Otherwise, exit the loop."

Each time this loop runs, it increases the value of `Counter` by one. As soon as the value of `Counter` equals 5, the condition `Counter < 5` suddenly becomes False and the Do-Loop While loop stops.

To avoid an endless Do-Loop While loop, make sure that at least one instruction inside your Do-Loop While loop changes the True or False value of the Boolean value that the loop checks. If your loop runs endlessly, it can freeze or crash the computer.

Comparing Your Loop Choices

Choose your loops carefully because loops may look similar but act differently. To avoid confusion, try to stick with one type of loop throughout your program so that it is easier for you to figure out how all your program's loops work.

If you need to loop zero or more times, use one of the following loops:

```
Do While BooleanValue        Do Until BooleanValue
  ' Instructions to repeat      ' Instructions to repeat
Loop                         Loop
```

If you need to loop at least once, use one of the following loops instead:

```
Do                           Do
  ' Instructions to repeat      ' Instruction to repeat
Loop Until BooleanValue      Loop While BooleanValue
```

All types of loops need some way of changing the Boolean value that they check so your loop will eventually end.

Chapter 25

For-Next Loops That Can Count

● ●

In This Chapter

▶ Using the For-Next loop

▶ Counting backward and forward

▶ Using the Step increment

● ●

The loops discussed in Chapter 24 run zero or more times and keep repeating themselves until or while a certain Boolean value is True or False. But what if you know you want to loop a specific number of times?

While you can still use a Do-While or Do-Until loop, a simpler solution is to use a For-Next loop, which looks like the following:

```
Dim Counter As Integer
For Counter = Start To End Step X
   Instructions
Next Counter
```

The Counter is a variable that represents an integer. Start represents the first number assigned to the value of the Counter. End is the last number assigned to the value of the Counter. Step is the interval to count by. If Step is omitted, Visual Basic .NET counts by 1.

How the For-Next Loop Works

If you want to loop exactly three times, you can use the following code:

```
Dim X As Integer
For X = 1 To 3
   ' Instructions to repeat
Next X
```

Here's what this code means:

1. The first line says, "Create a variable called X and make it an Integer data type."

2. The second line says, "Set the value of the X variable equal to 1. Keep looping as long as the value of X is 1, 2, or 3. The moment the value of X is no longer one of these values, stop looping."

3. The third line is where you can shove one or more instructions (including additional For-Next loops if you want).

4. The fourth line says, "Okay, get the next value of X (by adding 1 to the value of X) and go back to the first line. At this point, the value of X is now 2."

The following line tells Visual Basic .NET to loop three times:

```
For X = 1 To 3
```

By default, Visual Basic .NET counts by one. For grins and laughs, you can use any combination of numbers that you want, such as

```
For X = 1209 To 1211
   Instructions
Next X
```

This For-Next loop also loops three times, although it's not as easy to tell that just by looking at it:

The first time, X = 1209.

The second time, X = 1210.

The third and last time, X = 1211.

You can count by such bizarre numbers if these numbers somehow make sense to your program. For example, you can count by employee numbers:

```
For EmployeeNumber = 11250 To 11290
   ' Use the value of EmployeeNumber to search a database
   ' of employees and print their background information
Next EmployeeNumber
```

In this case, the instructions inside your For-Next loop use the value of EmployeeNumber to find a specific employee.

If you just need to loop a particular number of times, such as five, use the simplest and most straightforward method, as shown in the following:

```
For X = 1 To 5
   ' Instructions to repeat
Next X
```

Only if your numbers must be used inside your For-Next loop should you resort to bizarre, hard-to-read counting methods, such as

```
For Counter = 3492 To 12909
   Instructions
Next Counter
```

Counting Backward and Forward

Normally, the For-Next loop counts forward by 1s. However, if you want to count by 5s, 10s, 13s, or 29s, you can. To count by any number other than 1, you have to specify a Step increment. For example:

```
Dim counter As Integer
For counter = start To end Step increment
   Instructions
Next counter
```

Adding the Step increment instruction tells Visual Basic .NET, "Instead of counting forward by ones, count by the value of the increment that follows the word Step." If you wanted to count by 16s, you would use the following code:

```
Dim X As Integer
For X = 0 To 32 Step 16
   Instructions
Next X
```

This For-Next loop actually loops just three times:

The first time, X = 0

The second time, X = 16

The third time and last time, X = 32

If you want, you can even count backward. To count backward three times, you can use the following code:

```
Dim X As Integer
For X = 3 To 1 Step -1
   Instructions
Next X
```

Here's what the preceding code means:

1. The first line says, "Create a variable called X and make it an Integer data type."

2. The second line says, "Set the value of the X variable to 3, and count backward by –1."

3. The third line contains one or more instructions to follow.

4. The fourth line says, "Choose the next value of X. Because we're counting backward by –1, the new value of X will be X –2."

Although Visual Basic .NET doesn't care about how you count, always choose the simplest method whenever possible. That way, you and any other programmers can quickly see how many times a For-Next loop keeps looping.

Count backward or by unusual numbers (increments of 3, 5, 16, and so on) only if instructions in a For-Next loop need to use those numbers. Otherwise, you only make your program harder to read.

So what happens if you write a For-Next loop like the following?

```
Dim J As Integer
For J = 1 To 7 Step 5
   Instructions
Next J
```

Here's what this code means:

1. This For-Next loop repeats itself twice. The first time, the value of J is 1.

2. The second time, the value of J is 1 + 5 (remember, the value of Step is 5), or 6.

3. Before it can repeat a third time, the loop changes the value of J to 6 + 5, or 11. Because 11 is greater than the specified range of J = 1 To 7, the For-Next loop refuses to loop a third time and quits.

Use Caution When Using a For-Next Loop with the Step Increment

A For-Next loop must create its own variable to do its counting. For example, the following code creates a variable called XYZ that counts by 10s:

```
For XYZ = 1 To 50 Step 10
   Instructions
Next XYZ
```

And the next code creates a variable called TUV that counts by increments of 1.5:

```
For TUV = 1 To 7 Step 1.5
   Instructions
Next TUV
```

For-Next loops usually count by whole numbers, such as 1, 2, 5, or 58, so it's not difficult to determine the number of loops there will be. The first code example just shown counts by 10, so the number of times it will loop is pretty easy to figure out. (It loops five times.)

The second example, however, counts in increments of 1.5. Because of this decimal increment, it's harder to tell how many times it will loop. (It loops five times.) When using the Step increment, use whole numbers so that you can see the number of loops more easily.

When using a For-Next loop, *never* (and I repeat, *never*) change the value of the counting variable within the loop. The loop will get messed up, as the following example illustrates:

```
Dim X As Integer
For X = 1 To 5
   X = 3
Next X
```

Here's what happens:

1. The first line says, "Create a variable called X and make it an Integer data type."

2. The second line says, "Set the value of the X variable to 1."

3. The third line says, "Assign the value of 3 to a variable called X."

4. The fourth line says, "Add 1 to the value of X. Because X is equal to 3, now make X equal to 4."

Because X always equals 4 at the end of each loop, this For-Next loop becomes an endless loop, which never stops. So when using For-Next loops, make sure that none of the instructions inside the loop changes the counting variable. Otherwise, you'll be sorry. . . .

When to Use a For-Next Loop

Use a For-Next loop whenever you want to loop a specific number of times.

Just to show you that it is possible, you can also use other types of loops to count. The following two loops will loop exactly six times:

```
Dim X As Integer                Dim X As Integer
X = 0                           For X = 1 To 6
Do While X < 6                    ' Instructions to repeat
  X = X + 1                     Next X
  ' Instructions to repeat
Loop
```

Notice how simple and clean the For-Next loop is compared to the Do-While loop. There are an infinite number of ways to write a program that works (and an even greater number of ways to write programs that don't work), but the simplest way is usually the best.

Test your newfound knowledge

1. How many times will the following For-Next loop repeat itself?

```
For ID = 15 To 1 Step -1
          ' Instructions to
    repeat
Next ID
```

   a. Fifteen times.

   b. One time, but 15 times as fast.

   c. Zero or more times, or something like that. Wait a minute. I think I'm in the wrong lesson.

   d. None, because only history can repeat itself.

2. What is the main advantage of a For-Next loop over a Do-While loop?

   a. A Do-While loop is more complicated to use, and a For-Next loop doesn't work at all.

   b. It all depends on your point of view, man. Like, all things are good if we only love one another and live in peace and harmony.

   c. You can specify how many times you want a For-Next loop to repeat itself.

   d. There is no advantage to mastering Visual Basic .NET. You should be investigating C++ or Java instead.

Chapter 26

Nested Loops and Quick Exits

• •

In This Chapter

▶ Nesting loops

▶ Tips for using nested loops

▶ Quick exits from loops

• •

*F*or the ultimate in flexibility and complexity, you can jam loops inside other loops to create a mind-boggling series of loops. Whenever you have one loop stuffed inside another loop, it's called a *nested loop*. So which loop runs and completes first? The answer is simple.

Nesting Your Loops

When you have nested loops, the loop inside finishes first, as shown in the following example:

```
Dim J As Integer, Employee As String
Do While Employee = "Supervisor"
  For J = 1 To 5
    ' Instructions to repeat
  Next J
Loop
```

Now, here's what this code means:

1. The first line says, "Create a variable called J and make it an Integer data type. Then create a variable called Employee and make it a String data type."

2. The second line says, "Check the Employee variable to make sure its value is equal to "Supervisor". If it is, move to the third line. If it isn't, don't even bother looking at the For-Next loop inside; simply skip to the sixth line."

3. The third line says, "Set the value of the J variable to 1."

4. The fourth line says, "Follow these instructions, whatever they may be."

5. The fifth line says, "Increase the value of J by 1 and jump back to the first line again. Keep doing this until the value of J is greater than 5."

6. The sixth line says, "This is the end of the Do-While loop. Keep repeating as long as the variable Employee is equal to "Supervisor". (**Note:** Unless you had code inside the Do-While loop to change the value of the Employee variable, this Do-While loop will repeat itself endlessly, hanging up or crashing your computer.)

In the preceding example, the For-Next loop finishes before the Do-While loop. The For-Next loop also runs one complete time through for every time you go through the Do-While loop.

Tips for Using Nested Loops

Naturally, Visual Basic .NET gives you the complete freedom to cram as many loops inside one another as you want. When creating nested loops, indent each loop to make it easier to see where each loop begins and ends. For example, notice how confusing the following nested loops look without indentation:

```
Do While Name = "Sam"
Do
For K = 20 To 50 Step 10
Do
Do Until Sex = "Male"
' Change some variables here
Loop
Loop While Age > 21
Next K
Loop Until LastName = "Doe"
Loop
```

This is what the same code looks like with indentations:

```
Do While Name = "Sam"
   Do
      For K = 20 To 50 Step 10
         Do
            Do Until Sex = "Male"
               ' Change some variables here
            Loop
         Loop While Age > 21
      Next K
   Loop Until LastName = "Doe"
Loop
```

From the computer's point of view, both nested loops work the same. But from a programmer's point of view, the nested loops using indentation are much easier to read and understand. Visual Basic .NET's code editor can automatically indent your code for you, but you may still want to make sure the indentation clearly defines the start and end of your different loops.

With so many nested loops, make sure that the inside loops don't accidentally mess up the conditions or counting variables of the outer loops. Otherwise, you may create an endless loop and have to examine all your loops to find the problem.

Another problem that can prevent nested loops from running is if they are tangled, as in the following example:

```
For K = 1 To 4
   For J = 2 To 20 Step 2
Next K
   Next J
```

In this example, the two For-Next loops intertwine because the first For-Next loop ends before the second, inner For-Next loop can end. Fortunately, if you run the preceding BASIC code, Visual Basic .NET catches this mistake so this type of problem is easy to correct.

Making Quick Exits from Loops

A Do loop continues running until a certain condition becomes True or False. A For-Next loop continues running until it finishes counting. But what if you need to exit a loop prematurely? In that case, you can bail out of a loop by using the magic Exit command.

To bail out of a Do loop, use the Exit Do command, as shown in the following example:

```
Dim X As Integer
X = 0
Do While X < 6
   X = X + 1
   If X = 4 Then Exit Do
Loop
```

This Do-While loop continues looping as long as the value of a variable called X is less than 6. The moment the value of X equals 4, Visual Basic .NET runs the Exit Do command.

The Exit Do command bails Visual Basic .NET out of the loop, even though the value of X is still less than 6.

To bail out of a For-Next loop, use the following:

```
Exit For
```

For example:

```
For Y = 1 To 100
  If Y = 50 Then Exit For
Next Y
```

Normally this For-Next loop repeats 100 times, but the second line tells Visual Basic .NET to bail out of the For-Next loop as soon as the value of Y equals 50 — even if the value of Y is still less than 100.

Use the Exit command sparingly, just in case the user needs to do something else. However, make sure that using Exit Do or Exit For doesn't kick you out of the loop before you want it to. Otherwise, you'll have another bug to hunt and track down.

If you use the Exit Do/For commands within a loop nested inside another loop, the Exit Do/For command only exits out of the current loop and then returns control to the outer loop.

Test your newfound knowledge

1. What is the limit to the number of loops you can nest?

   a. Theoretically, the number is infinity. Practically, the number is as many as you feel like typing, although the more nested your loops are, the harder it is to see what each one does.

   b. The number of loops is limited to your yearly allotment, as defined by Microsoft when you send in your registration card.

   c. Five.

   d. Discovered by Einstein, the limit to the number of nested loops is equal to the same value that represents the speed of light.

2. To make nested loops easier to read and understand, what should you do?

   a. Avoid using loops, control structures, variables, or anything else that requires thinking.

   b. Absolutely nothing. If people can't understand my nested loops, that's their problem.

   c. Avoid indentation, because only amateurs need to rely on such editing tricks to write programs.

   d. Use plenty of indentations to make the beginning and ending of each loop easy to find.

Part VI
Writing Subprograms (So You Don't Go Crazy All at Once)

The 5th Wave   By Rich Tennant

"HERE ON ALTAIR-14, WE'VE IMPLEMENTED ANYTHING-TO-ANYTHING INTEGRATION."

In this part . . .

Now is the time to find out how to divide your Visual Basic .NET program into smaller programs so you can create programs that are easier to write, modify, and understand. Rather than write one huge, monolithic program (which is like carving a mansion out of a single piece of granite), subprograms let you create miniature programs and paste them together to make one larger program (which is more like using bricks to build a house).

By dividing one large program into several smaller ones, you can test each part of your program before moving on to writing another part of the program. By conquering each task of your program one by one, you can also maintain your sanity so that you don't go nuts trying to create one monster program in one sitting.

Chapter 27

General Procedures (Subprograms That Everyone Can Share)

*P*rocedures are small programs that make up a single larger program, much like bricks make up an entire wall. Visual Basic .NET has two types of procedures: event-handling procedures and general procedures.

An *event-handling procedure* is part of a user interface object, such as a radio button, check box, or scroll bar. Event-handling procedures are stored within a form file and run only when a certain event occurs to a certain object, such as clicking the mouse on a radio button or pull-down menu command.

A *general procedure* isn't attached or connected to any specific objects on the user interface. A general procedure doesn't do anything until an event-handling procedure (or another general procedure) specifically tells it to get to work.

So do you need event-handling procedures? Yes. Event-handling procedures make your user interface respond to the user. Do you need general procedures? No. General procedures exist solely for the programmer's convenience.

But if two or more event-handling procedures contain nearly identical instructions, typing the same instructions over and over would be repetitive. Even worse, if you needed to modify the instructions, you would have to change these instructions in every event-handling procedure that used those same instructions.

To save yourself from typing the same instructions again and again, store them in a general procedure. A general procedure can hold commonly used instructions in one place. That way, if you need to modify the instructions, you change them in just that one place.

Understanding Module Files

Every Visual Basic .NET program consists of at least one form file, and every form file contains the event-handling procedures needed to make your program work. So when you want to create general procedures, you can also store them in your form files.

But mixing event-handling procedures and general procedures in the same form file can make your program messy and harder to understand, much like mixing your socks in the same drawer as your underwear and shirts, and then wondering why you can't find anything you want in a hurry. As an alternative to storing general procedures in form files, Visual Basic .NET gives you the option of storing your general procedures in separate files called module files instead.

Many programmers like to store related general procedures in the same module file, such as all general procedures involved in printing in one module file and all general procedures involved in saving files in another module file. That way, if your program doesn't save files correctly, you can isolate the problem to the module file that contains general procedures for saving files.

Figure 27-1 shows what happens if you store different chunks of code scattered in a single file. If anything goes wrong with your program, trying to understand, let alone find, the BASIC code that doesn't work can be difficult and time-consuming. But if you organize related BASIC code into separate module files, as shown in Figure 27-2, you can quickly find and understand all the BASIC code used by your entire program.

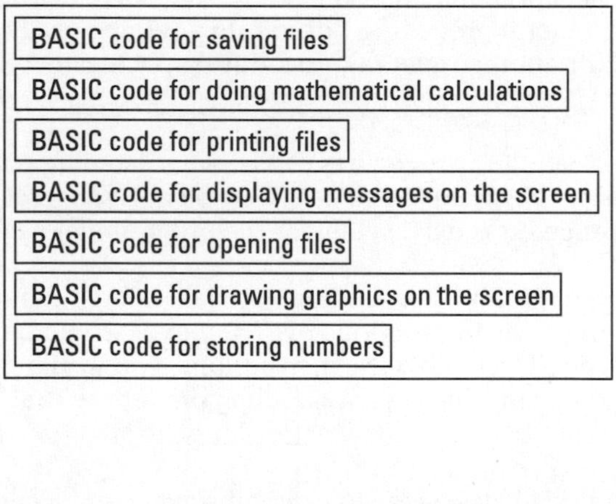

Figure 27-1:
If you store BASIC code in a single file, trying to understand and modify your BASIC code can be difficult.

> BASIC code for saving files
>
> BASIC code for doing mathematical calculations
>
> BASIC code for printing files
>
> BASIC code for displaying messages on the screen
>
> BASIC code for opening files
>
> BASIC code for drawing graphics on the screen
>
> BASIC code for storing numbers

Module1

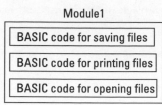

| BASIC code for saving files |
| BASIC code for printing files |
| BASIC code for opening files |

Module2

| BASIC code for drawing graphics on the screen |
| BASIC code for displaying messages on the screen |

Module3

| BASIC code for doing mathematical calculations |
| BASIC code for storing numbers |

Figure 27-2:
If you store related BASIC code in separate module files, you can quickly identify and find the BASIC code that performs specific functions.

A Visual Basic .NET program can have zero or more module files.

To create a new module file, follow these steps:

1. Choose Project⇨AddModule.

An Add New Item dialog box appears, as shown in Figure 27-3.

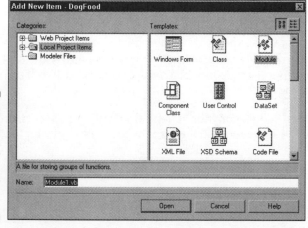

Figure 27-3:
Adding a module file to your Visual Basic .NET program.

2. **Click on the Module icon and then click in the Name text box.**

3. **Type a name for your module file.**

   Make sure you leave the .VB file extension as part of your module file name.

4. **Click Open.**

   Visual Basic .NET displays your module name in the Solution Explorer window (if it's visible) and displays an empty module file in the code window that looks something like this, where `Module1` is the name you chose in Step 3 for your module file:

```
Module Module1

End Module
```

Creating General Procedures

A general procedure looks like this:

```
Public Sub ProcedureName()
  ' Instructions to run
End Sub
```

Notice that a complete general procedure consists of five parts:

- ✔ Public (or Private)
- ✔ Sub
- ✔ Your general procedure name
- ✔ A pair of parentheses ( )
- ✔ End Sub

The word `Public` tells Visual Basic .NET that the general procedure is public. If you store the general procedure in a module file, event-handling or general procedures stored in either form or module files can use it.

If you want to limit the use of your general procedures only to those procedures stored in the same module file, use the word `Private` instead, such as:

```
Private Sub ProcedureName()
  ' Instructions to run
End Sub
```

When you store a general procedure in a form file, only event-handling and general procedures stored in that same form file can use that general procedure.

The word Sub identifies your subroutine as a procedure. (If you replace the word Sub with the word Function, you can create a general function, which is covered later in Chapter 29.) Your procedure name is the name that event-handling procedures and other general procedures use to call your general procedure. *Calling* a procedure means telling a particular procedure, "Okay, do something now!"

The pair of parentheses is called the *argument list* (which you can read about in Chapter 28). The simplest general procedures have an empty argument list, represented by an empty pair of parentheses.

The End Sub words identify the end of the general procedure.

You can create and save general procedures in one of two places:

- ✔ Form files (the same file that contains your user interface objects such as buttons and pull-down menus)
- ✔ Module files

If you save your general procedures in a module file, you can create a library of useful general procedures that you can plug into any other Visual Basic .NET programs you write. Ideally, you should always store general procedures in module files and only store event-handling procedures in form files. That way you can keep the code for your user interface separate from the code that does the actual calculations.

Creating a general procedure in a form file

If you store general procedures in a form file, you risk making your program harder to understand and modify, especially if you write a program containing lots of BASIC code.

To create and save a general procedure in a form file, follow these steps:

1. **Click on a form file in the Solution Explorer window and then press F7; choose View⇨Code; or click on the View Code icon to open the code window.**

2. **Scroll through your code until you see a box that says Windows Form Designer generated code, as shown in Figure 27-4.**

3. **Click directly underneath the Windows Form Designer generated code text and type your general procedure.**

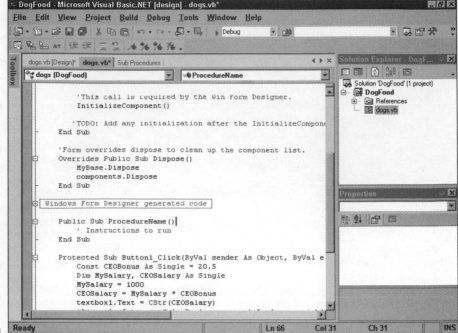

Figure 27-4:
You can
type your
general
procedures
directly
under the
Windows
Form
Designer
generated
code portion
of your
program.

Creating and saving a general procedure in a module file

If you haven't created a module file yet, follow the steps for creating a module in the earlier section in this chapter called "Understanding Module Files."

To create a general procedure in a module file, follow these steps:

1. **Choose <u>V</u>iew⇨Solution Explorer, or press Ctrl+Alt+L.**

   The Solution Explorer window appears.

2. **Double-click on the module file where you want to store your general procedure.**

   Visual Basic .NET displays an empty module file in the code window that looks something like this, where `Module1` is the name of your module file:

   ```
   Module Module1

   End Module
   ```

3. **Type your general procedure anywhere in between the `Module` and `End Module` lines.**

Use the `Public` keyword to create a general procedure that can be used outside of your module file. Use the `Private` keyword to create a general procedure that can only be used inside of your module file.

Naming a General Procedure

Unlike with event-handling procedure names (which identify the object name and the event), you can name general procedures anything you want, with the following restrictions:

- ✔ The name must be no longer than 40 characters in length.
- ✔ The name must begin with a letter and can consist of only letters, numbers, and the underscore character (_).
- ✔ The name can't be a reserved word that Visual Basic .NET already uses such as `End`, `Sub`, or `Private`.

Ideally, you want to use names for your general procedures that describe what they do. For example:

```
CubeRoot
Ask4Password
DisplayWindow
```

These complete procedure names would appear in the code window as follows:

```
Public Sub CubeRoot()

End Sub
```

and

```
Public Sub Ask4Password()

End Sub
```

and

```
Public Sub DisplayWindow()

End Sub
```

Calling a General Procedure

A general procedure contains one or more instructions. When another procedure wants to run the instructions stored in a general procedure, it needs to call that particular general procedure by name.

You can call a procedure in two ways. You can state the procedure's name:

```
ProcedureName ()
```

Or, you can state the procedure's name along with the word Call:

```
Call ProcedureName ()
```

Visual Basic .NET doesn't care which method you use. But whatever method you choose, use it consistently — your program's easier to read that way.

By using the Call keyword, you can make it easier to identify when your BASIC code calls or runs a general procedure that may be stored in another file.

Stating only the procedure name is simpler than using the word Call, but the latter helps identify all procedure calls in your program. For example, consider the following general procedure:

```
Public Sub Warning()
   MsgBox ("Your computer will blow up in 3 seconds!", ,
           "Warning!")
End Sub
```

This general procedure simply displays a dialog box with the message "Your computer will blow up in 3 seconds!", as shown in Figure 27-5.

To run this general procedure, you just need to type the general procedure name, such as:

```
Public Sub cmdAlert_Click()
   Warning ()
End Sub
```

If the event-handling procedure used the Call method of calling a procedure, it would look like this:

```
Public Sub cmdAlert_Click()
   Call Warning ()
End Sub
```

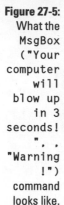

Figure 27-5:
What the
MsgBox
("Your
computer
will
blow up
in 3
seconds!
", ,
"Warning
!")
command
looks like.

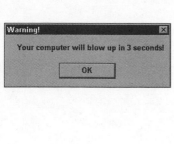

Both of these event procedures are equivalent to the following:

```
Public Sub cmdAlert_Click()
    MsgBox ("Your computer will blow up in 3 seconds!", ,_
            "Warning!")
End Sub
```

Although this example is simple, you can see that, if you cram two or more instructions inside a general procedure, you won't have to type these same instructions over and over again in multiple places. Instead, you can just call a single general procedure.

Test your newfound knowledge

1. Why would you need to use a general procedure?

   a. Because a more specific procedure won't do the job.

   b. To store commonly used instructions in one place so that the procedure is easy to modify.

   c. To keep your event-handling procedures from getting lonely.

   d. There's no reason to use general procedures — cool programmers have no need of such crutches.

2. How can you call a general procedure?

   a. Use a telephone.

   b. Type the general procedure's name in your code or put the word Call in front of the general procedure name.

   c. See your favorite psychic and participate in a séance.

   d. Get your local hog-calling contest winner to shout really loud for you.

Chapter 28

Passing Arguments

● ●

In This Chapter

▶ Sending arguments to a procedure

▶ Problems with passing arguments

▶ Quitting a procedure early

● ●

*W*hen a procedure calls a general procedure, it does so by name. Calling a general procedure by name essentially tells that general procedure, "Hey, get busy and start doing something."

Many times, the called general procedure needs no further instructions when its name is called. Sometimes, though, the called general procedure needs additional information before it can do anything.

Any procedure can call a general procedure and give it data to work with. This data is called an *argument*. Essentially, the first procedure is saying, "Don't argue with me. Here's all the information you need to get busy. Now get to work."

Why Use Arguments?

An *argument* is data — numbers, strings, or variables, (which represent a number or string) — that a general procedure needs to work with. By using arguments, you can write a single, nonspecific procedure that can replace two or more specialized general procedures.

For example, you can create two general procedures, as follows:

```
Public Sub DisplayWarning()
  txtReadMe.Text = "Warning! Nuclear meltdown has occurred!"
End Sub
```

and

```
Public Sub DisplayCaution()
  txtReadMe.Text = "Caution! Turn off the reactors now!"
End Sub
```

To use either procedure, you call them in one of two ways:

- ✔ DisplayWarning() **or** Call DisplayWarning()
- ✔ DisplayCaution() **or** Call DisplayCaution()

However, creating two procedures that do almost the same thing is tedious and wasteful. So instead of writing near-duplicate copies of the same procedure, you can replace both of those procedures with a single generic one, such as the following:

```
Public Sub Display(ByVal Message As String)
   txtReadMe.Text = Message
End Sub
```

This new procedure says, "Create a variable called Message that holds a string that another procedure will give to me. Whatever this string may be, stuff it in the Text property of the text box called txtReadMe.

To call a general procedure that requires data, you stuff that data in the parentheses. For example, to call the preceding Display general procedure, you can choose different text for that procedure to use, such as:

```
Display ("Warning! Nuclear meltdown has occurred!")
```

or

```
Display ("Caution! Turn off the reactors now!")
```

or

```
Call Display ("Warning! Nuclear meltdown has occurred!")
```

or

```
Call Display ("Caution! Turn off the reactors now!")
```

Sending Arguments to a Procedure

To call a procedure and send data (called an argument) to it, you can use one of two methods:

- ✔ ProcedureName (Argument)
- ✔ Call ProcedureName (Argument)

Suppose you had the following general procedure:

```
Public Sub Display(ByVal Message As String)
   txtReadMe.Text = Message
End Sub
```

To call the preceding procedure and display the message "Warning! Nuclear meltdown has occurred!", you can use one of two methods:

✔ Display ("Warning! Nuclear meltdown has occurred!")

✔ Call Display ("Warning! Nuclear meltdown has occurred!")

Both methods are equivalent, so you can use whichever one you prefer. Ideally, you should stick to one method of calling procedures and use that method consistently throughout your program.

Now here's what calling the Display general procedure does:

1. First it tells Visual Basic .NET, "Find a general procedure named Display and send it one argument." In this case, the one argument is the string, "Warning! Nuclear meltdown has occurred!"

2. Visual Basic .NET finds a general procedure called Display. The Display procedure says to assign whatever argument it gets to the variable Message.

3. Then the Display procedure says, "Stuff the value of Message into the Text property of the text box called txtReadMe. Because the value of Message is the string "Warning! Nuclear meltdown has occurred!", stuff this value into the Text property."

If you call the procedure in the following way:

```
Display ("Caution! Turn off the reactors now!")
```

the Text property of the text box called txtReadMe gets stuffed with the string "Caution! Turn off the reactors now!".

By using the same procedure but feeding it different arguments, you can replace two or more specialized general procedures with a single, generic general procedure.

Accepting Arguments

Before a general procedure can accept arguments, you have to define the procedure's argument list. Essentially, this list defines how many arguments the general procedure can take.

For example, to define a general procedure that won't take any arguments, you use a pair of empty parentheses, as follows:

```
Public Sub NoBackTalk()

End Sub
```

To call this procedure, you can choose one of two ways:

- ✔ NoBackTalk ()
- ✔ Call NoBackTalk ()

To define an argument list that takes one argument, you do the following:

```
Public Sub BackTalk(ByVal Something As Integer)

End Sub
```

In this case, you defined a variable named Something and the data type that it holds is an Integer data type. To call this procedure and give it the argument 4, you can do one of the following:

- ✔ BackTalk (4)
- ✔ Call BackTalk (4)

If you try to call this general procedure and feed it data that is not the proper data type (in this case an Integer data type), Visual Basic .NET will scream and refuse to run your program.

Passing arguments by value

To protect your procedures from messing around with data from the rest of your program, Visual Basic .NET forces you to pass arguments by value, hence the odd term ByVal in a procedure's argument list.

When you pass an argument by value, you're giving the general procedure a copy of the original data. That way if the general procedure messes up the data, that same data used elsewhere in your program won't be affected.

If you forget to type the ByVal keyword in your procedure's argument list, Visual Basic .NET will automatically type it in for you.

You actually have a choice of passing arguments by value or by reference. When you pass an argument by value, you give the procedure a separate copy of data. When you pass an argument by reference, you allow the procedure to manipulate the actual data. Passing arguments by reference increases the chance that your procedures will accidentally mess up data needed by other parts of your program. By default, Visual Basic .NET always assumes that you want to pass arguments by value. If you want to live dangerously, you can pass arguments by reference by using the ByRef keyword instead of the ByVal keyword, such as:

```
Public Sub BackTalk(ByRef Something As Integer)

End Sub
```

Defining multiple arguments

Instead of just accepting a single argument, a general procedure can accept two or more arguments. Each time you specify a variable, you have to specify the data type for each argument and separate each by a comma. For example, the following defines three arguments, I, S, and D:

```
Public Sub Chatty(ByVal I As Integer, ByVal S As String,
         ByVal D As Double)
End Sub
```

To call this procedure and give it the arguments 30, "Hello", and 12.9, you must do one of the following:

- Chatty (30, "Hello", 12.9)
- Call Chatty (30, "Hello", 12.9)

There is no practical limit to the number of arguments that a procedure can accept. However, the longer your argument list is, the more complicated your procedure must be and the more likely you may get confused trying to understand exactly what your procedures do.

Problems with Sending Arguments

Two common problems may occur when calling procedures. One problem is when the number of arguments sent doesn't match the number of arguments defined by the procedure. The other problem occurs when the types of arguments sent don't match the types of arguments defined by the procedure.

Giving the wrong number of arguments

When you define a procedure with an argument list, the argument list defines the number of arguments it needs to run. If you call this procedure and don't give it the correct number of arguments, the procedure doesn't work. For example:

```
Public Sub ArgueWithMe(ByVal Flame As Integer)

End Sub
```

This procedure expects one argument, which is an integer. None of the following calls to this procedure work, because the number of arguments is not one:

- ArgueWithMe ()
- ArgueWithMe (9, "Shut up!")
- Call ArgueWithMe("Why?", "Go away!", 4500, "Okay.")

Giving the wrong type of arguments

Likewise, when calling a procedure, always make sure that the arguments have the same data types as the types defined in the argument list. For example:

```
Public Sub ArgueWithMe(ByVal Flame As String)

End Sub
```

This procedure expects one argument, which must be a String data type. None of the following calls to this procedure work because the arguments aren't String data types:

- ArgueWithMe(78.909)
- ArgueWithMe(9)
- Call ArgueWithMe(34)

Quitting a Procedure Prematurely

Normally, a procedure runs until all its instructions are followed. However, you may want to exit a procedure before it finishes.

To exit a procedure prematurely, you have to use the following code:

```
Exit Sub
```

For example, you may have a procedure like the one that follows:

```
Public Sub EndlessLoop()
   X = 0
   Do
      X = X + 1
      If (X = 13) Then
         Exit Sub
      End If
   Loop Until X = 25
End Sub
```

Normally, this loop would keep repeating until the value of X equals 25. However the If-Then statement inside the Do-Loop causes this procedure to end when X equals 13.

Test your newfound knowledge

1. Explain why argument passing is useful in writing programs.

   a. Argument passing is like passing the buck. Programmers do this all the time to avoid taking responsibility when their project is behind schedule.

   b. Passing arguments lets you write one general-purpose procedure to replace two or more specialized procedures.

   c. Arguments let you give wrong information to your procedures, so they have twice as many chances of wrecking your entire project.

   d. Argument passing is like scream therapy. Each side argues for its own point until both sides are exhausted, which prevents people from shooting each other at work.

2. Explain what the following argument list means:

   ```
   Public Sub Confusion_
   (ByVal Catch As String,_
   ByVal X As Integer, ByVal_
   Z As Integer)

   End Sub
   ```

   a. Crud, I have to review this section all over again.

   b. Now I finally understand why programmers look and act the way they do, if they have to spend eight hours a day deciphering cryptic commands like this.

   c. Someone didn't comment the code correctly to make this argument easy to understand.

   d. The procedure expects three arguments. The first argument is called Catch, is passed by value, and must be a String data type. The second and third arguments are called X and Z, and must be an Integer data type.

Chapter 29

Functions, a Unique Type of Subprogram

- -

In This Chapter

▶ Calling functions

▶ Defining argument types

▶ Quitting a function early

- -

Functions are miniature programs that accept data, calculate a result, and then return a single value. Visual Basic .NET includes a bunch of built-in functions with odd names such as Sqr (which accepts a number and returns that number's square root) and LCase (which accepts a string and returns that string all in lowercase). Table 29-1 lists some of Visual Basic .NET's many available functions.

Table 29-1	Some Commonly Used Visual Basic .NET Functions
Built-In Visual Basic .NET Function	*What It Does*
Abs (number)	Returns the absolute value of a number
Date	Returns the current system date
LCase (string)	Converts a string to lowercase
Sqr (number)	Returns the square root of a number

Naturally, Visual Basic .NET allows you to create your own functions as well. A typical function looks like the following:

```
Public Function FunctionName(ArgumentList)As DataType
  FunctionName = SomeValue
End Function
```

The word `Public` tells Visual Basic .NET that if the function is stored in a module file, that this function can be used by all event-handling and general procedures in your Visual Basic .NET program. (If you store a function in a module file and substitute the word `Private` for `Public`, your function can only be used by other functions or general procedures stored in that same module file.)

If the function is stored in a form file, this function can be used only by event-handling and general procedures stored in that same form file.

The word `Function` defines the subprogram as a function. The `FunctionName` can be any valid Visual Basic .NET name, preferably one that describes what the function does. The `ArgumentList` can contain zero or more arguments. The `DataType` defines what type of data the function returns, such as an integer or a string.

As an alternative to the above, you can also use the following:

```
Public Function FunctionName(ArgumentList)As DataType
   Return SomeValue
End Function
```

The only difference in this alternate way of creating functions is that instead of specifically assigning a value to the function name, you just use the Return statement instead, which automatically assigns the value to the function name.

How to Create a Function

You can create and save functions in two types of files:

- ✔ Form files
- ✔ Module files

When you save a function in a form file, that function can be used only by procedures or functions stored in that same form file. When you save a function in a module file, the function can be used by any procedures or functions that make up your Visual Basic .NET program.

Ideally, you should store all your functions in a module file to keep your user interface BASIC code from getting mixed up with the BASIC code that does the actual calculations of your program.

Creating a function in a form file

To create and save a function in a form file, follow these steps:

1. **Click on a form file in the Solution Explorer window and then press F7; choose View⇨Code; or click on the View Code icon to open the code editor.**

2. **Scroll through your code until you see a box that says Windows Form Designer generated code.**

3. **Click directly underneath the Windows Form Designer generated code text and type your general procedure.**

Creating and saving a function in a module file

(In case you need to create a module file, refer to Chapter 27 and read the section "Understanding Module Files.")

To create and save a function to a module file, follow these steps:

1. **Choose View⇨Solution Explorer, or press Ctrl+Alt+L.**

   The Solution Explorer window appears.

2. **Double-click on the module file where you want to store your function.**

   Visual Basic .NET displays an empty module file in the code window that looks something like this, where `Module1` is the name of your module file:

```
Module Module1

End Module
```

3. **Type your function anywhere in between the** `Module` **and** `End Module` **lines.**

Assigning a Value to a Function

Somewhere inside every function, you must either assign the function's name to a value or an expression, or use the Return statement, such as one of the two following examples:

```
Public Function YardsToMeters(ByVal Yards As Single) As_
          Single
  Const Conversion = 0.9
  YardsToMeters = Yards * Conversion
End Function
```

or

```
Public Function YardsToMeters(ByVal Yards As Single) As_
          Single
  Const Conversion = 0.9
  Return Yards * Conversion
End Function
```

If you don't assign a value to a function's name or use the Return keyword, the function can't return any value — and the whole point of using functions is to return a value.

You can also define the specific data type of the value that a function returns, such as Integer, String, or Boolean. For everything you've ever wanted to know about data types, check out Chapter 15.

The three main differences between a function and a procedure are as follows:

- A function calculates and returns one (and only one) value. A procedure performs a specific task.

- Somewhere inside the function, the function's name must be assigned a value. You never need to do this with a procedure.

- You must define the data type that a function represents. You never define a procedure to represent a data type.

Calling Functions

Calling a function is different than calling a procedure. Because functions represent a single value, you call a function by assigning the function name to a variable:

```
Public Function YardsToMeters(ByVal Yards As Single) As_
          Single
  Const Conversion = 0.9
  YardsToMeters = Yards * Conversion
End Function

Private Sub Button1_Click(ByVal sender As System.Object,_
          ByVal e As System.EventArgs) Handles Button1.Click
  Dim Meters As Single
  Meters = YardsToMeters(CSng(txtYards.Text))
  txtMetric.Text = CStr(Meters)
End Sub
```

This event-handling procedure says, "When the user clicks on a button called Button1, do the following:"

1. Create a variable called Meters and define this variable to hold only Single data type.

2. Take whatever value is stored in the Text property of a text box called txtYards and use the value as an argument for the YardsToMeters function.

3. The YardsToMeters function takes txtYards.Text as its argument, multiplies the argument by 0.9, and stores this new result in the YardsToMeters function name. The result stored in the YardsToMeters function name gets stuffed into the Meters variable.

4. The value stored in the Meters variable gets converted into a string and stuffed into the Text property of a text box named txtMetric.

Note the differences in calling procedures and calling functions. When calling a procedure, you can use one of two methods:

```
ProcedureName(ArgumentList)
```

or

```
Call ProcedureName(ArgumentList)
```

To call a function, you typically assign a variable to that function such as:

```
Variable = FunctionName(ArgumentList)
```

If the function returns a Boolean value, you can also call a function within a Boolean expression, such as:

```
If FoundGuilty(CongressmanName) Then
  ' BASIC code here
End If
```

Because a function name represents a single value, you can use a function name in any mathematical expression, such as

```
Variable = FunctionName(ArgumentList) + Variable
```

So a procedure that calls a function called `YardsToMeters` may look like this:

```
Private Sub cmdConvert_Click()
  Dim Meters As Single, NewValue As Single
  NewValue = (YardsToMeters (Meters) + 32) * 4
End Sub
```

Defining a Function as a Certain Data Type

Because a function returns a single value, you can specify what data type that value represents.

Take a look at the following, for example:

```
Public Function YardsToMeters(ByVal Yards As Single) As_
          Single
  Const Conversion = 0.9
  YardsToMeters = Yards * Conversion
End Function
```

This defines the value of `YardsToMeters` as a Single data type. You can define a function to represent a variety of data types, such as the following:

- Integer
- Long
- Boolean
- Single
- Double
- Decimal
- String

No matter what data type a function represents, any variables assigned to the function must be of the same data type. For example:

```
Public Function YardsToMeters(ByVal Yards As Single) As_
          Single
  Const Conversion = 0.9
  YardsToMeters = Yards * Conversion
End Function

Private Sub Button1_Click(ByVal sender As System.Object,_
          ByVal e As System.EventArgs) Handles Button1.Click
  Dim Meters As Single
  Meters = YardsToMeters(CSng(txtYards.Text))
  txtMetric.Text = CStr(Meters)
End Sub
```

In this example, the variable Meters is defined as a Single data type, and the YardsToMeters function is also defined as a Single data type.

If Meters is defined as the following:

```
Dim Meters As String
```

the line

```
Meters = YardsToMeters(CSng(txtYards.Text))
```

can't work because Meters is a String data type, and YardsToMeters returns a Single data type value. Because Meters expects a string but YardsToMeters gives Meters a number, Visual Basic .NET will refuse to run the program.

Defining argument types

Arguments are data (numbers, strings, or variables, which represent a number or a string) that a function needs to be able to work.

In addition to defining the number of arguments in an argument list, you have the option of defining the type of data each argument must represent.

For example, you can define an argument to represent different data types such as:

- ✔ Integer
- ✔ Long
- ✔ Boolean
- ✔ Single

- ✔ Double
- ✔ Decimal
- ✔ String

To define an argument type, you have to define the type in the argument list:

```
Public Function Convert(ByVal Fahrenheit As Integer, ByVal_
          Celsius As Integer) As Single
```

This example defines a function (which returns a Single data type) and two arguments (which must be Integer data types). The following shows the only procedure call that can work:

```
Private Sub Button1_Click(ByVal sender As System.Object,_
          ByVal e As System.EventArgs) Handles Button1.Click
  Dim X, Y, Z As Integer
  Dim A, B, C As String
  Dim L, M, N As Single
  L = Convert(X, Y)   ' This would work
  C = Convert(A, B)   ' Neither A nor B are Integers
  Z = Convert(M, N)   ' Neither M nor N are Integers
  Y = Convert("Hello", X)   ' "Hello" is not an Integer
End Sub
```

Problems sending arguments

Two types of problems may occur when calling functions. One problem is when the number of arguments sent doesn't match the number of arguments defined by the function.

Another problem is when the types of arguments sent don't match the types of arguments defined by the function.

Giving the wrong number of arguments

When you define a function with an argument list, the list specifies the number of arguments that the function needs to run. If you call this function and don't give the function the right number of arguments, the function isn't going to work. For example:

```
Public Function Flame(ByVal Mail As String) As Single

End Function
```

Test your newfound knowledge

1. When do you want to use a function and when do you want to use a procedure?

   a. In Chapter 27, I read about procedures, so that's where you use a procedure. In this chapter, you use only functions, because that's what this chapter covers.

   b. Use a function when you need to calculate a single value. Use a procedure to calculate zero or more values.

   c. Functions and procedures are identical except that they use different names, have different purposes, and don't look the same.

   d. You use a function only if you're too wimpy to use a procedure, like a real programmer does.

2. Which line is a function call and which line is a procedure call?

   ```
   Dim Alex, Pete, George As_
   Double
   Pete = 3
   George = 0
   ```

   ```
   Alex =_
   ClockworkOrange(Pete,
   George) ' Line 4
   ConditionedBehavior(Alex)
   ' Line 5
   ```

   a. Line four is a function call, because a variable is assigned to the value represented by the function name. Line five is a procedure call.

   b. Both lines four and five are procedure calls, because I think this is a trick question and because guessing wrong 99 percent of the time since I started answering these question sections of this book still hasn't convinced me that the right answer is always the most obvious one.

   c. Line five is a function call because this line looks different from line four, which is also a function call.

   d. I don't know the answer, but this question looks like something organic that's really mechanical, much like a clockwork orange. Have you read the book, with the original ending, by Anthony Burgess?

This function expects one argument, which must be a string. None of the following calls to this function work, because the number of arguments is not one:

✔ X = Flame

✔ X = Flame(9, "Shut up!")

✔ X = Flame("Why?", "Go away!", 4500, "Okay.")

Giving the wrong type of arguments

Likewise, when calling a function, always make sure that the arguments have the same data types as the types defined in the argument list:

```
Public Function Flame(ByVal Mail As String) As Single

End Function
```

This function expects one argument, which must be a String data type. None of the following calls to this function can work because the arguments are not String data types:

- ✔ X = Flame(78.909)
- ✔ X = Flame(9)
- ✔ X = Flame(34)

Quitting a Function Prematurely

Normally, your function runs until all the function's instructions have been followed. However, you may want to exit a function before it's finished.

To exit a function prematurely, you have to use the following code:

```
Exit Function
```

Before you exit a function, make sure that you also assign a value to the function name; otherwise, your program may not work correctly.

Part VII

Understanding Object-Oriented Programming

The 5th Wave   By Rich Tennant

YOU KIDDING!! TRUE INTERACTIVE CONTENT?! ME CAN'T WAIT, PULL LEVER, OPEN SCREEN!

In this part . . .

If you believe the hype, object-oriented programming can help you write programs faster, make your programs more reliable, and give you fewer cavities at your next dental checkup. Essentially, object-oriented programming is a method for organizing programs so they're easier to write and debug.

This part of the book gives you a brief introduction to object-oriented programming, so you can use it when you write your own Visual Basic .NET programs. Object-oriented programming won't make you a better programmer overnight, but when used wisely, it can help you write programs that actually work, which is a worthy goal that even folks in major corporations and governments never quite achieve in their lifetime.

Chapter 30

What the Heck Is Object-Oriented Programming?

In This Chapter
▶ Working with structured programming
▶ Solving problems with object-oriented programming

*I*n an attempt to keep up with the latest programming trends, Visual Basic .NET gives you the ability to use object-oriented programming to develop your next killer application. Of course, unless you know what object-oriented programming is and what this form of programming can do for you, this latest feature is about as useful as giving a chain saw to a monkey and expecting the monkey to build a tree house.

So before you get all excited about using object-oriented programming with Visual Basic .NET, take some time to find out what the heck object-oriented programming is supposed to do for you in the first place.

One reason that computer scientists created object-oriented programming was that despite the rigors of college computer science curricula, programming is still more an art than a science. Even if you have a Ph.D. in computer science, there's still no guarantee that you can write better programs than a high school dropout.

So to make programming easier, computer scientists have developed a variety of different programming techniques. The ultimate goal is to help people write programs quickly that work and run efficiently, but most of the time people are just happy having a program written quickly (regardless of whether it works or runs efficiently).

The Divide and Conquer Method of Structured Programming

In the early days of programming, programmers often wrote programs without any prior planning. Instead, they just started writing code and adding on new features wherever they felt like it, which often resulted in a program that might work, but was disorganized and hard to understand. Such convoluted programs soon got the unwanted reputation of *spaghetti coding* because trying to understand the way the program worked was as difficult as trying to untangle a pile of spaghetti.

Having a disorganized program that worked wasn't the problem. The problem occurred when the time came to modify the existing program to add new features. But with a program so disorganized, adding new code often meant accidentally introducing bugs that suddenly kept the program from running at all.

A more serious problem occurred when programmers would start writing programs without any previous planning, and then lose track of so many details that their program never worked in the first place. Because trying to fix this original mess was too difficult and confusing, most programmers simply threw away their previous program and started from scratch all over again — often running into the same problems and abandoning their new version of the program until nothing ever got done at all.

One of the first solutions that computer scientists introduced was to create guidelines for making large programs easier to understand using a method called *structured programming*. Structured programming introduced three ideas:

- Divide a large program into a lot of smaller programs
- Define variables and the data type each variable can hold
- Divide a small program into sequential, branching, or looping commands

Dividing a large program into multiple subprograms

Creating a large program that does multiple tasks is much harder than writing a single tiny program that solves one problem. So theoretically, you could create a bunch of little programs that solve one problem, then paste them together to create a larger program that ultimately solves a lot of problems.

Not only should this help you write a large program that works, but it should also make modifying that large program easier because any time you want to debug or update your program, you just need to debug or update one of the tinier programs that make up your larger program.

Visual Basic .NET encourages this practice by dividing your user interface into separate event-handling procedures. When you need to write BASIC code that calculates a result, Visual Basic .NET encourages you to write general procedures and store them in separate module files (see Chapter 27).

Declaring variables and data types

In the early days, programs could create variables at any time and store any type of data in them, which made understanding how the program worked almost impossible. So structured programming forced programmers to declare their variables. That way other programmers would know the exact variable names used in the program.

As further insurance against bugs, structured programming also forced programmers to declare the type of data a variable could hold. If you tried to run a program that stored the wrong type of data in a variable, the computer would halt and refuse to run your program. That way you wouldn't accidentally distribute a program that would store the wrong type of data in a variable and crash somebody else's computer.

By forcing you to declare your variables and the data type those variables represent, Visual Basic .NET helps force you to write programs that are easy to understand and modify. (For more information about variables, see Chapter 15.)

Using sequential, branching, or looping commands

The biggest problem in early programs was the improper use of a special command called a GOTO command. This command essentially told the computer, "Jump to the end of the program and run those instructions, then jump to the middle of the program and run those instructions, then jump to the front, then to the back, then to the middle, and so on."

By jumping from one set of instructions to another, early programs were nearly impossible to understand. So structured programming introduced the idea of confining the flow of a program in one of three ways: in a sequence, in a branch, or in a loop.

When a program follows commands in a sequence, the computer just follows one instruction after another.

When a program follows commands in a branch, the computer runs one of many possible sets of instructions. That's the whole idea behind If-Then and Select-Case statements (see Chapter 22 and 23).

When a program follows commands in a loop, the computer repeats one or more instructions. That's why Visual Basic .NET offers looping commands (see Chapters 24 and 25).

By limiting your program to run sequential, branching, or looping commands, structured programming forces you to isolate programming instructions in distinct groups that are easy to find, understand, and modify later.

Object-Oriented Programming to the Rescue (Sort of)

While structured programming helped people create programs that were easier to write and modify, two major problems still remained. Although the different parts of the program might be physically isolated from one another, each part of a program could still access data used by another part of the program. So now if one part of your program started messing up data used by another part of your program, trying to find the source of the problem might mean searching through your entire program.

Even worse, if you wanted to change the way your program accessed certain data such as a file on a hard disk, you had to exhaustively search through the entire program and find all the commands that accessed that data. Miss one command and you've just introduced a bug into your program.

The second big problem with structured programming was that writing a lot of little programs took time. To save time, many programmers simply copied parts from an existing program and pasted it into their own program.

This solution worked, except that part of another program might need some minor editing to make it work in your own program. Even worse, if you found this particular chunk of code useful, you might be tempted to modify it to use in multiple places in your own program. Pretty soon you might have several variations of the same subprogram scattered throughout your entire program.

But what if you suddenly wanted to update that subprogram? Now you had to update it everywhere you copied and modified that subprogram elsewhere in your program.

So to solve both of these problems, computer scientists created a new guideline called object-oriented programming, often abbreviated as OOPs (as in "Oops, you just wasted four years of college studying structured programming").

Object-oriented programming techniques keep all the good programming principles of structured programming but add some new principles to help make programming faster, more reliable, and easier to update. Two main principles of object-oriented programming are known as encapsulation and inheritance.

Encapsulation: Isolating your data and commands

Like structured programming, object-oriented programming encourages programmers to divide a large program into several smaller ones. But in structured programming, subprograms simply organize related instructions together, while object-oriented programming organizes related instructions and the data they manipulate together. In case you understand pictures better than text, Figure 30-1 shows the difference between the way an object-oriented program works and a nonobject-oriented program works.

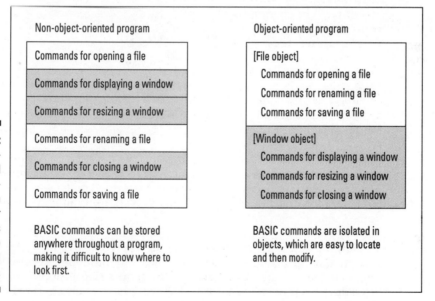

Figure 30-1: Object-oriented programming can make your programs easier to understand and modify.

Non-object-oriented program

| Commands for opening a file |
| Commands for displaying a window |
| Commands for resizing a window |
| Commands for renaming a file |
| Commands for closing a window |
| Commands for saving a file |

BASIC commands can be stored anywhere throughout a program, making it difficult to know where to look first.

Object-oriented program

[File object]
Commands for opening a file
Commands for renaming a file
Commands for saving a file

[Window object]
Commands for displaying a window
Commands for resizing a window
Commands for closing a window

BASIC commands are isolated in objects, which are easy to locate and then modify.

By encapsulating both commands and the data they manipulate into an object, object-oriented programming keeps one part of your program from accidentally messing up another part of your program. So instead of pasting lots of little subprograms together to make a large program, object-oriented programming allows you to paste lots of little objects together to make a large program.

Inheriting reusable code

If you want to copy and reuse code in structured programming, you have to make a physical copy of that code and paste it everywhere in your program. But in object-oriented programming, if you want to copy and reuse code, you can create a new object based on an existing object.

Essentially this new object is a copy of another object but with a twist. Instead of containing a copy of the source code from the original object, the new object *inherits* code from the original object, which means it points to the location of the original source code. So when the computer tries to run BASIC code in an object that has inherited code, the object tells the computer, "The BASIC code you want to run is actually stored in another object. I'll point you to that other object that contains the BASIC code you need to follow."

The main advantage of inheritance is that you can borrow code from another object without copying the source code. Now if you ever need to change the code, you only need to change it in a single location instead of multiple locations.

Overloading existing code

Another fancy feature of object-oriented programming is something called *overloading*. An object can inherit code from another object. Naturally, you can add your own code to an object, which means that your object can contain two sets of code: the code it inherited from another object and any additional code you add to it.

So what if you create a new object that inherits code that you don't want to use? You can just ignore it, but object-oriented programming gives you the option of *overloading* it instead. When you overload code, you create a new subprogram that has the identical name as a subprogram inherited from another object.

Normally Visual Basic .NET would scream and refuse to run your program if you gave two procedures identical names, but under object-oriented programming, you can give a subprogram the same name as another subprogram stored in another object. That way you don't have to create nearly identical names for subprograms that essentially perform the same task.

For example, one object in your program might represent an airplane and one subprogram in that airplane object might be named Move, which simply tells that object (in this case, an airplane) to move on the screen.

Test your newfound knowledge

1. Name three ways structured programming can make programs easier to write and modify.

   a. It forces programmers to use cryptic languages like C++, pay obscene salaries for programmers who don't have any experience, and throw as many people on a project as possible.

   b. It divides a large program into several smaller ones, declares variables and data types, and uses sequential, branching, or looping instructions.

   c. Structured programming doesn't make programs easier to write or modify. That's why programs like Windows have so many bugs in them and crash your computer every day or two.

   d. By giving you stock options so you can hire someone to do your work for you, pay to buy another program, or bribe someone to steal a program from a rival company.

2. Name three unique features of object-oriented programming.

   a. Larry, Curly, and Moe.

   b. Object-oriented programming is more complicated, harder to master, and impossible to put into practice.

   c. Encapsulation of commands and data, inheritance of existing code, and overloading.

   d. Object-oriented programming has the funny acronym of OOPs, it sounds cool like you know what you're talking about, and it still won't make programs any faster or more reliable in the long run anyway.

Now suppose you want to create an object that represents a spaceship. Although you can rewrite an entirely new object from scratch, you may find it easier just to inherit the existing code from the airplane object instead.

Of course, airplanes move a lot differently than spaceships, so you'll have to write a new Move subprogram to move the spaceship. With overloading, you can also name your spaceship's subprogram Move. Your spaceship's Move subprogram essentially replaces the Move subprogram from the airplane object. Best of all, you now have two separate but identically named Move subprograms: one to move the airplane object and one to move the spaceship object.

So when your program runs the Move subprogram, the first thing the computer does is ask, "Which object am I supposed to move?" If the object is the airplane, use the airplane's Move subprogram. If the object is the spaceship, use the spaceship's Move subprogram.

By allowing you to use the same names for subprograms that manipulate different objects, object-oriented programming helps you reuse descriptive names as many times as you need to.

Object-oriented programming helps make programming easier by keeping your code and data separated and by making it easy to reuse code without copying it to another location and risk messing it up by mistake.

Chapter 31

Getting Some Class with Object-Oriented Programming

*T*he main idea behind object-oriented programming is to divide your program into separate objects that interact with one another. So if you were designing a video game where players shoot monsters in a maze, two logical types of objects would be a weapon object and a character object.

The weapon object would represent any type of gun that the monsters or the player used, and the character object would represent the player and one or more monsters.

Object-oriented programming is being credited with making programs easier to write, modify, and reuse. However, it alone won't make your program useful or bug free in any way. A poor programmer using object-oriented programming will still be less efficient than a great programmer who doesn't use object-oriented programming.

Using Object-Oriented Programming in Visual Basic .NET

Now that you have a general idea how objects work, you may be curious how objects work in Visual Basic .NET. Creating objects in Visual Basic .NET involves a three-step process:

1. **Create a class file.**

2. **Type BASIC code into this class file.**

3. **Declare a variable elsewhere in your Visual Basic .NET program that represents your class file.** When a variable represents a class file (as opposed to a data type such as an Integer or String), that variable is known as an object, which is where the term object-oriented programming comes from.

A class file acts like a template that defines the way an object works. After you've created a class file, you still need to declare a variable to create an object.

Creating a class file

A class file defines how a single object behaves. To create a class file, follow these steps:

1. **Choose Project⇨Add Class.**

   An Add New Item dialog box appears.

2. **Click on the Class icon and then click in the Name text box.**

3. **Type a name for your class file.**

   You don't need to type the .VB file extension as part of the class file name; Visual Basic .NET will add the .VB file extension automatically.

4. **Click Open.**

   Visual Basic .NET displays your class name in the Solution Explorer window (if it's visible) and displays an empty class in the code window that looks something like this, where `Class1` is the name you chose in Step 3 for your module file:

```
Public Class Class1

End Class
```

At this point, you have an empty class file that won't do a thing. You still need to type BASIC code in between the `Public Class Class1` line and the `End Class` lines.

Defining an object

After you've created a class file, the next step is to write BASIC code that makes that object actually do something. A typical class module consists of three parts:

- Variable declarations
- Property (data) declarations

  ✔ Methods, which are BASIC procedures (see Chapter 27 for more informa-
    tion about procedures) that manipulate variables and properties

```
Public Class Class1
   ' Variable declarations

   ' Property declarations

   ' Methods
End Class
```

Each object encapsulates (isolates) its own data (properties) from the rest
of the program. The only way to manipulate that data is through a command
(method) stored inside that particular object. That way, your program never
needs to directly access the data itself. Figure 31-1 shows how an object-
oriented program accesses data compared to the structure of an ordinary
program.

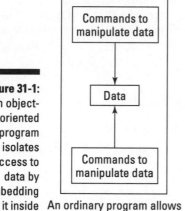

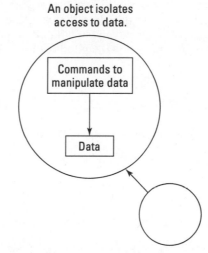

An object isolates
access to data.

Figure 31-1:
An object-
oriented
program
isolates
access to
data by
embedding
it inside
an object.

An ordinary program allows
access to data from
anywhere in the program.

If you ever need to change the way your program accesses specific data, you
just need to modify the commands inside that object instead of modifying
commands scattered throughout your entire program. In this way, object-
oriented programming helps isolate the commands that affect specific data,
thereby reducing the chance of introducing new bugs into your program
when you need to modify your program.

There is no right or wrong way to define objects, but the more the objects in
your program correspond to actual objects that your program manipulates,
the easier your program will be for others to understand and modify later.

Declaring your variables

Declaring all the variables used by your class at the beginning of your class is a good idea so you know what type of information your class is using. If you want to declare a variable that only your class needs to use, you can declare a private variable, such as:

```
Private Counter As Integer
```

Variables are often used for temporarily storing the value of an object's properties as explained in the following section, "Defining an object's properties."

Although not recommended, you can also declare a public variable that any part of your program can use to store or retrieve information. To declare a public variable, you just substitute the word `Public` for `Private` such as:

```
Public Counter As Integer
```

If you declare a public variable, any part of your program (including other objects) can put data into that variable, which means that debugging your program can be extremely difficult. In general, don't declare a public variable unless you have a really good reason to do so.

Defining an object's properties

A property represents data that the rest of your program can access by storing data into that property or retrieving data back out of it again. A typical property declaration looks like this:

```
Dim VariableName As DataType

Public Property PropertyName() As DataType
  Get
    PropertyName = VariableName
  End Get

  Set (ByVal Value As DataType)
    VariableName = Value
  End Set
End Property
```

To create your own property declaration, you need to create a private variable (`VariableName`) to represent the value of your property. You can choose any name you wish in place of `VariableName`.

The data type (`DataType`) of this variable must be the same data type as the property's data type. So if the variable is a String data type, the property declaration must be a String data type as well.

Finally, you need to choose a name for your property (`PropertyName`).

So if you created a property named `Direction` to represent an Integer data type, your complete property declaration might look like this:

```
Private mWay As Integer

Public Property Direction() As Integer
  Get
    Direction = mWay
  End Get

  Set
    mWay = Value
  End Set
End Property
```

Visual Basic .NET interprets the preceding code as follows:

1. The first line defines a private variable, called `mWay`, that can hold an integer value.

2. The second line tells Visual Basic .NET, "Create a property called `Direction`, which represents an Integer data type."

3. The third, fourth, and fifth lines tell Visual Basic .NET, "When another part of the program wants to retrieve (`Get`) a value from the `Direction` property, set the `Direction` property value to the value of the `mWay` variable."

4. The sixth, seventh, and eighth lines tell Visual Basic .NET, "When another part of the program wants to store (`Set`) a value into the `Direction` property, store this value in the `mWay` private variable."

5. The ninth line tells Visual Basic .NET, "This is the end of the property definition."

Writing an object's methods

After you declare any variables your object may need and define your object's properties, the next step is to write methods (procedures or functions) that do something with the data stored inside of your object.

Writing a procedure or function is fairly straightforward (for more information check out Chapters 27, 28, and 29). The main difference is that instead of using the `Private` keyword in front of your procedure or function declarations, you use the `Public` keyword, such as:

```
Public Function XLocation () As Integer
 ' Some useful BASIC code goes here
End Function
```

When you want to call an object's methods, you just use the object's name plus the object's method such as:

```
m_Object.Move
```

The preceding code tells Visual Basic .NET, "Find an object called m_Object and call the procedure named Move." As far as your main program is concerned, the program has no idea how the Move procedure works because the Move procedure is isolated inside your object.

Designing a class on paper

Although you could rush right into writing the BASIC code that makes up a class module, you should take some time to design your class module first. What's the best way to design a class module? None. (Now aren't you glad you bought a book that told you that?)

Actually, the optimum design for a class module depends on how you plan to use the class module. The optimum design of a class module for one program may be horrible for another type of a program. To give you some pointers in designing classes, consider the following tips:

✔ To determine a class module's properties, decide the basic building block of data your program needs to manipulate. If you're writing a program to store information about employees, your class module needs to include properties that contain names, addresses, phone numbers, IQs, or felony records. If you're writing a video game where cartoon aliens pop up on the screen so you can shoot them, your class module may contain the X- and Y-coordinates of your cartoon alien's position on the screen.

✔ To determine a class module's methods, decide what your main Visual Basic .NET program needs to do with the information stored in your class module. For example, a class module containing employee names and addresses may need methods that allow the main program to search, sort, and print employee data. Likewise, a class module containing cartoon alien X- and Y-coordinates may need methods that allow the main program to move, display, and blow up the alien.

✔ After you sketch out the type of properties and methods your class module needs to include, you're ready to create an actual class module.

Using a Class Module in a Visual Basic .NET Program

After going through all this trouble creating a class module, you still have to write BASIC code in your main program to actually use your class to create an object. Before you can use an object, you have to create one. After you create an object, you can use that object's methods or store or retrieve information in that object's properties.

Creating an object

Even though you may have gone through the trouble of creating and defining your class module, you still have to create an object based on the design of your class module. In the world of object-oriented programming, creating an object is called creating an *instance*.

To create an instance of an object, you have to create an object to represent your class module using the Set and New keywords, such as:

```
Dim ObjectName As New ClassName
```

This is how Visual Basic .NET interprets this single line of code:

1. The Dim keyword tells Visual Basic .NET, "Get ready to create an object."
2. The ObjectName variable is the name of your object.
3. The New keyword tells Visual Basic .NET, "Create a new object based on the class module defined by ClassName."

The ClassName is the name you gave your class file when you first created it. If you didn't give your class a unique name, Visual Basic .NET gives it a generic name such as Class1.

Using an object

After you create an object, the final step is to use that object to

- ✔ Stuff a value into an object's property
- ✔ Retrieve a value out from an object's property
- ✔ Use an object's method to do something with the object's data

To stuff a value into an object's property, you just have to use the following code:

```
ObjectName.Property = Value
```

To retrieve a value out from an object's property, you have to use the following code:

```
Variable = ObjectName.Property
```

To use an object's method, you can use the following code:

```
ObjectName.Method
```

Try Class Modules Yourself

Naturally the best way to understand anything is to do what you don't understand yourself, so in case this entire chapter doesn't make a whole lot of sense, try the following program. This sample program, as shown in Figure 31-2, demonstrates how a main program can create an object from a class module, call an object's method to manipulate the data, and then retrieve the data afterwards.

Figure 31-2: Create a program that consists of a form with three buttons and two picture boxes.

In this particular program, you use a class file to represent the location of a smiley face and a frowning face on the screen. Each time you click on the Move Smiley or Move Frown button, the smiley or frowning face moves. The following table lists the objects and the properties you need to change to make the program.

If you get nothing else out of this chapter, just remember that object-oriented programming is supposed to help you organize your programs so that you have fewer chances of introducing bugs into any programs that you write or modify.

Object	Property	Setting
PictureBox1	Image	FACE02
	Name	picSmile
	SizeMode	StretchImage
PictureBox2	Image	FACE04
	Name	picFrown
	SizeMode	StretchImage
Button1	Text	Move Smiley
	Name	btnSmile
Button2	Text	Exit
	Name	btnExit
Button3	Text	Move Frown
	Name	btnFrown

Double-click on the three buttons on the form and create the following event procedures:

```
Private Sub btnSmile_Click(ByVal sender As System.Object,_
          ByVal e As System.EventArgs) Handles_
          btnSmile.Click
   Dim Smile As New Class1()
   Smile.xspot = picSmile.Location.X
   Smile.Move()
   picSmile.Left = Smile.xspot
End Sub

Private Sub btnFrown_Click(ByVal sender As System.Object,_
          ByVal e As System.EventArgs) Handles_
          btnFrown.Click
   Dim Frown As New Class1()
   Frown.yspot = picFrown.Location.Y
   Frown.Move()
   picFrown.Top = Frown.yspot
End Sub

Private Sub btnExit_Click(ByVal sender As System.Object,_
          ByVal e As System.EventArgs) Handles btnExit.Click
   Me.Close()
End Sub
```

Create a separate class file and type the following:

```
Public Class Class1
    Dim x, y As Integer
    Const Increment = 10

    Public Property xspot() As Integer
        Get
            xspot = x
        End Get
        Set(ByVal Value As Integer)
            x = Value
        End Set
    End Property

    Public Property yspot() As Integer
        Get
            yspot = y
        End Get
        Set(ByVal Value As Integer)
            y = Value
        End Set
    End Property

    Public Sub Move()
        x = x + Increment
        y = y - Increment
    End Sub
End Class
```

Chapter 32

Using Inheritance and Overloading

In This Chapter

▶ The advantage of using inheritance

▶ Visual inheritance: Cloning your forms

▶ Code inheritance: Cloning your code

▶ Overriding your methods and properties

Programmers tend to be a fairly lazy bunch. Rather than write a brand new subprogram, they'd rather copy somebody else's subprogram that has already proven to work. By copying an existing subprogram, you can save time and (hopefully) use a reliable chunk of code that won't have bugs in it.

But in the old days, reusing code meant making a separate copy of that code and pasting it in every new project where you needed it. Pretty soon you wound up with several copies of the same code, and if you wanted to modify that subprogram in one project, you'd have to modify that same subprogram everywhere else as well.

Even worse was that copying the source code to a subprogram meant that other programmers might accidentally (or deliberately) modify it without your knowledge. So the major advantage of object-oriented programming is something called *inheritance,* which allows you to reuse existing code while protecting the original source code from modification.

Why Use Inheritance?

A class file defines a single object. You can create any number of objects based on the same class file, but each object will have identical characteristics. So what happens if you want to create two objects that share most, but not all, the same characteristics?

You could create a second class file to define your new object, but that would take time and risk introducing bugs. (Any time you write code, you risk introducing bugs, so the trick is to write as little code as possible and still get paid as much as possible for doing it.)

To save time and reduce the risk of introducing new bugs, object-oriented programming allows you to use inheritance, which means you create a new object based on an existing object. So instead of writing code to define a new object in a separate class file, you can inherit the existing object and add new BASIC code to define different characteristics (known as properties and methods).

That way your new object contains all the proven code from the previous object and you can add your own code. So if anything goes wrong with your inherited object, chances are the bug is in the new code you wrote.

By reusing proven code, inheritance reduces the risk of introducing new bugs into a program.

Visual Inheritance: Copying a Form

A simple form of inheritance is inheriting an existing form. When you inherit a form, you essentially copy another form. But when you make any changes to the original form, Visual Basic .NET automatically makes those same changes in your inherited form.

Inheriting a form allows you to duplicate a form that includes all user controls on that form (such as buttons and pull-down menus) and all BASIC code trapped inside any event-handling procedures.

Before you can inherit a form, you (obviously) need to create an initial form in the first place. To inherit a form that already exists, follow these steps:

1. **Choose Project➪Add Inherited Form.**

   An Add New Item dialog box appears, as shown in Figure 32-1.

2. **Click on the Inherited Form icon.**

3. **Click in the Name text box and type a name for your inherited form.**

   Whatever name you choose, do not type a file extension other than .VB. Otherwise Visual Basic .NET may not recognize your form as part of your program.

4. **Click Open.**

Figure 32-1:
The Add
New Item
dialog box
is where
you can
name your
inherited
form.

An Inheritance Picker dialog box appears, as shown in Figure 32-2.

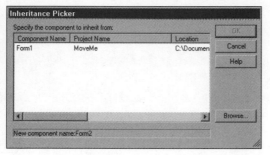

Figure 32-2:
The Inheri-
tance Picker
dialog box
allows you
to choose a
base form
to inherit.

5. Click on the form that you want to use and click OK.

Visual Basic .NET creates your new form and displays the form name in
the Solution Explorer window.

If you make any changes to your base form (the one you chose in Step 5), you
need to choose Build⇨Rebuild All to see those changes reflected in your
inherited forms.

Inheriting Code

Inheriting forms (and their accompanying event-handling procedures) can
simplify the process of designing your user interface. But for additional
flexibility, Visual Basic .NET gives you the option of inheriting BASIC code
stored in another class file.

To inherit code, you need to create a separate class file and insert a line using the `Inherits` keyword and the class file name that you want to inherit, such as:

```
Public Class Class1
   Inherits ClassName
End Class
```

This is how Visual Basic.NET interprets the above BASIC code:

1. The first line tells Visual Basic .NET, "This is a class file named `Class1`."

2. The second line tells Visual Basic .NET, "Inherit BASIC code from a class named `ClassName`."

3. The third line tells Visual Basic .NET, "This is the end of the BASIC code that defines this new class."

To see how code inheritance works, suppose you had a class file named `MainClass` that looked like this:

```
Public Class MainClass
  Private mWay As Integer

  Public Property Direction() As Integer
    Get
      Direction = mWay
    End Get

    Set (ByVal As Integer)
      mWay = Value
    End Set
  End Property
End Class
```

Now if you want to create a new class file that inherits code from the `MainClass` file, your new class file (named `CopyClass`) might look like this:

```
Public Class CopyClass
   Inherits MainClass
End Class
```

Although this class file might look empty, it's equivalent to filling it in with identical BASIC code from the `MainClass` file, such as:

```
Public Class CopyClass
  Private mWay As Integer

  Public Property Direction() As Integer
    Get
      Direction = mWay
    End Get
```

```
   Set (ByVal As Integer)
      mWay = Value
   End Set
 End Property
End Class
```

Overriding Properties and Methods

If you've inherited a bunch of BASIC code from another object, a problem might arise. Suppose a method name from an inherited object is identical to a method name you want to use in your new object.

You can avoid this problem by always choosing distinct names for every method used by your objects. However, this can be clumsy so Visual Basic .NET offers an alternative called *overriding*.

Overriding means that an inherited object can modify a method without affecting the original object. So if you created one object that had a method named KillHardDisk and created an inherited object, that inherited object would also have a method named KillHardDisk with the identical BASIC code to make it work.

However with overriding, an inherited object can reuse a method name but replace its guts with completely different BASIC code.

When you want an object to manipulate data, you have to name the object and the method you want to use, such as:

```
ObjectName.MethodName
```

So if you wanted to run a method named KillHardDisk in an object called Payload, you would use this command:

```
Payload.KillHardDisk
```

Now if you inherited a new object called BombsAway from the Payload object and wanted to run the KillHardDisk method, you would use a similar command such as:

```
BombsAway.KillHardDisk
```

So overriding allows you to reuse the same descriptive method name for use with inherited objects.

Test your newfound knowledge

1. What is the main reason to use inheritance?

   a. To reuse existing, proven code.

   b. To get a lot of money without having to work for any of it.

   c. Inheritance forces your relatives to be nice to you until you die.

   d. There is no reason to use inheritance. You should give all your money to charity.

2. What does overriding do?

   a. Nothing that you can't do using good ol' COBOL code and a ball peen hammer.

   b. Overriding means you put the saddle on top of the horse instead of underneath.

   c. Overriding allows an object to modify an inherited method or property without affecting the way the original method or property behaves.

   d. Overriding makes your processor run faster than it's supposed to, which can burn up your computer and cause it to blow up in an explosive fireball that will visible to everyone within a three-mile radius.

To override a method or property, you need to follow these steps:

1. **Click on the class file in the Solution Explorer window that you want other classes to inherit.**

   Visual Basic .NET highlights your chosen class file.

2. **Press F7, choose <u>V</u>iew⇨<u>C</u>ode, or click on the View Code icon in the Solution Explorer window.**

   Visual Basic .NET displays the BASIC code for your chosen class file.

3. **Substitute the keyword** `Overrridable` **for the keyword** `Public` **for each property or method you want to override.**

   So if you had the following properties and method:

```
Public Class CopyClass

    ' Variable declarations here

    Public Property MyProperties() As String
        ' Property declarations here
    End Property

    Public Sub MyMethod()
        ' BASIC code here
    End Sub

End Class
```

You can replace the `Public` keyword with the `Overridable` keyword, such as:

```
Public Class CopyClass

    ' Variable declarations here

    Overridable Property MyProperties() As String
        ' Property declarations here
    End Property

    Overridable Sub MyMethod()
        ' BASIC code here
    End Sub

End Class
```

If you don't use the Overridable keyword to define a property or method, an inherited object cannot override that property or method.

4. **Choose Project➪Add Class.**

   An Add New Item dialog box appears.

5. **Type a name for your class file in the Name text box (be sure to leave the .VB file extension) and click Open.**

   Visual Basic .NET displays a blank class in the code window, where `ClassName` represents the name you typed in this step, such as:

```
Public Class ClassName

End Class
```

6. **Type the keyword** `Inherits` **followed by the class file name that you want your new class to inherit.**

   For example, if you want to inherit from a class named `Class1`, you would type the following:

```
Public Class ClassName
    Inherits Class1
End Class
```

7. **Type the property or methods that you want to override, but instead of using the keyword** `Public`**, use the keyword** `Overrides`**.**

   The following BASIC code shows the use of the `Overrides` keyword to redefine a method and property:

```
Public Class ClassName
    Inherits CopyClass

    Overrides Property MyProperties() As String
         ' Property declarations here
    End Property

    Overrides Sub MyMethod()
         ' BASIC code here
    End Sub
End Class
```

At this point, you just need to write BASIC code to redefine the way your overridden properties and methods work differently.

Don't worry if the rationale behind inheritance and overriding still seems a bit fuzzy. The important point to know is that both inheritance and overriding are ways that (hopefully) make programming easier, faster, and more reliable by allowing you to selectively reuse the names and code of inherited properties and methods or just the names instead.

Try Inheritance and Overriding Yourself

To see how Visual Basic .NET works with inheritance and overriding, try the following simple program and study the BASIC code so you can better understand how the whole thing works. This example uses the form and class that you created in Chapter 31.

Edit the Class1.vb class file from Chapter 31 and substitute the `Overridable` keyword for the `Public` keyword, such as:

```
Public Class Class1
    Dim x, y As Integer
    Const Increment = 10

    Public Property xspot() As Integer
        Get
            xspot = x
        End Get
        Set(ByVal Value As Integer)
            x = Value
        End Set
    End Property
```

```
    Public Property yspot() As Integer
        Get
            yspot = y
        End Get
        Set(ByVal Value As Integer)
            y = Value
        End Set
    End Property

    Overridable Sub Move()
        x = x + Increment
        y = y - Increment
    End Sub

End Class
```

Next, create a separate class file named `CopyClass` and type the following code into the `CopyClass` class file, substituting the `Overrides` keyword for the `Public` keyword, as follows:

```
Public Class CopyClass
    Inherits Class1

    Overrides Sub Move()
        MsgBox("Overridden the Move method")
    End Sub

End Class
```

Finally, edit the code in your form file to use both the original class file (`Class1`) and the inherited class file (`CopyClass`) as follows:

```
Public Class Form1
    Inherits System.Windows.Forms.Form

    Private Sub btnSmile_Click(ByVal sender As_
            System.Object, ByVal e As System.EventArgs)_
            Handles btnSmile.Click
        Dim Smile As New Class1()
        Smile.xspot = picSmile.Location.X
        Smile.Move()
        picSmile.Left = Smile.xspot
    End Sub

    Private Sub btnFrown_Click(ByVal sender As_
            System.Object, ByVal e As System.EventArgs)_
            Handles btnFrown.Click
        Dim Frown As New CopyClass()
        Frown.yspot = picFrown.Location.Y
        Frown.Move()
        picFrown.Top = Frown.yspot
    End Sub
```

```
     Private Sub btnExit_Click(ByVal sender As_
             System.Object, ByVal e As System.EventArgs)_
             Handles btnExit.Click
         Me.Close()
     End Sub
End Class
```

If you click on the Move Smiley button, the smiley face icon moves on the screen as before. But if you click on the Move Frown button, Visual Basic .NET uses the inherited code in the CopyClass file, and the Move method in the CopyClass file displays a message box with the message, "Overridden the Move method" on the screen.

Part VIII
The Part of Tens

The 5th Wave   By Rich Tennant

"We're here to clean the code."

In this part . . .

Now that you've made it this far in the book (or maybe you're one of those readers who jumps to the end of a great book), you're looking for a few ideas to help you write the best Visual Basic .NET programs possible without losing your mind in the process.

With the help of this book and Visual Basic .NET, you can now write your own programs or get a job writing programs for others. But no matter what you may plan to do with your programming skills, browse through this part of the book to pick up tips for making the most of your newly acquired Visual Basic .NET programming skills.

Chapter 33

Ten Visual Basic .NET Topics That Didn't Fit Anywhere Else

* *

In This Chapter

▶ Finding magazines and newsletters

▶ Visiting Visual Basic .NET Web sites

▶ Joining a user group

▶ Attending technical conferences

▶ Working with C#

▶ Writing programs for the Macintosh, Linux, Palm OS, and PocketPC

* *

*N*ow that you've reached the end of this book (even if you just skipped to this section while browsing through this book in the bookstore), you may be wondering what to do next to continue your Visual Basic .NET education without going through the process of trial and error and driving yourself crazy in the process.

So to give you a hand, here are some random topics to help you get the most out of Visual Basic .NET so you can continue using one of the most powerful programming languages on the face of the Earth.

Buy, Read, or Steal Visual Basic Programmer's Journal

Every month, look for a fresh copy of *Visual Basic Programmer's Journal* at your favorite magazine stand or bookstore. This magazine comes loaded with articles exploring the intricate details of Visual Basic .NET, reviews of Visual Basic .NET add-ons, and samples of Visual Basic .NET code that you can copy (steal) for your own use.

Unlike other magazines, one of the more useful features is the advertising. If you need an ActiveX control to make your programming task easier, browse through the ads and you'll probably find what you need. For more information about this magazine, contact

✔ **Visual Basic Programmer's Journal,** Fawcette Technical Publications, 209 Hamilton Avenue, Palo Alto, CA 94301-2500; Tel: 650-833-7100 Fax: 650-853-0230; www.vbpj.com.

Spend a Bundle of Money and Get a Visual Basic .NET Newsletter

Pinnacle Publishing, Inc. publishes a Visual Basic monthly newsletter, *Visual Basic Developer,* which comes with source code examples that you can copy and use in your own Visual Basic .NET programs. Of course, this newsletter costs a bit more (about $149 a year), but if you can get your company to buy this for you, who cares about the price?

For more information about the *Visual Basic Developer* newsletter, contact

✔ **Visual Basic Developer,** Pinnacle Publishing, Inc., 1000 Holcomb Woods Parkway, Building 200, Suite 280, Roswell, GA 30076; Tel: 770-992-9401 Fax: 770-993-4323; www.pinpub.com.

Visit a Web Site Dedicated to Visual Basic .NET

If you have access to the Internet, you can often find entire Web sites devoted to Visual Basic .NET programming. Although the number of specialized Visual Basic .NET Web sites continues to grow, here's a short list of the more popular Web sites you may want to visit:

✔ Carl and Gary's Visual Basic Home Page: www.cgvb.com

✔ Planet Source Code's Visual Basic section: www.planet-source-code. com/vb

✔ Visual Basic Explorer Home Page: www.vbexplorer.com

✔ VB Tips & Tricks Home Page: www.vbtt.com

You can find plenty more Visual Basic .NET Web sites by visiting your favorite search engine and typing in **Visual Basic .NET**.

Attend a Visual Basic .NET Technical Conference

Every few months, Microsoft and *Visual Basic Programmer's Journal* sponsor a Visual Basic Technical Summit somewhere in the United States, Europe, or Asia. These conferences are great places to discover techniques from real-life Visual Basic .NET programming experts, listen to the latest propaganda talks from Microsoft representatives, buy Visual Basic .NET add-ons cheaply from vendors, and make lots of contacts in the Visual Basic .NET world. For more information about these technical conferences, contact

> ✔ *Visual Basic Programmer's Journal,* Fawcette Technical Publications, 209 Hamilton Avenue, Palo Alto, CA 94301-2500; Tel: 650-833-7100 Fax: 650-853-0230; www.vbits.net.

Shop from Mail-Order Dealers

Don't buy Visual Basic .NET or any Visual Basic .NET add-on programs direct from the publisher. Most software publishers cheerfully charge full retail price for their programs, which makes as much sense as paying full sticker price for a used car.

Rather than buy direct from the software publisher, shop by mail order instead. Mail-order dealers give you even deeper discounts (up to 50 percent in some cases), with the added advantage of saving you from having to pay sales tax.

Three popular mail-order dealers are Programmer's Paradise, Provantage, and VBxtras. All three companies specialize in selling programming tools, including Visual Basic .NET add-ons at substantial discounts, so give them a call and ask for a free catalog.

For more information on these mail-order companies, contact

> ✔ **Programmer's Paradise,** 1157 Shrewsberry Avenue, Shrewsberry, NJ 07702; Tel: 732-389-8950 Fax: 732-389-0010; www.programmersparadise. com.

> ✔ **Provantage,** 7249 Whipple Avenue NW, North Canton, OH 30339; Tel: 330-494-8715 Fax: 330-494-5260; www.provantage.com.

> ✔ **VBxtras,** 1905 Powers Ferry, Suite 100, Atlanta, GA 30339; Tel: 770-952-6356 Fax: 770-952-6388; www.vbxtras.com.

Combine Visual Basic .NET with C# (and Other Programming Languages)

One of the main features of Microsoft's .NET framework is that you can write a single program using multiple languages and they can all share data seamlessly. That way multiple programmers can use their favorite language and .NET provides the foundation.

So if you're already familiar with another programming language or just want to exercise your programming skills, try writing your next program using a variety of programming languages. For example, you might use Visual Basic .NET to create your user interface, and then use C# to write the underlying code that actually makes your program do something useful.

Although using multiple programming languages might seem like a nightmare to maintain, there are several advantages to combining Visual Basic .NET with other languages. For instance, if you have an existing program written in C or COBOL, you can copy the entire program to .NET and then use Visual Basic .NET to slap a friendly user interface on it.

By giving you the ability to mix Visual Basic .NET with other programming languages, Microsoft hopes you'll have the flexibility to create anything you want, just as long as you don't write any programs that threaten anything that Microsoft is already trying to sell.

Participate in a Visual Basic .NET Open Source Project

One of the best ways to master any programming language is to study plenty of real-life, actual working programs written in the language you want to learn. Although you can find plenty of Visual Basic .NET source code floating around the Internet, one of the best ways to study Visual Basic .NET code is to participate in an open source project that uses it.

Open source projects provide the complete source code for anyone to examine and study. The idea is that the more minds working on a given project, the more likely the project will as be bug-free as possible.

Naturally, open source projects welcome all people, so if you want to find out about Visual Basic .NET programming from experienced Visual Basic .NET programmers, join a Visual Basic .NET open source project today.

To help you find an open source project that uses Visual Basic .NET, visit SourceForge (`http://sourceforge.net`). SourceForge can not only help you find a Visual Basic .NET project to join, but it can also help you find a particular category of open source projects as well, such as an open source video game, multimedia program, or communications utility. Whatever type of program you want to study, chances are somebody's already running an open source version of that program that you can help build and learn from as well.

Buy a Program to Create Help Files

Every good Windows program has an online help system so that panicky users can browse through a hypertext reference on the screen instead of wading through hundred-page manuals that don't make any sense anyway. If you're serious about writing Visual Basic .NET programs, you are going to need to provide a help system with your programs, too.

Creating a help system isn't difficult, just incredibly dull and tedious. Fortunately, you can get a special program to make the process a little more enjoyable. Two popular help file creation programs are RoboHelp and ForeHelp, which let you design help screens as easily as writing a document in a word processor. When you're finished, each of these programs lets you test your creations by showing you exactly how your help screens are going to look when added to your own Visual Basic .NET programs.

In today's competitive world of software development, a good help file is crucial to your program's professional appearance. Then again, if you don't care about making your programs easier to use, go work for any of the major software companies instead.

For more information on RoboHelp and ForeHelp, contact

✔ **RoboHelp,** eHelp Corporation, 7777 Fay Avenue, La Jolla, CA 92037; Tel: 858-459-6365 Fax: 858-459-6366; `www.ehelp.com`.

✔ **ForeHelp,** ForeFront, Inc., 4710 Table Mesa Drive, Suite B, Boulder, CO 80305; Tel: 303-499-9181 Fax: 303-494-5446; `www.ff.com`.

Buy a Program to Create Installation Disks

After you finish creating a program in Visual Basic .NET, the final step is to distribute your program to others. Although you can just copy your Visual Basic .NET program onto a floppy disk and trust that the other person knows how to use the disk, you are better off using a special installation program instead.

Installation programs can guide someone, step by step, through the often confusing process of copying a program onto another computer. By using a special installation program, you can simplify this process for your customers and display your own corporate logo, advertisements, or sound effects during the installation process as well.

Two popular installation programs are InstallShield and Wise. Both programs can help you create foolproof installation programs for all your Visual Basic .NET programs.

For more information on these installation programs, contact

✔ **Wise Installer,** Wise Solutions, 5880 North Canton Center Road, Suite 450, Canton, MI 48187; Tel: 734-456-2100 Fax: 734-456-2345; www. wisesolutions.com.

✔ **InstallShield,** InstallShield Corporation, 900 National Parkway, Suite 125 Schaumburg, IL 60173-5108; Tel: 847-240-9111 Fax: 847-619-0788; www. installshield.com.

Write BASIC Programs for the Macintosh, Linux, Palm OS, and the PocketPC

When Microsoft first introduced Visual Basic back in 1991, programmers went nuts over it because they could design applications quickly and easily. So Microsoft promised that they would port Visual Basic to other operating systems so you could write Visual Basic programs for other computers.

After releasing Visual Basic for MS-DOS and then letting it die, Microsoft has pretty much ignored releasing Visual Basic for any other platforms except for Windows CE (also known as the PocketPC operating system). If Microsoft ever ports their .NET framework to other operating systems, such as Linux or the Macintosh, you'll (theoretically) be able to write and run your Visual Basic .NET programs on multiple operating systems without rewriting your programs.

Until this theoretical happy day arrives though, you'll still be stuck writing Visual Basic .NET programs just for Windows. So if you want to use Visual Basic .NET to write a Macintosh program, you can't.

However, you can use a Macintosh Visual Basic clone called REALBasic. Like Visual Basic, REALBasic lets you visually draw your user interface and then write BASIC code to make it do something useful.

REALBasic includes many similar features as Visual Basic and can even take programs written in earlier versions of Visual Basic and convert them into REALBasic. Best of all, you can use REALBasic to write Macintosh programs and then recompile that same program to run on Windows. That way you can write both a Windows and Macintosh program from a single collection of source code.

Two similar Visual Basic clones allow you to design a program visually and then write BASIC code to make it work on a Palm OS or a PocketPC handheld computer. With NSBasic, you can write your program on a desktop or laptop computer, test it using a Palm OS or PocketPC emulation program, and then download your program to a handheld computer to make sure it runs properly before you distribute or sell it to others.

Finally, don't overlook XBasic, which is an open source BASIC compiler that runs under both Windows and Linux. Not only can you see the source code that makes XBasic work, but you can write programs in XBasic and compile them to run under both Windows and Linux.

- ✔ **REALBasic,** Real Software, Inc., PMB 220, 3300 Bee Caves Road, Suite 650, Austin, TX 78746; Tel: 512-263-1233 Fax: 512-263-1441; www. realbasic.com.

- ✔ **NSBasic,** NS Basic Corporation, 77 Hill Crescent, Toronto, Canada M1M 1J3; Tel: 416-264-5999 Fax: 416-264-5888; www.nsbasic.com.

- ✔ **XBasic,** www.xbasic.org.

Chapter 34

(Almost) Ten Tips for Using the Visual Basic .NET User Interface

*B*ecause a computer monitor can only display a limited amount of information on the screen at any given time, Visual Basic .NET provides several different windows for displaying vital information about your Visual Basic .NET program. After you understand the purpose of each window, you can use some of the tips listed in this chapter to make programming in Visual Basic .NET easier than before.

Playing with the Properties Windows (F4)

The Properties window allows you to modify the way objects, such as a button or a check box, look and behave. To help you find properties to change, the Properties window can display information alphabetically or by categories.

To display properties alphabetically, click on the Alphabetic icon in the Properties window. To display properties organized by category, click on the Categorized icon.

The Properties window displays all properties for a single object. If you want to view the properties for another object, you can click on that object or use the Object list box. Just click on the downward-pointing arrow of the Object list box to display a list of all objects and then click on the object that you want to modify.

Using the Solution Explorer (Ctrl+Alt+L)

The Solution Explorer displays all the files used to create a single Visual Basic .NET project. From within the Solution Explorer, you can edit a form, edit the code stored in a file, remove a file from a project, or delete that file altogether by right-clicking on the file you want to change and then clicking on one of the following:

- ✔ View Code (to edit BASIC code)
- ✔ View Designer (to modify your user interface)
- ✔ Exclude From Project (to remove a file from the project without deleting that file)
- ✔ Delete (to remove a file from a project and erase that file at the same time)

Customizing the Toolbox (Ctrl+Alt+X)

The Toolbox displays all the different types of objects you can add to your user interface such as radio buttons, check boxes, or text boxes, which are stored under the Windows Forms tab. For quick access to your most commonly used objects, you can create your own tab and store your favorite objects on that tab.

Customizing a Tab in the Toolbox

To create a tab in the Toolbox, follow these steps:

1. **Right-click on any tab (such as the Windows Forms tab) in the Toolbox.**

   A pop-up menu appears.

2. **Click on Add Tab.**

   The Toolbox displays a blank tab.

3. **Type a descriptive name for your tab and press Enter.**

   The Toolbox displays your tab name in the Toolbox.

Adding Objects to a Custom Tab in the Toolbox

To add objects to your custom tab in the Toolbox, follow these steps:

1. **Right-click on an object that you want, such as TextBox or RadioButton.**

   A pop-up menu appears.

2. **Click on Copy.**

3. **Click on the tab where you want to store the object you chose in Step 1.**

4. **Right-click and choose Paste.**

   The Toolbox displays your chosen object under your Toolbox tab.

Deleting a Tab in the Toolbox

To delete a tab in the Toolbox, follow these steps:

1. **Right-click on the tab you want to delete.**

   A pop-up menu appears.

2. **Click on Delete Tab.**

   If you have any objects stored under your chosen tab, a dialog box appears, asking if you want to continue.

3. **Click Yes.**

   Visual Basic .NET deletes your chosen Toolbox tab.

Looking at the Class View (Ctrl+Alt+C)

The Class View lists all the variables, methods, and properties used by class files that make up your Visual Basic .NET project, as shown in Figure 34-1. By using the Class View window, you can quickly jump to the part of a class file that you need to examine or modify.

Variable

Property

Method

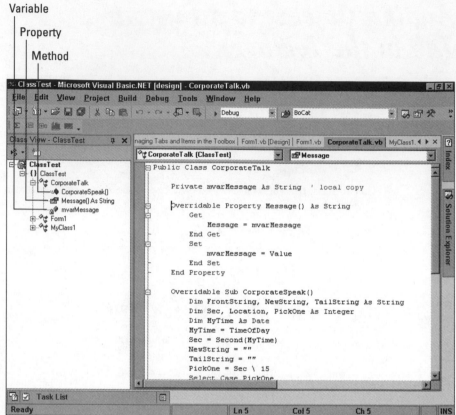

Figure 34-1:
Using the
Class View
window.

To view a variable, method, or property, follow these steps:

1. **Choose View⇨Class View (or press Ctrl+Alt+C) to open the Class View window.**

   The Class View window appears.

2. **Double-click on the variable, method, or property that you want to examine or modify.**

   Visual Basic .NET displays your chosen variable, method, or property in the Code Editor.

Index

● *T* ●

Notes

Notes

Notes

Notes

Notes